IMAGES
of America

ECHO SUMMIT

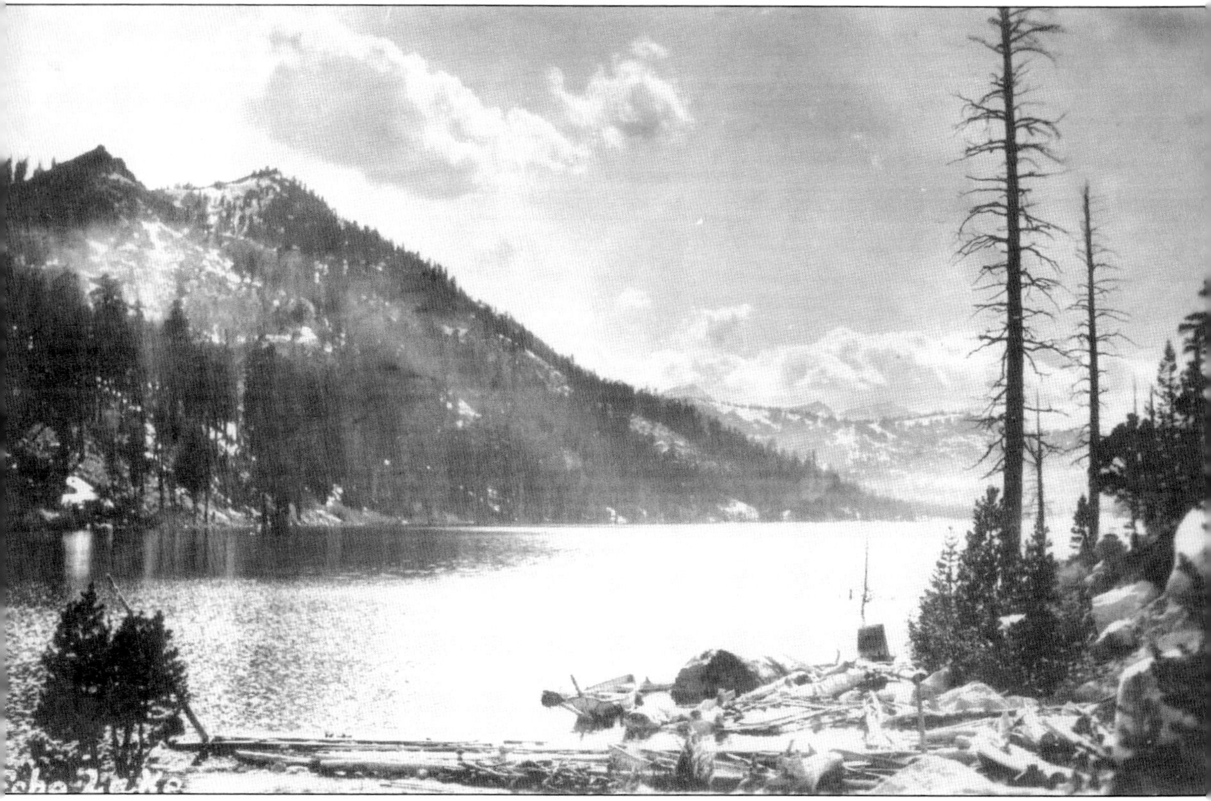

This c. 1895 photograph looks west from Lower Echo Lake's dam and natural outlet toward Desolation Valley. Boats are tethered amid storm debris. A boat has a cloth sail attached to its mast, crafted from a small tree. This storm approached from the west, bringing with it a rare fog of ice crystals suspended in the air. Nevada Washoe and Paiute tribes call this type of ice fog *pogonip*. (Courtesy of Dorothy De Mare)

ON THE COVER: Men observe teamsters leading horse teams and freight wagons through cut snow over Johnson Pass—once called Mickey Free Point and now called Echo Summit—where the 50 milestone marker and Echo Summit Lodge now stand. Wagons and coaches followed each other closely traveling the steep, winding Osgood Grade now called Meyers Grade. There were few places to pass wagons moving in the opposite direction. Coordination of traffic was a major concern. When stages and wagons reached the bottom of Osgood Hill, they paid their tolls at the Osgood Toll House then headed to Yanks Station, the Kingsbury Grade and beyond. There were 61 milestones marking the Placerville-to-Tahoe route, each playing a major role in early commerce marking the exact distances traveled. Murderer Mickey Free's Echo Summit hideout was located at 51 milestone. Sixty-Mile House, also called Summit Station, was at 52 milestone, and Osgood's Toll Station was at 53 milestone. (Courtesy of Dorothy De Mare.)

IMAGES
of America

ECHO SUMMIT

Paul DeWitt and Dorothy De Mare

ARCADIA
PUBLISHING

ISBN 978-1-4671-3200-8

Published by Arcadia Publishing
Charleston, South Carolina

Printed in the United States of America

Library of Congress Control Number: 2014940808

For all general information, please contact Arcadia Publishing:
Telephone 843-853-2070
Fax 843-853-0044
E-mail sales@arcadiapublishing.com
For customer service and orders:
Toll-Free 1-888-313-2665

Visit us on the Internet at www.arcadiapublishing.com

For 20th-century pioneers Shirley and Ralph King and Harriet and Carleton '"Duke" DeWitt for their years of dedication and services to the Echo Summit communities.

Contents

ACKNOWLEDGMENTS

Extraordinary individuals shared personal collections and oral histories. Deep appreciation is extended to them and to Jared Nelson, Arcadia Publishing acquisitions editor, for interest and support of our project. Thanks go to the following: Audrey Alber, Rae Anino, Joe Cagwin Beach, Loie Bonser, Robin Kling Brilliant, Alice Busick, Bernice Cagwin, George Cagwin, Louisa Cagwin, Tom Cagwin, Peter Caldwell, Chris and Tom Celio, Miles Celio, Bev Cola, Alice Cagwin Cook, Jim Crain, FA Darrington, Peter De Mare, Al DeWitt, Harriet and Carlton "Duke" DeWitt, Jayne DeWitt, Rick Donaldson, Ramona Douglass, Katherine Bishop Dunlap, John Durien, Joy Elkinton, Kathleen and Tom Fashinell, Margaret Gray, John Hannum, Ed Herny, Jim Hubbard, Carol Jensen, Sybil Swissler Jones, Jeannie and Haven "Jorgy" Jorgensen, Bob Kaspar, Patricia Keats, Beverly King, Ralph King, Robert King, Shirley King, Imogene Gray Kling, Marylee King Larson, Lori Cagwin Leavy, Rodi Lee, Fran Leonard, Joe Little, Laura Vail Lyman, Jon McCabe, Nancy and Maury McLaughlin, Doug Noble, Ellen Osborne, Dee Owens, Marge and Alan Patera, Fran and Darrel Pierce, Floyd Poole, Dorothy Riebe, Blanche Rocca, Curt Rocca, Mildred Royle, Norm Sayler, Lynn and Tom Schaefer, Dan Schell, Susan Seminoff, Ralph Shaw, Margaret and Robert Shorrock, Mike Shorrock, Jack Smith, Gordon Stangland, Todd Voorheis Skinner, Art Sommers, Shirley Taylor, Joyce Thompson, Margaret Edith "Mees" Trussell, Jane Voiles, Nancy Von Pohle, George Wheeldon, Rosemary Whitesides, Patricia and Lyman Wilbur, Dennis Witcher, Theadore Clemens Wohlbruck, and Mary Lou Zec.

Warm appreciation goes to the following organizations and staff for generously providing use of their images and collections: Berkeley Echo Lake Camp; California Alpine Club; California Department of Transportation, Diane Voll; California Historical Society, North Baker Research Library, San Francisco's Ralph Cross, Sr. Collection; Center for Sacramento History, Dylan McDonald; City of Berkeley Human Resources Department, Rorry Dean-Evans; Davies Photo Service; Douglas County Historical Society; Echo Chalet, Inc.; Echo Lakes Association; Echo Lakes Community; Echo Portals; Echo Summit Lodge; El Dorado County History Museum, Mary Cory; *El Dorado Gazette*; El Dorado Research, Betty Laarveld; Frasher's Fotos; Genoa Court House Museum; Highway 50 Association, *Wagon Train* magazine; Historic Environment Consultants; Lake Tahoe Historical Society Museum, Diane Johnson; *Lake Tahoe News*; *Mountain Democrat-Times: Reminiscing*; Pacific Gas and Electric Company; *Placerville Times*; *Reno Gazette Journal;* San Francisco Bay Area Postcard Club (www.postcard.org); Society of California Pioneers; *Tahoe Daily Tribune*; *Tahoe Tattler*; and USFS El Dorado National Forest, Tom Fuller, Devin Maher, and John Maher.

INTRODUCTION

This book is a historical look at the Echo Summit ridge, which sits atop of the Sierra Nevada Mountains. The summit overlooks the Lake Tahoe and Lake Valley basin to the east and the canyon of the South Fork of the American River toward the west.

For more than 1,000 years, Washoe and Paiute Indians climbed the Echo Summit ridge and hiked to Echo Lake for fishing and hunting. John "Cockeyed" Johnson used one of their trails in the late 1840s to make a shortcut to Placerville from the Carson Valley. His trail became known as the Johnson Cutoff. The first white migrants to travel extensively over Echo Summit came in the 1850s, when the discovery of gold in California brought a rush of miners overland seeking their fortunes. When silver and gold were discovered in 1859 in Virginia City, Nevada, the traffic flow was reversed, as thousands of people and tons of supplies headed toward the new strikes in stagecoaches and freight wagons drawn by horse and mule teams. The most-traveled route to Virginia City was over Echo Summit. When the transcontinental railroad was finished in 1869, travel along the Echo Summit road dwindled to a much smaller number of travelers and commerce. Travel toward Echo Summit on the dirt and rocky road was made easier with the addition of roadhouses, hotels, restaurants, and watering holes. As automobiles were introduced and the roads were improved with paving, reconfiguring, and widening, many of these roadside businesses closed and disappeared as the cars traveled faster and rarely made stops on their way to Lake Tahoe. Today, over one million tourists a year use Echo Summit to travel into the Lake Tahoe basin.

Echo Lake was first visited by fur trappers and commercial fishermen in the 1870s. Before coming to Echo Lake in 1896, Hamden Eldorado Cagwin built a cabin on Tahoe's Stateline shore and trapped for the markets. To curtail Cagwin's fishing proficiency, merchant Charles Ramsey of Bijou petitioned California's legislature against wholesale taking of fish; legislation enacted in 1917. At Echo Lake, Ham Cagwin began a boat rental business and became the caretaker of a dam built at the lake's outlet to divert water from Lake Tahoe to the American River. In the 1920s, the US Forest Service encouraged the public to apply for summer home leases. There are about 120 such cabins on Echo Lake and about 130 cabins built along the Echo Summit ridge. Ralph King came to Echo Lake in 1925 to work at a camp on Upper Echo Lake. He stayed at the lake until 1936, working on cabins and operating a boat concession. In 1939, the Echo Chalet was built to provide cabin owners, hikers, and backpackers going into the Desolation Wilderness Area with groceries, supplies, and boat services. It still exists today.

The City of Berkeley opened Berkeley Echo Camp in 1922 as a family camp on US Forest Service land. Families slept in tents, ate in the dining hall, participated in hikes to various scenic areas, such as the Desolation Wilderness Area, and took part in recreational activities, such as archery, mountain golf, crafts, folk dancing, volleyball, and campfires. Carlton "Duke" DeWitt and Harriet DeWitt managed Berkeley Camp from 1935 to 1945. Besides serving as a family camp today, Berkeley Camp also has specialized programs for youth camps and adult camps. For parts of the summer, it serves as the center for cross-country running programs, religious gatherings, and other groups and organizations that want to visit the rustic area.

Echo Portals was built in 1926 on US Forest Service land at the junction of Echo Lakes Road and the Placerville-Lake Tahoe Highway going over Johnson Pass at Echo Summit. It was part of the US Forest Service efforts to encourage people to come into the wilderness areas. The Echo Portals business had a wooden alphabetized mail rack hanging on the inside wall for sorting mail, a soda fountain, and groceries and supplies for local cabin owners and travelers along the road to Lake Tahoe. Ralph and Shirley King acquired Echo Portals in 1936 after they left Echo Lake. When the highway was changed, bypassing Echo Portals in the 1940, it slowly declined in business and eventually closed.

Echo Summit Lodge was built by Thomas Wohlbruck on US Forest Service land in 1922. Located at the edge of the Echo Summit ridge, it gives travelers spectacular views of the Lake Tahoe and Lake Valley basins. The lodge provided rooms, cabins, meals, a soda fountain, and a store with postcards, books, and souvenirs for the travelers who stopped to enjoy the scenery. When the direction of Highway 50 was changed in 1940, bypassing the lodge, its business also declined. In 1952, the California Alpine Club purchased the lodge and still operates it today.

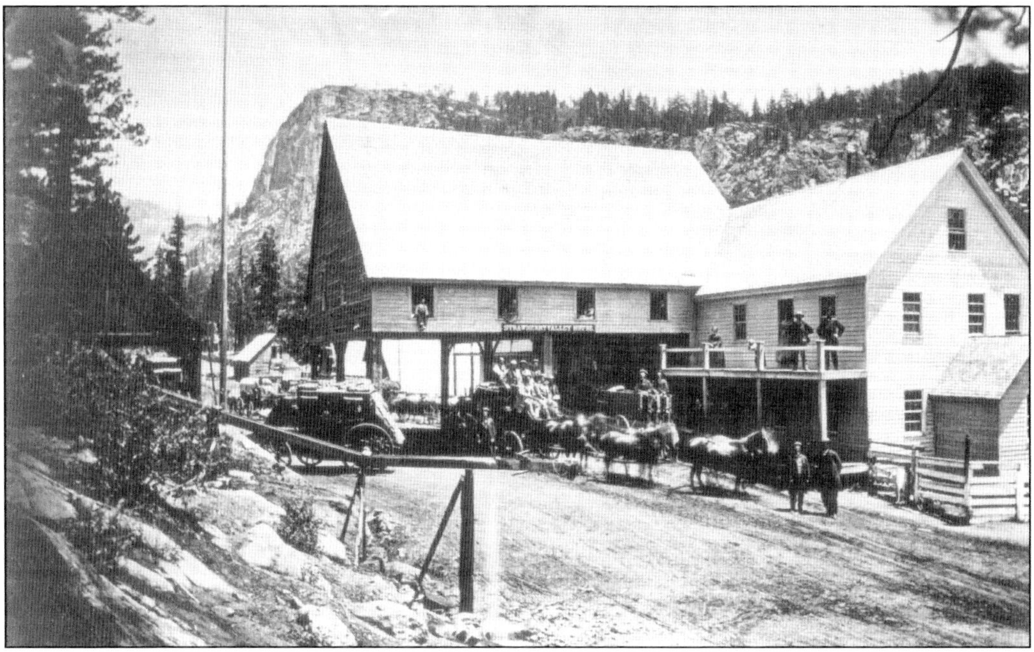

Strawberry Valley House was one of the many establishments built along the road between Placerville and Echo Summit in the 1850s and 1860s. Teamsters, packers, and peddlers entering the station were wretched from the dirt of the road and the stench of their sweaty bodies. The bar served numerous drinks to quench the thirst of guests who wanted to party. Dinners were served every half hour in six shifts. Manners did not exist! When sleeping, travelers shared the floor of a large room with 100 other smelly souls. Yet, Strawberry Valley House was considered one of the most popular places to stay along the road. (Courtesy of the Society of California Pioneers.)

One

Approaching Echo Summit From Genoa and the Tahoe Basin

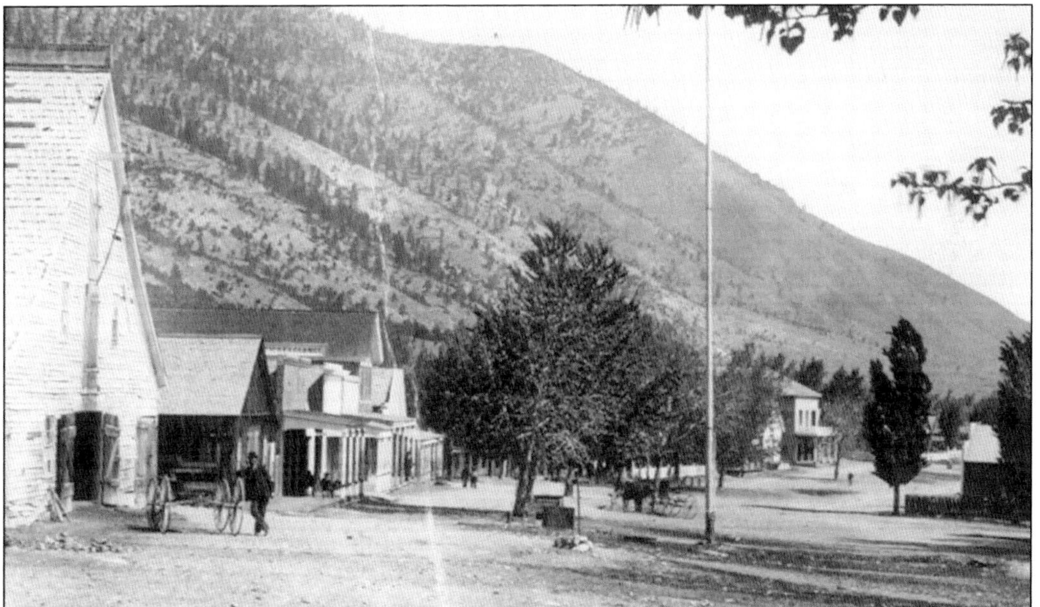

Genoa, the oldest town in Nevada, was settled in 1849 by a small group of Mormons from Salt Lake City who established a trading post to sell supplies to the pioneers traveling to the gold fields of California. The trading post was known as Mormon Station. In 1851, John Reese and about 20 other Mormon businessmen arrived to build a small community. The name of the town was changed to Genoa in 1855, when it became the county seat of Carson County in the Utah Territory. Genoa is seen here in 1875. (Courtesy of the Douglas County Historical Society.)

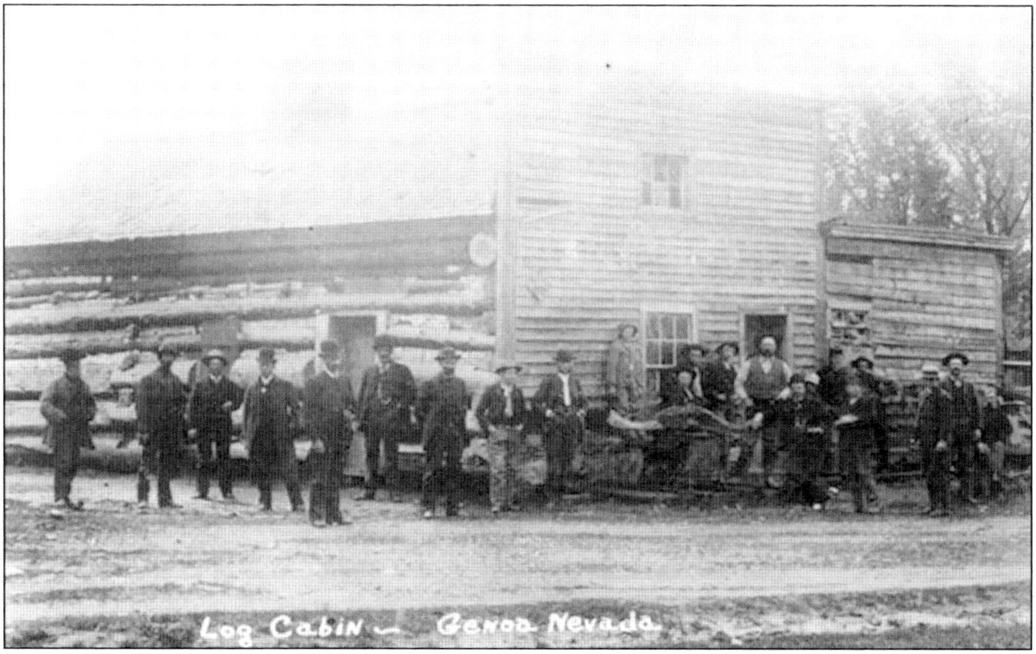

In 1859, a territorial convention was held in Genoa to organize the Territory of Nevada. Statehood was achieved in 1864. Genoa became the county seat of Douglas County in the new territory and the new state. This photograph of the old Mormon Station shows teamsters standing around waiting for their wagons to be ready to take on the trail to California or to Virginia City. (Courtesy of the Douglas County Historical Society.)

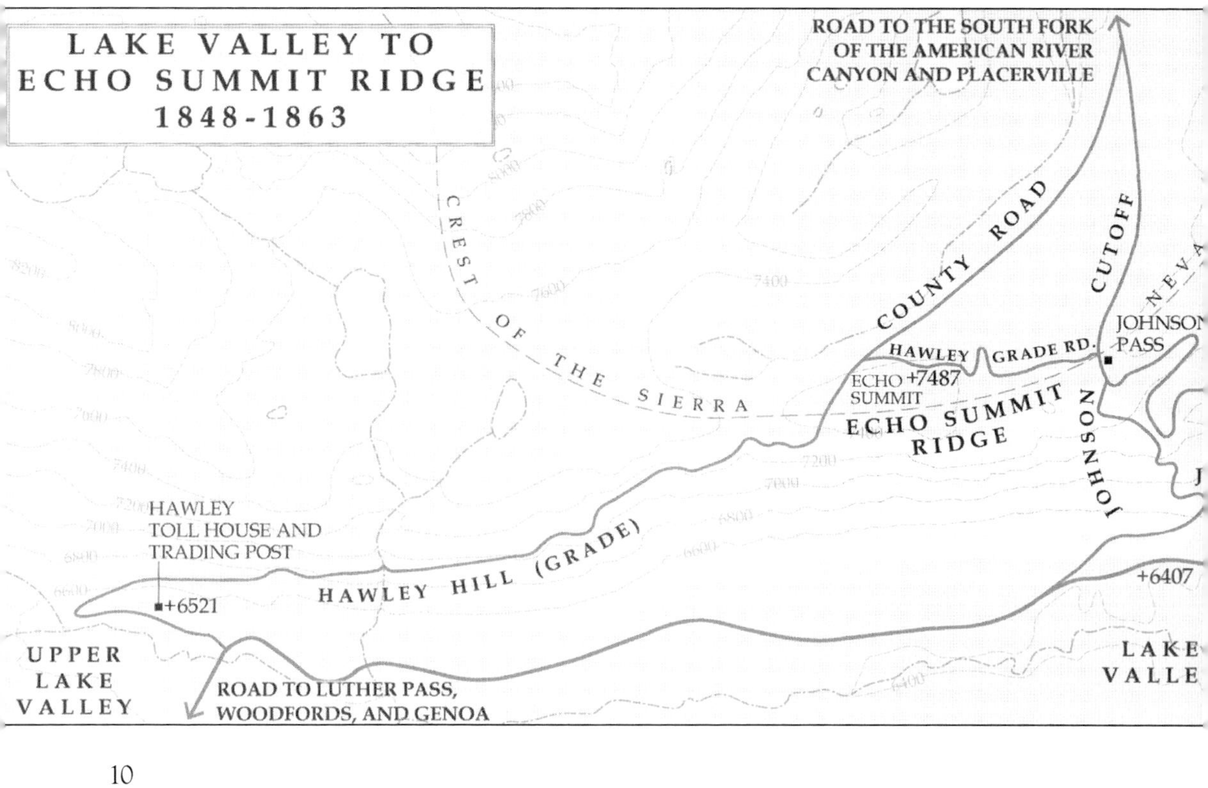

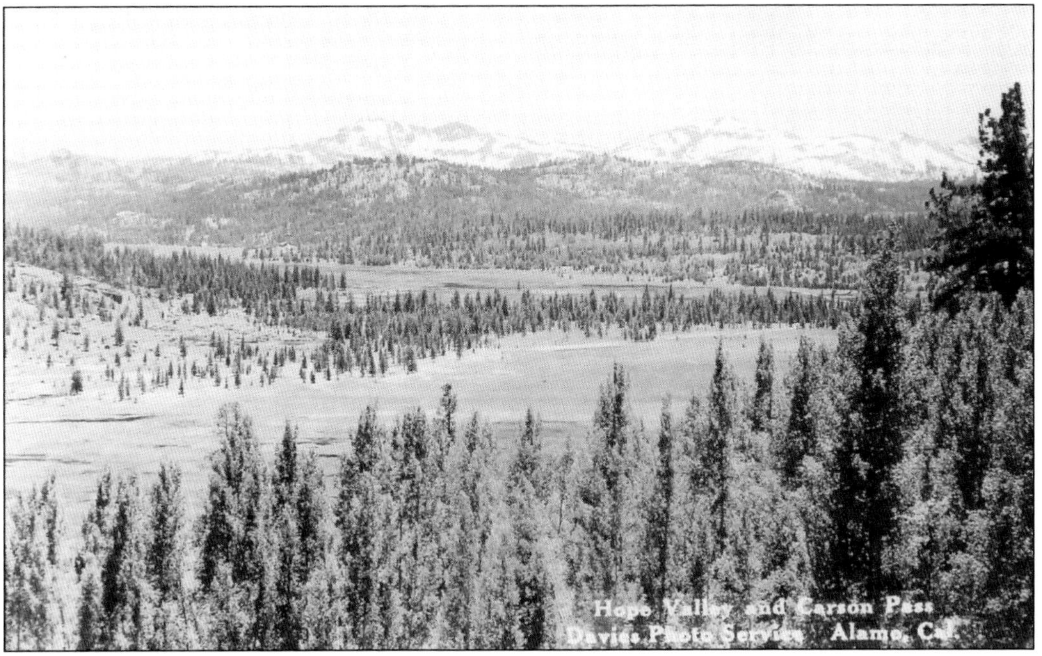

Pioneers taking a southern route from Utah in the early 1840s and the 1850s would travel south up the Carson Valley, through the Carson River Canyon, and into Hope Valley. They would cross the Sierra Nevada crest at Carson Pass, 8,500 feet in elevation, and West Summit Pass at 9,300 feet. The travelers would then proceed down the Emigrant Trail to the area of what is today Pollock Pines and Camino. (Courtesy of Paul DeWitt.)

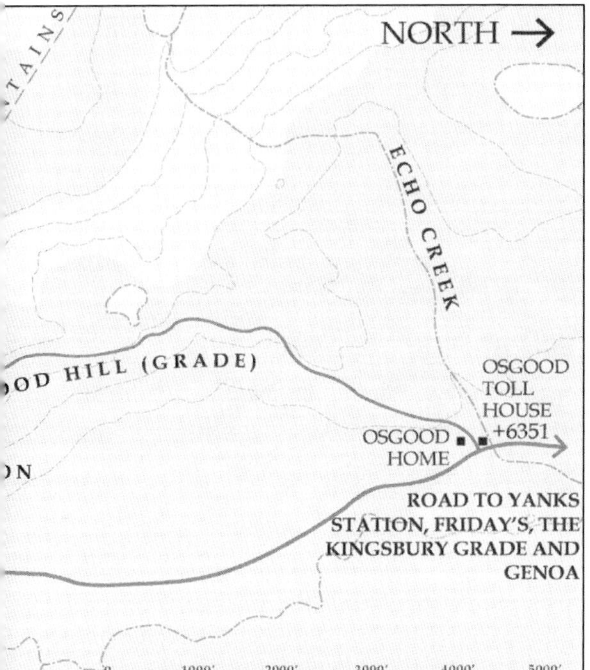

John "Cockeyed" Johnson was quite a trailblazer in the late 1840s. He wanted to shorten the route from Carson Valley to Placerville and to cross the Sierra Nevada Mountains at a lower elevation. His trail became known as the Johnson Cutoff. It crossed two passes, one at 7,200 feet and one at 7,400 feet. When Johnson came to the valley below Echo Summit, he followed old Indian trails to reach the top. This part of his trail is known as Johnson Hill. (Courtesy of Al DeWitt.)

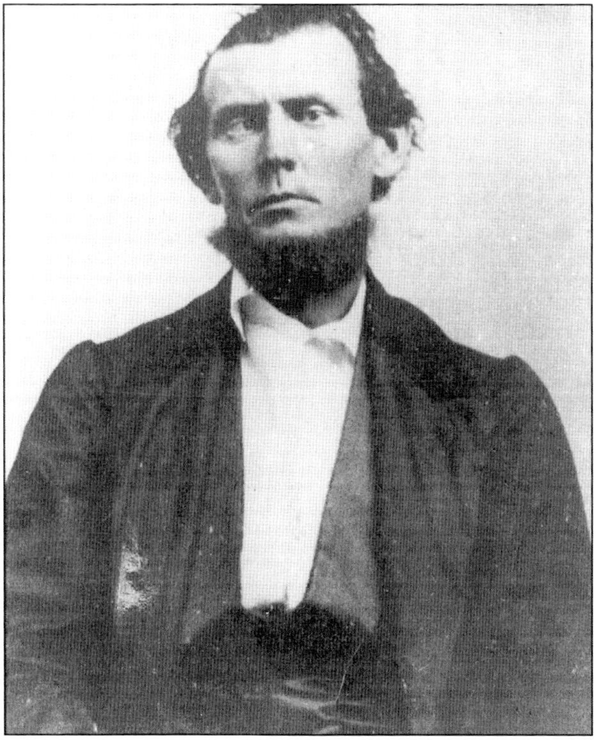

The climb up Johnson Hill was almost 1,000 feet, with a grade in some places at more than 40 degrees. Sometimes, riders would dismount and pull their horses up the slope. Pack animals could make it with difficulty. Wagons were usually unloaded, their oxen unhitched, and everything was hauled up the grade by manpower, hoists, pulleys, and block and tackle. In some cases, it took two days to make it to the summit. John "Cockeyed" Johnson settled on a ranch near Camino in about 1850 and raised a family of seven children. In 1876, he went to Arizona to purchase land for another ranch. On September 13, 1876, John and a friend were attacked and killed by Apache Indians. (Courtesy of the El Dorado County Historical Museum.)

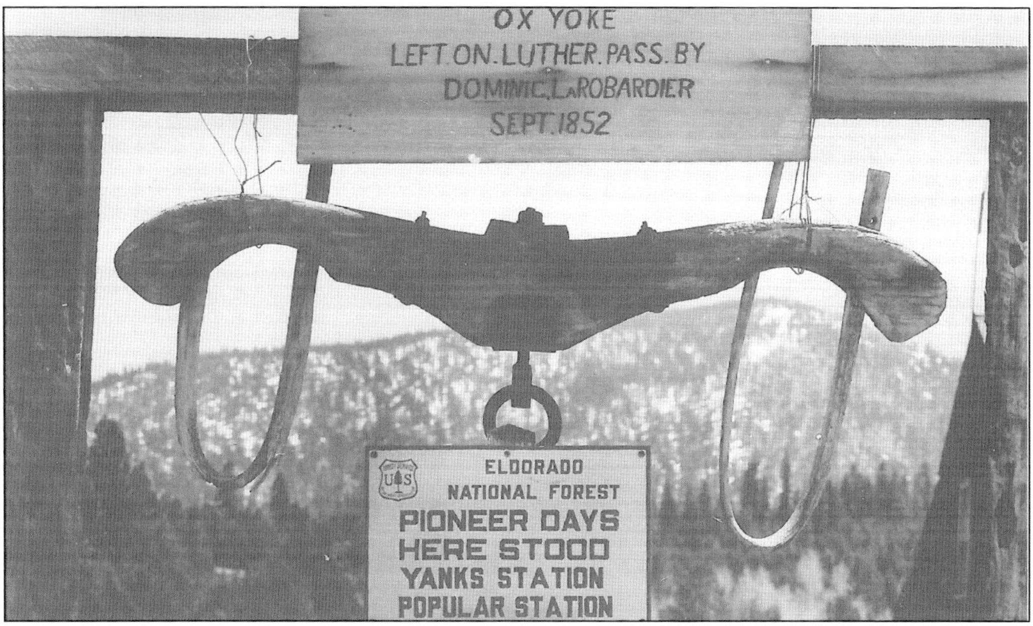

In 1851, two men were carrying mail from Placerville to Genoa. They took the Johnson Cutoff to Lake Valley. They turned south to go up the valley and over a pass to meet the Carson Valley trail in Hope Valley and headed to Genoa. In 1852, Ira M. Luther was going to the gold fields of El Dorado County by the Carson Valley and Pass. When he reached Hope Valley, he made a right turn and headed his covered wagon over a low plateau and into Upper Lake Valley. This route became known as Luther Pass. (Courtesy of Paul DeWitt.)

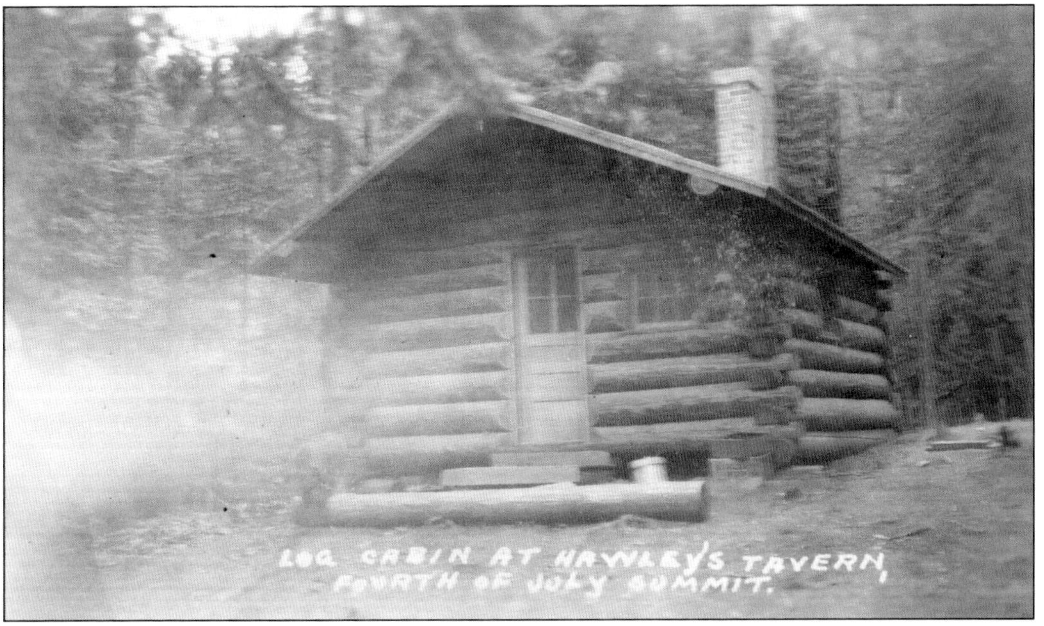

Asa Hawley was the second pioneer to settle in the Lake Valley area of the Lake Tahoe Basin. He arrived in 1855 and opened a trading post. Hawley soon built a two-story lodge with an immense fireplace and dining room in the back. Upstairs were sleeping accommodations for 20 people. He also had stables and a barn. His establishment was known as Lake Valley House. (Courtesy of Dorothy De Mare.)

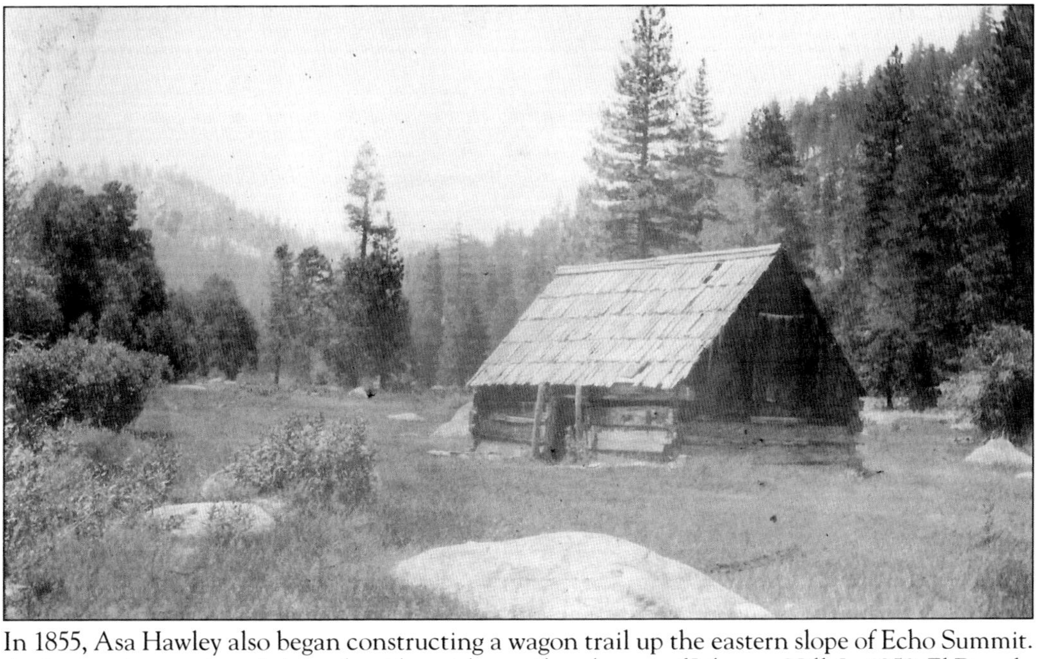

In 1855, Asa Hawley also began constructing a wagon trail up the eastern slope of Echo Summit. At the top, he continued along the ridge with a trail to the top of Johnson Hill. In 1858, El Dorado and Sacramento Counties paid to build a road to the top of Hawley's Grade. Wagons began using the grade to get to Lake Valley, Luther Pass, and Genoa until 1860. Photographed above in 1916 is Hawley's barn. (Courtesy of Miles Celio.)

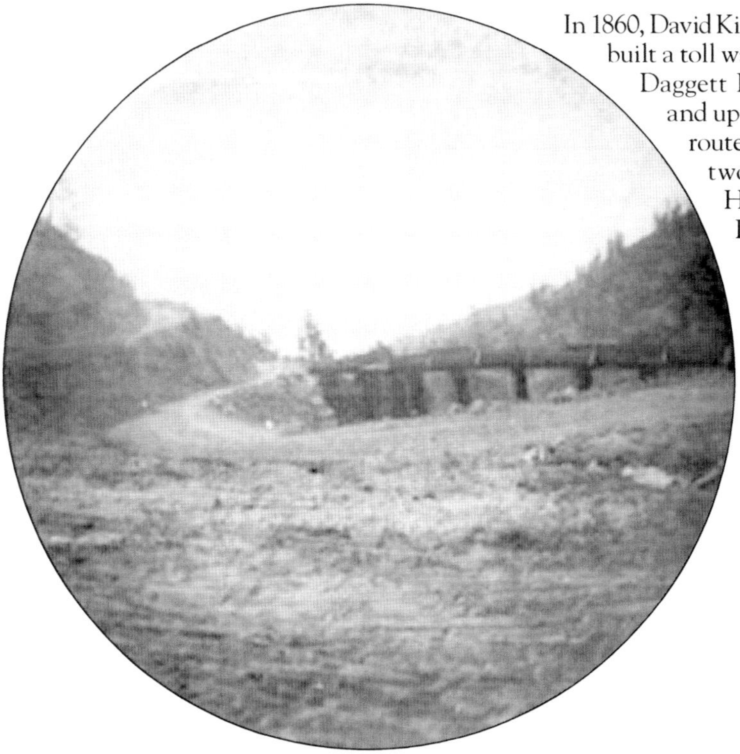

In 1860, David Kingsbury and John McDonald built a toll wagon trail from Genoa, over Daggett Pass, through Lake Valley, and up to Echo Summit. This new route cut 15 miles and a day or two of travel time from the Hawley Grade and Luther Pass road. This photograph shows the early Kingsbury Grade climbing out of Genoa and a flume to send logs from the Daggett Pass area to the sawmill in Genoa. (Courtesy of Douglas County Historical Society.)

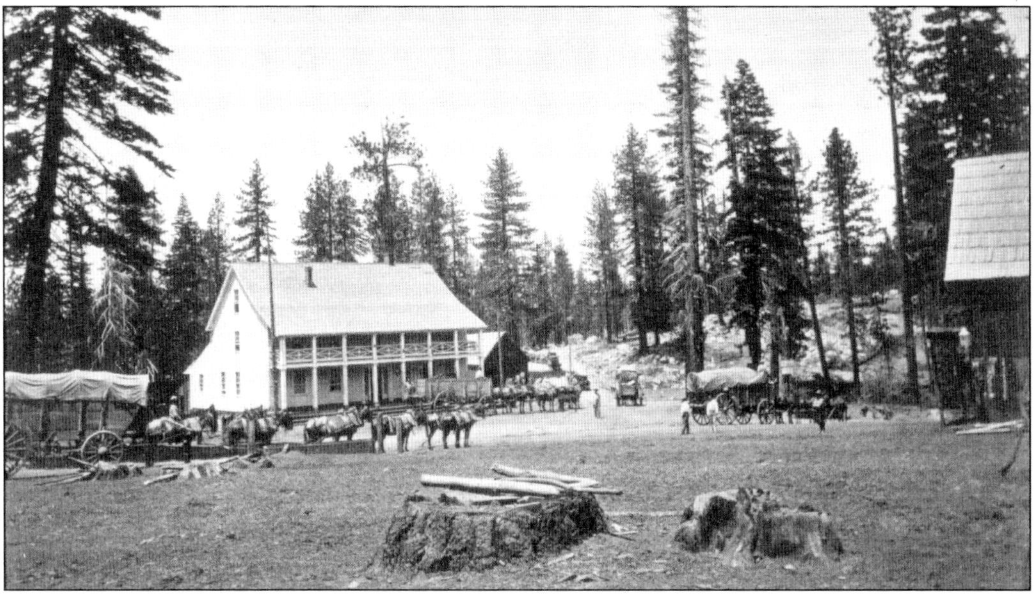

Friday's Station was the first way station that travelers would come to after going over Daggett Pass on the Kingsbury Grade. Martin K. "Friday" Burke and James Washington Small built Friday's Station in 1859. It provided meals and sleeping arrangements for teamsters and stagecoach passengers, and stables, grain, and hay for livestock. Today, Friday's is known as Edgewood, a private, gated estate on Highway 50, near the Kingsbury Grade exit. (Courtesy of the Society of California Pioneers.)

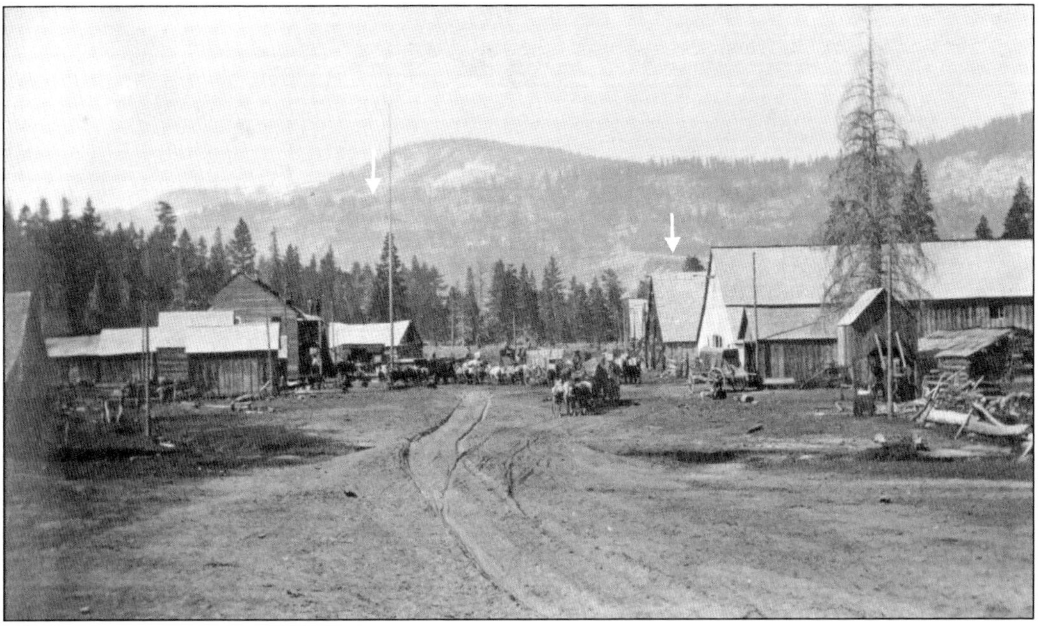

Martin Smith was the first pioneer to settle in Lake Valley, in 1851. In 1859, Ephraim "Yank" Clement purchased Smith's property, which became known as Yank's Station. It was located on the toll road from the Kingsbury Grade to Echo Summit. The Echo Summit ridge is seen in the background of this 1864 photograph. The arrow on the left indicates Johnson Pass; the right arrow is pointing to Osgood Grade. (Courtesy of the Society of California Pioneers.)

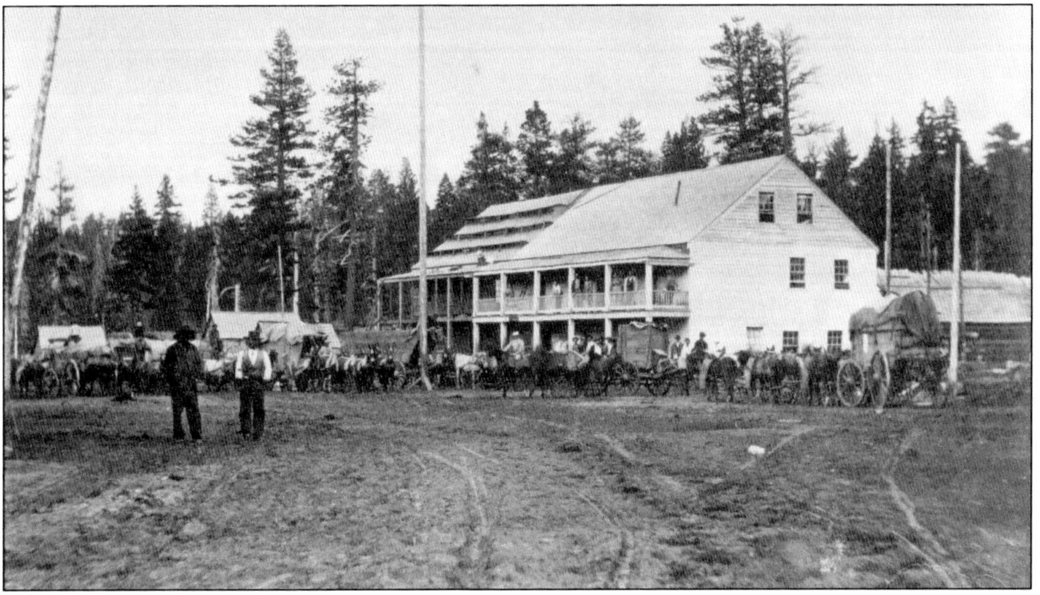

Yank's Station was one of the most popular places in Lake Valley. Drivers of stagecoaches and freight wagons coming down Osgood Grade and heading to Virginia City would stop for meals and a place to spend the night. Local residents would come to Yank's for parties and conversation. Yank's Station declined in business after 1869. Ephraim Clement sold the station to George Meyers, a local farmer, in 1873. The name of the station was changed to Meyers. (Courtesy of the Society of California Pioneers.)

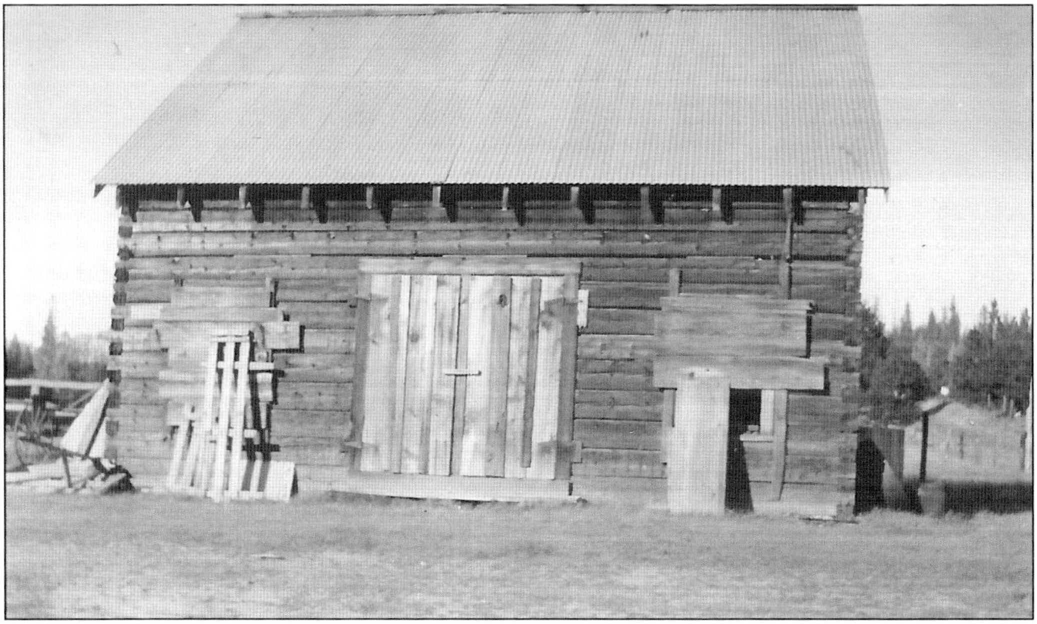

Nehemiah Osgood came to Lake Valley in 1859 and was employed by David Kingsbury and John McDonald to build the Osgood Grade from Lake Valley to Echo Summit and to operate the Osgood Toll House at the base of the grade. The tollhouse was situated between the grade and Echo Creek, next to the Luther Pass road. Osgood built his home on the other side of the grade. This photograph shows the tollhouse in Meyers in 1916. (Courtesy of Miles Celio.)

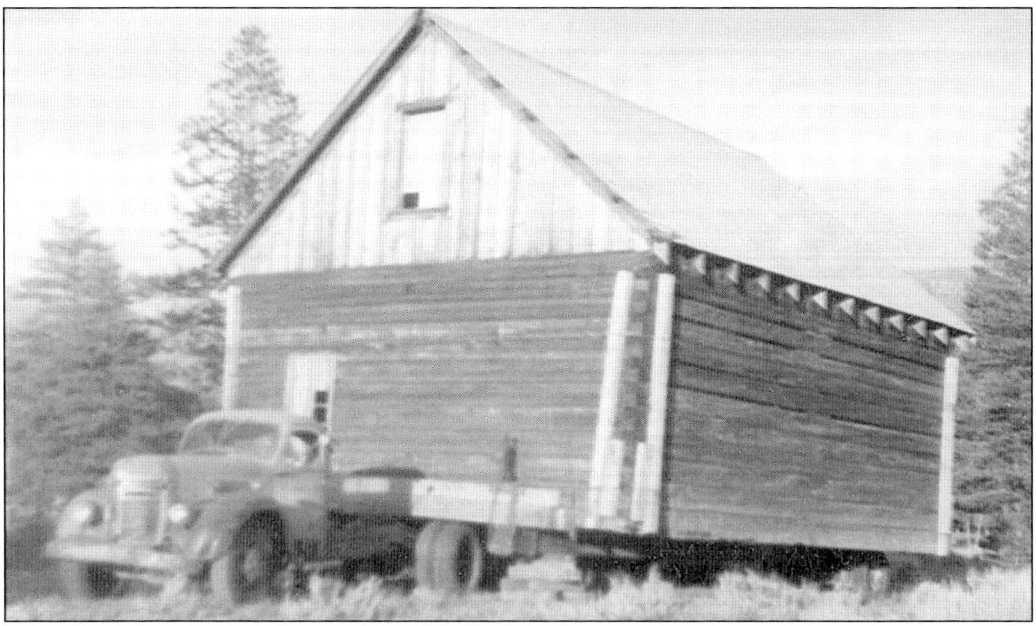

In 1866, Osgood was named superintendent of the Kingsbury-McDonald Toll Road, from North America House, just west of Johnson Pass, to Genoa. California bought all of the toll roads and made them free public roads in 1892. In 1911, the dam on Echo Lake collapsed and flooded Lake Valley, washing the old Osgood Toll House off its foundation. The Celio family moved the tollhouse to Meyers. (Courtesy of the Lake Tahoe Historical Society.)

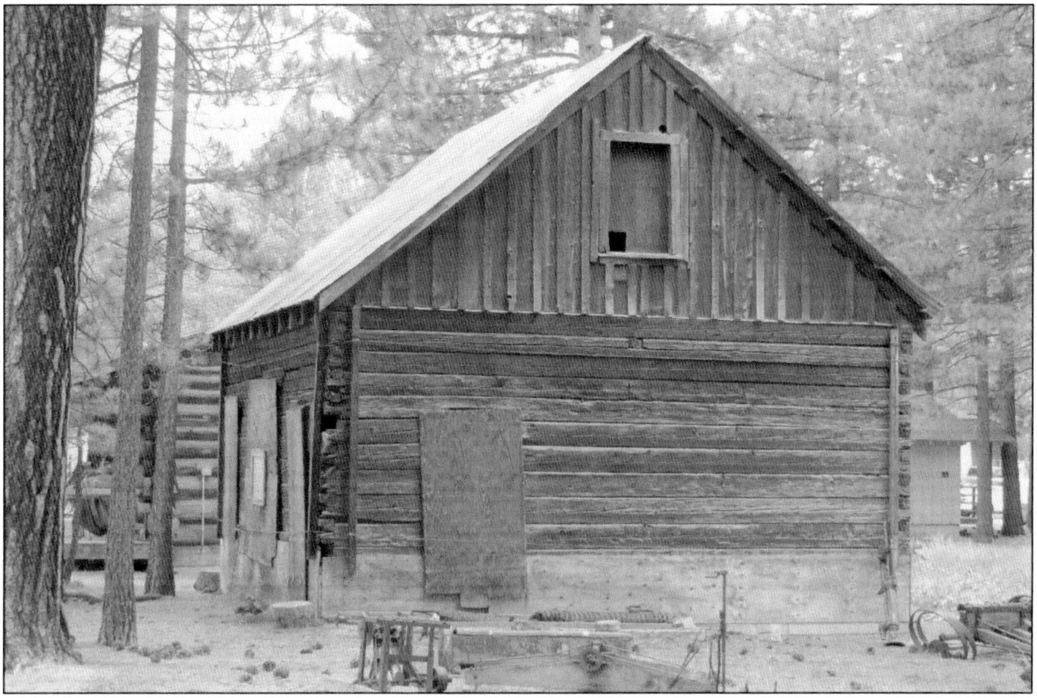

The Celio family donated the Osgood Toll House to the Lake Tahoe Historical Society in 1975. Local citizens loaded the tollhouse onto a truck and moved it to the museum in South Lake Tahoe. Unlike Friday's Station, which is an immaculate estate, the tollhouse has weathered extensively over the years. What holds it together are the large interlocking timbers that make up the walls, and the vertical braces and cables supporting the structure. (Courtesy of Paul DeWitt.)

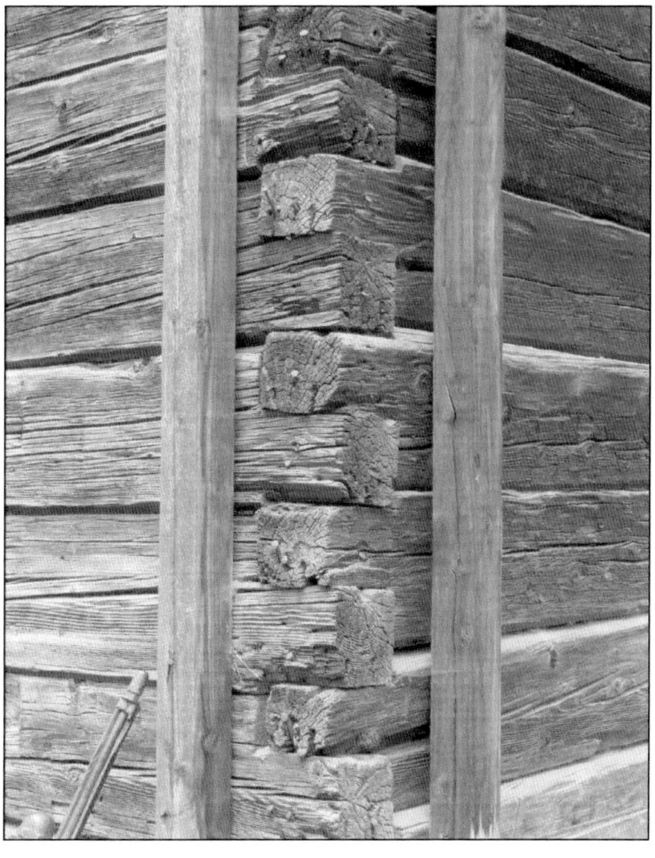

The Osgood Toll House is the oldest building in South Lake Tahoe, on the California side of the state line. Although the structure looks dilapidated, the Lake Tahoe Historical Society hopes to refurbish it and turn it into a community hall and an assembly center. (Courtesy of Paul DeWitt.)

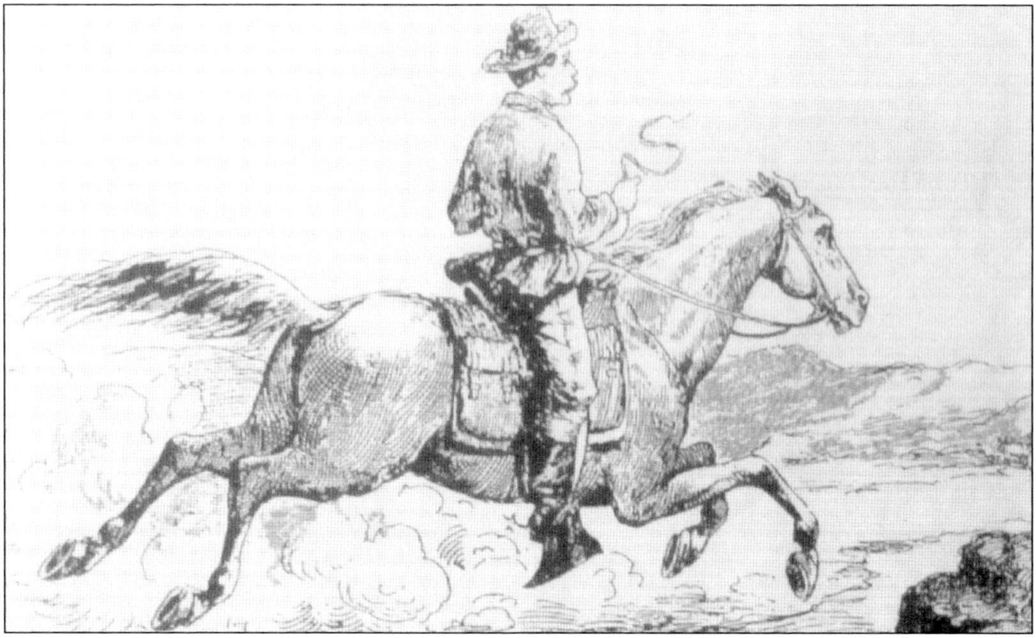

The Pony Express carried mail from St. Joseph, Missouri, to Sacramento, California, from April 3, 1860, to November 20, 1861. The first rider from Sacramento entered Lake Valley by coming down the Hawley Grade to change horses at Lake Valley Station and then headed off for Luther Pass, Woodfords, and Genoa. The Pony Express route was shortened with the opening of the Kingsbury Grade in late 1860. (Courtesy of the Genoa Court House Museum.)

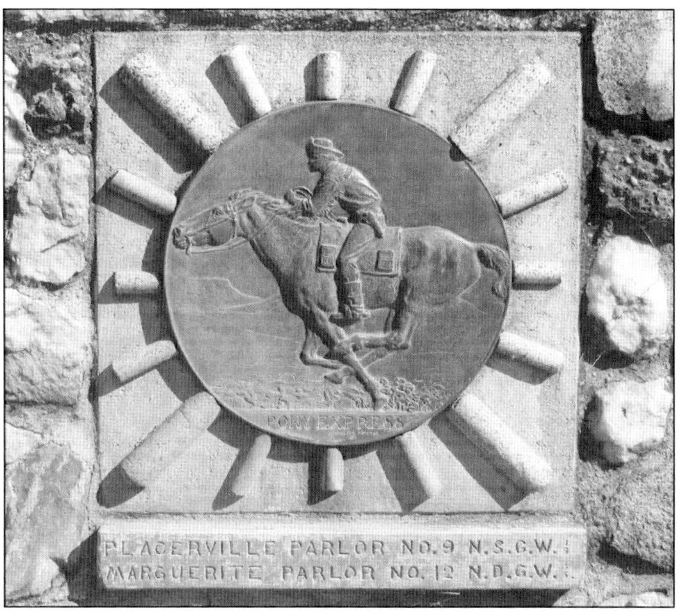

Pony Express riders took the Kingsbury Grade into the Tahoe Basin. At Friday's, a home station, riders and horses were changed. They rode on to Yank's Station for another change of horses. From Yank's, the riders galloped up the Osgood Grade and crossed Echo Summit at Johnson Pass. This plaque was placed at all Pony Express stations in California in 1935. There are still two plaques between Placerville and South Lake Tahoe, at Sportsman's Hall and at Pacific House. (Courtesy of Paul DeWitt.)

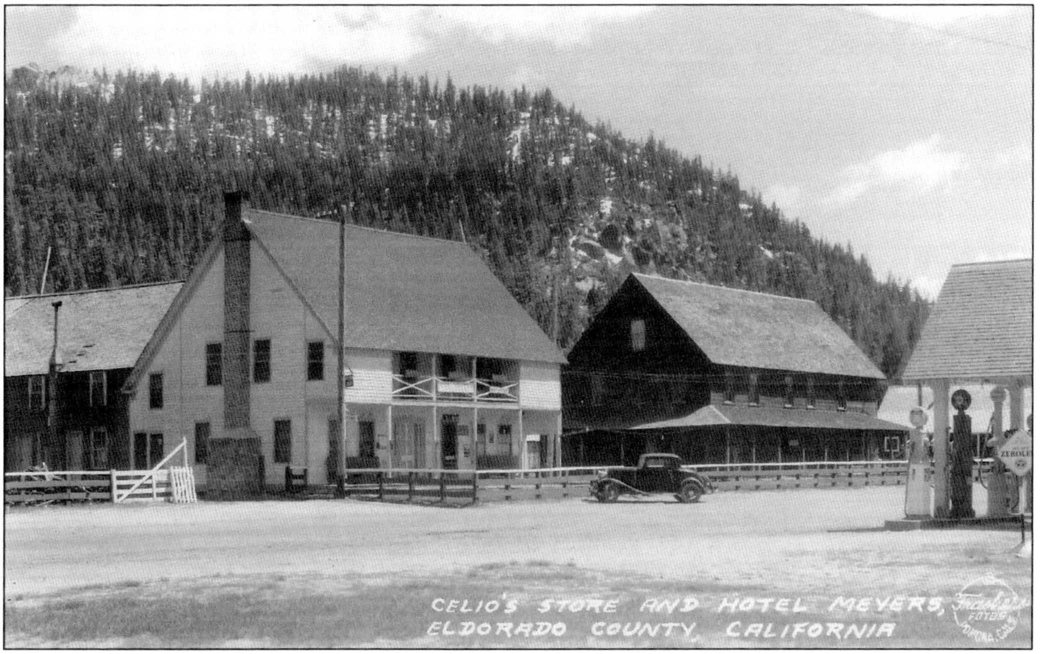

George Meyers owned the town of Meyers for 30 years. In 1903, he sold it and 1,400 acres to C.G. Celio & Sons, Inc. The Celio family tried to change the name to Celio Station, but the new name was never accepted. The post office kept the Meyers name, and the highway department has always identified the town as Meyers. Ephraim Clements erected the two buildings facing the road in the 1860s. They were destroyed by fire in November 1938. (Courtesy of Paul DeWitt.)

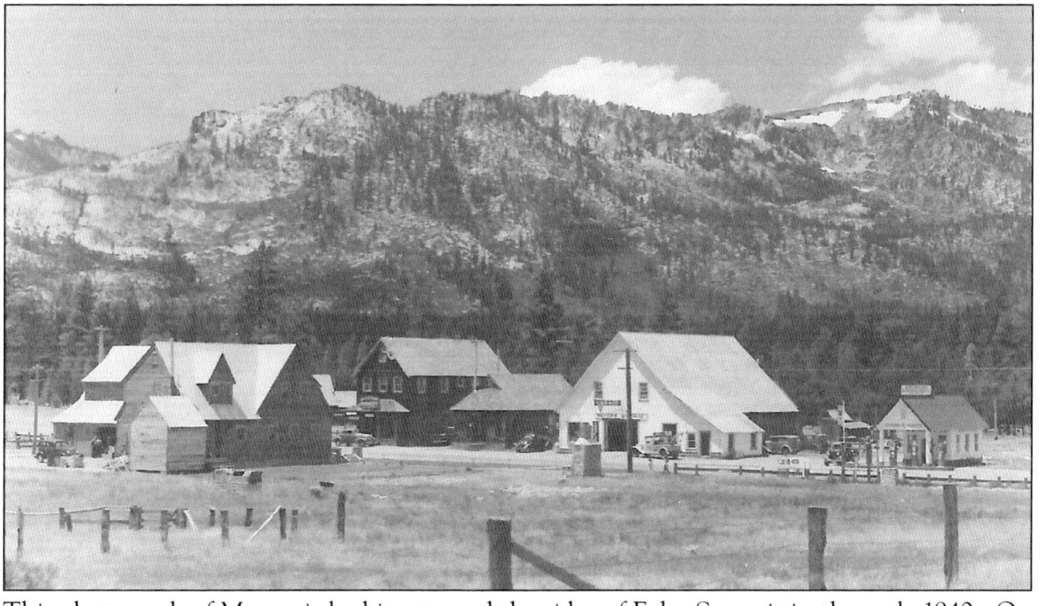

This photograph of Meyers is looking toward the ridge of Echo Summit in the early 1940s. On the right is the gas station, and next to it is the garage that was originally built as a stable in the 1860s. The next building is the former post office, and the two-story structure at center is the meat market. The back of the new Meyers store, the post office, and the hotel are on the left. (Courtesy of Miles Celio.)

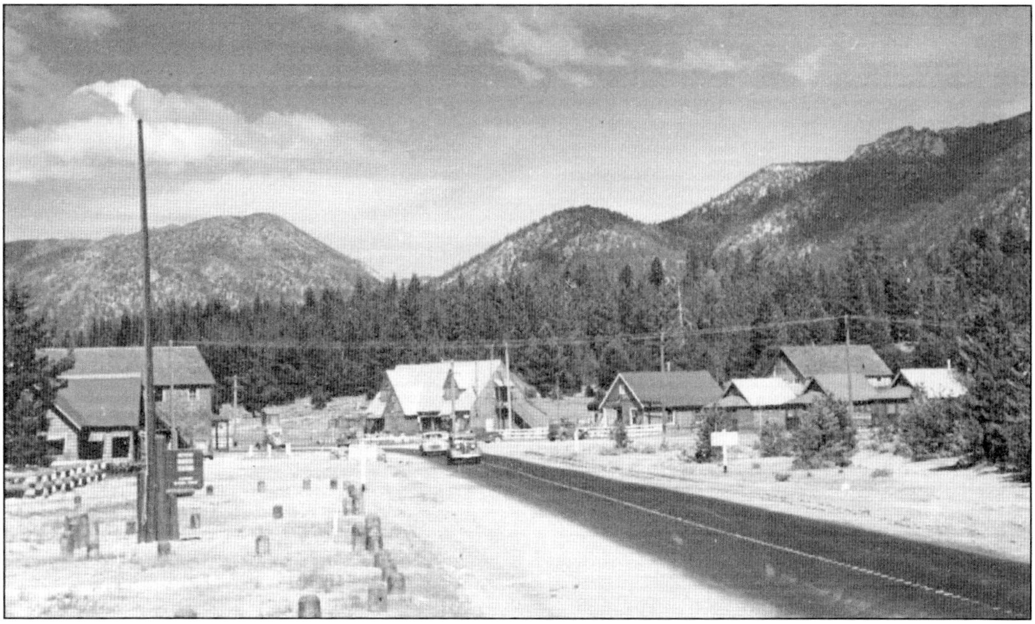

A visitor driving into Meyers from Echo Summit in the 1940s would see many other buildings as part of the community. Several private homes are on the right. The flagpole on the left marks the entrance to the Forest Service Lake Tahoe headquarters for El Dorado National Forest. (Courtesy of Shirley Taylor.)

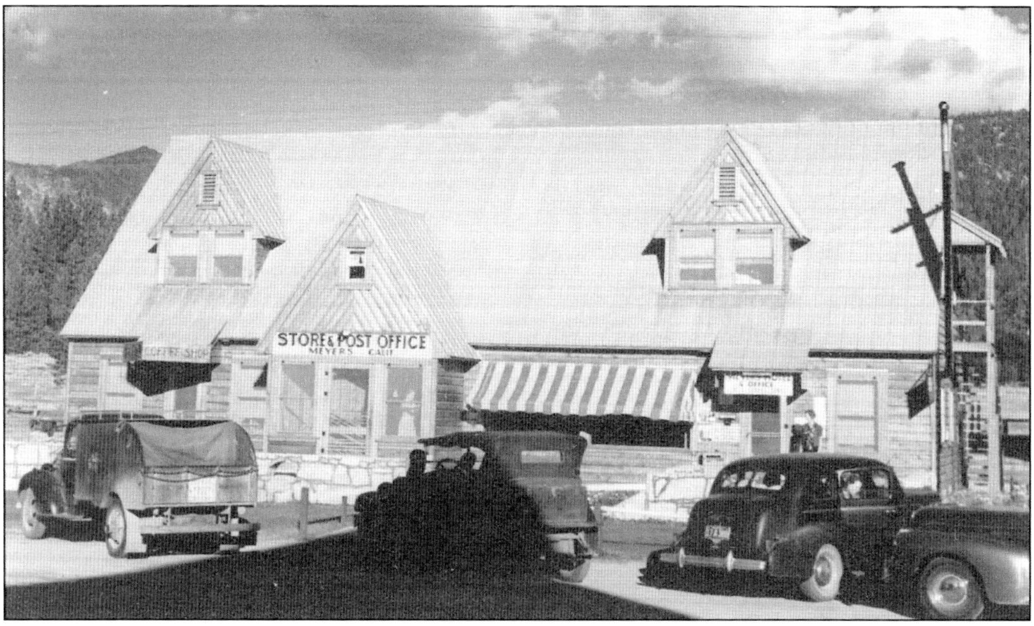

By 1950, the Celio family was getting older and decided to sell all of its properties to real estate developers, who tore down Meyers to create their own community, Tahoe Paradise. The post office name was even changed to Tahoe Paradise. The developers' venture was not too successful. The highway department still called the community Meyers. In 2002, the Tahoe Paradise Post Office was closed and a new post office was built with the new name of Meyers, named after the Meyers community. (Courtesy of Shirley Taylor.)

Two

Approaching Echo Summit from Placerville and the South Fork of the American River

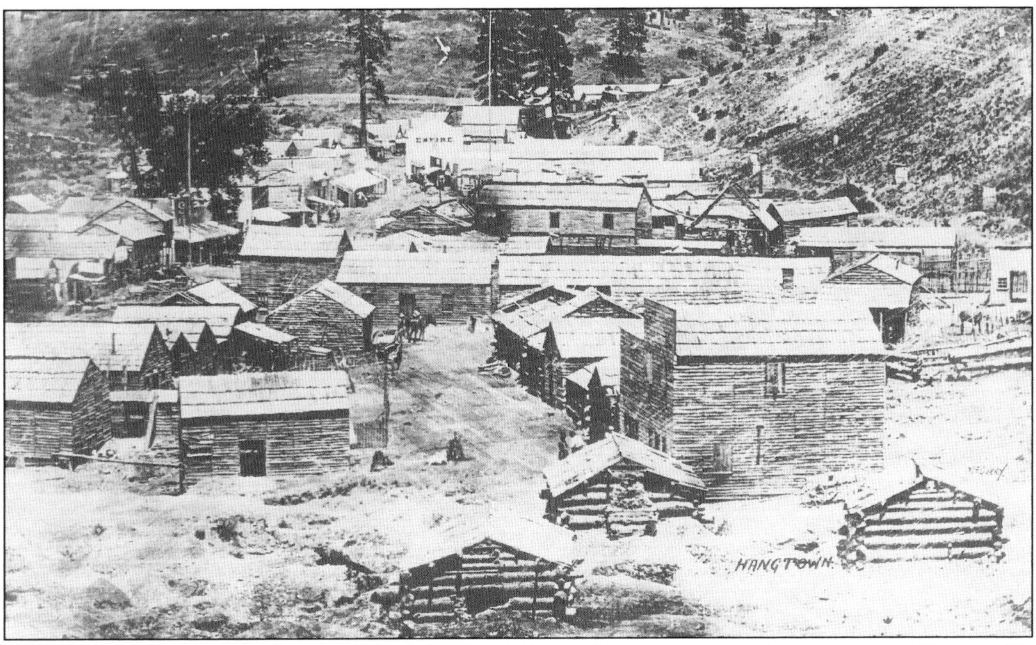

After the discovery of gold in 1849 in the foothills of the Sierra Nevada Mountains, Placerville (Hangtown, as it was known then) became the western terminus of the emigrant trek from Genoa, over Echo Summit, down the American River Canyon, and into the gold-mining regions of western El Dorado County. This direction of travel was reversed in 1859, when thousands of people traveled east after the discovery of silver and gold in the Comstock Lode of Virginia City. (Courtesy of Paul DeWitt.)

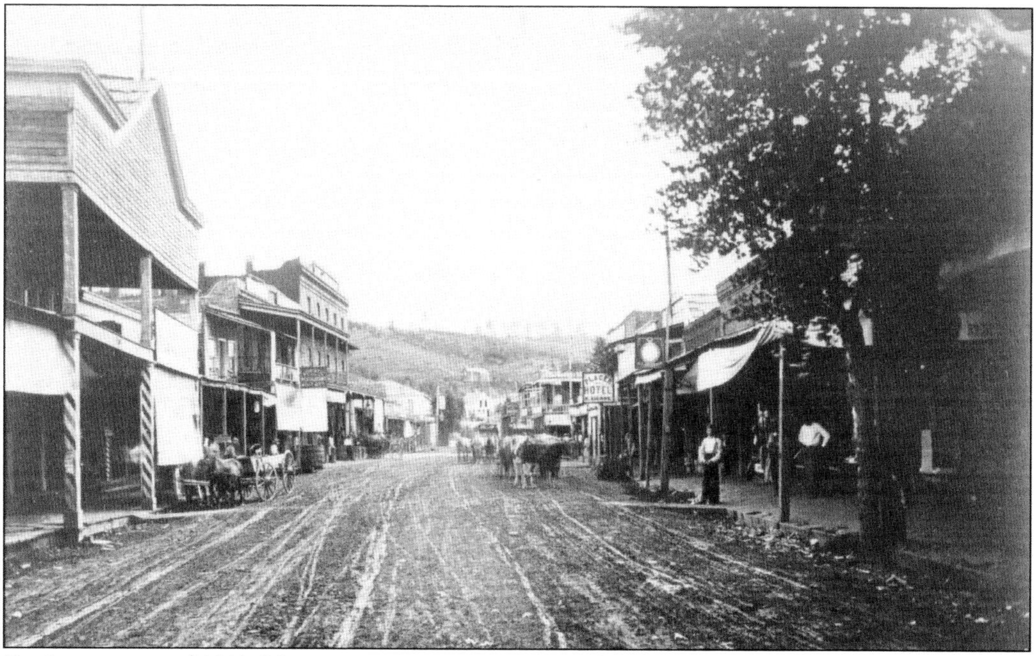

By the summer of 1849, Hangtown was a major center for gold mining. In 1852, Placerville was incorporated as the third-largest town in the state, with 4,000 people by 1853. It became the county seat in 1857. A major fire wiped out most of the business area in 1856. In 1857, William Cary built the Cary Hotel (far left) on Main Street. With all the new construction, Placerville began rising from the ashes of old Hangtown. (Courtesy of the Society of California Pioneers.)

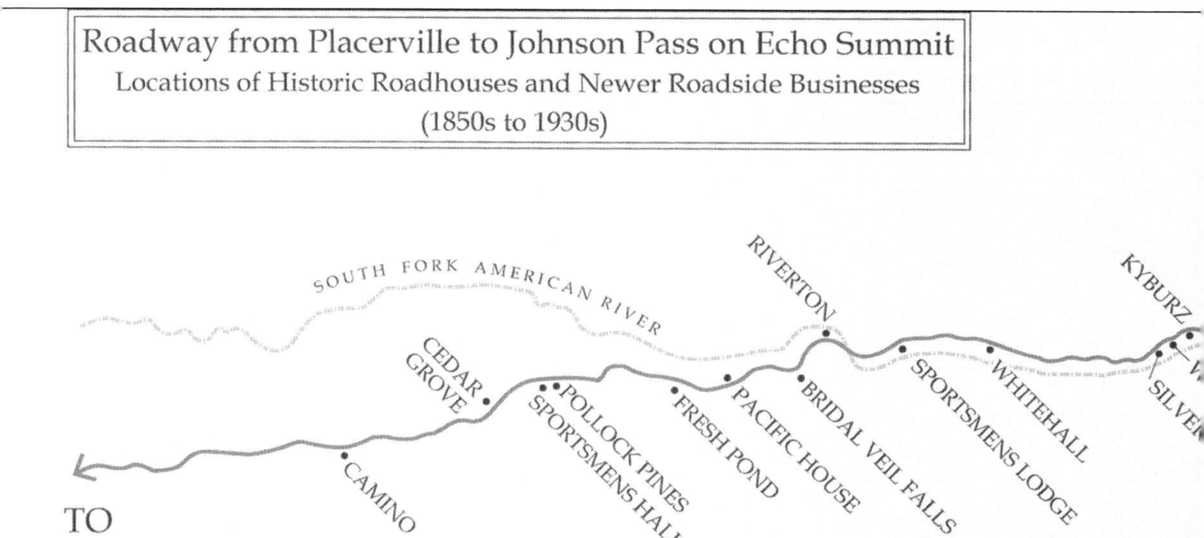

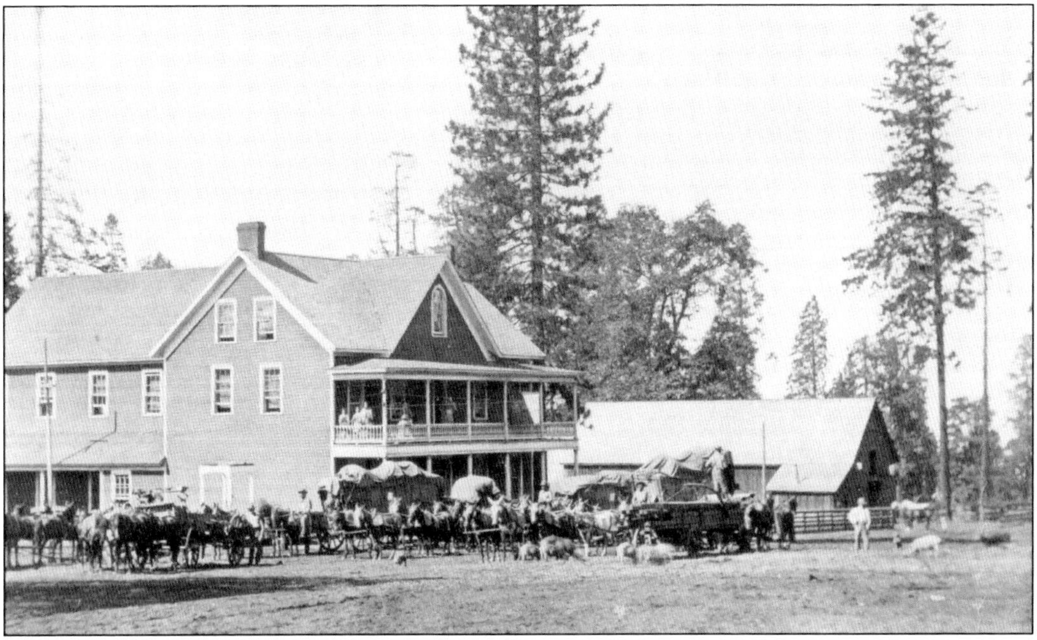

Built in about 1853 by John and James Blair, this 1864 photograph of the original Sportsman's Hall shows a very ornate, three-story structure serving stagecoaches and teamsters headed for the Comstock Lode. At times, there were up to 1,000 horses and mules in the stables and corrals during the early spring to the late fall. This Sportsman's Hall burned down in 1868. It was rebuilt as a much smaller structure. Today, it is a shuttered bar and restaurant that is for sale. (Courtesy of the Society of California Pioneers.)

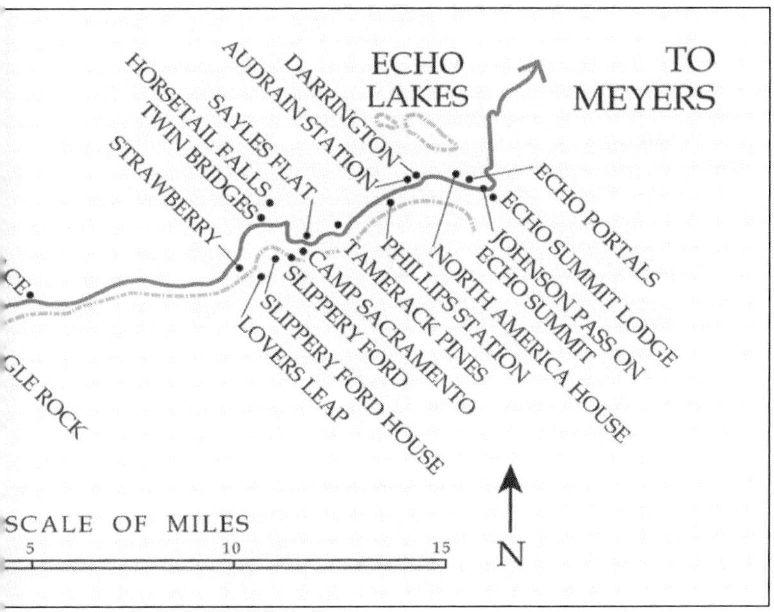

The direction of travel from Placerville over Echo Summit to Genoa became the main route for stagecoaches, freight wagons, and peddlers to the Comstock Lode until 1868 when the Central Pacific Railroad completed its tracks from Sacramento to Reno making a quicker route to Virginia City. Travelers on the Placerville-Genoa road dwindled to a small number. Many of the roadhouses and way stations disappeared in the 1870s. (Courtesy of Al DeWitt.)

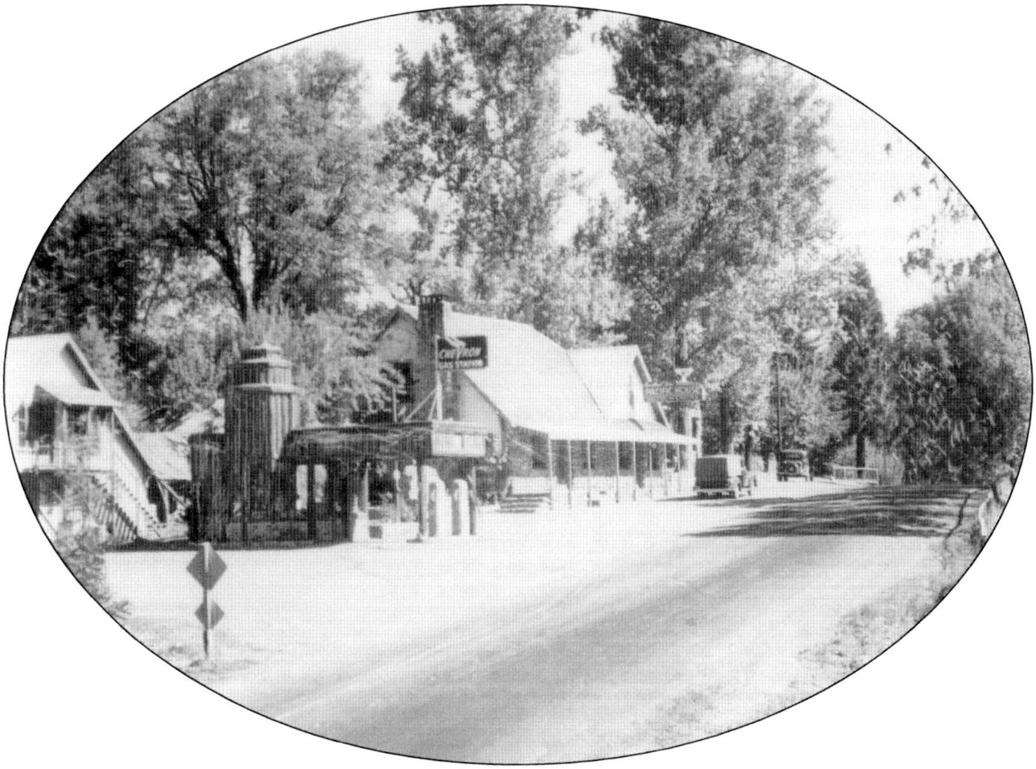

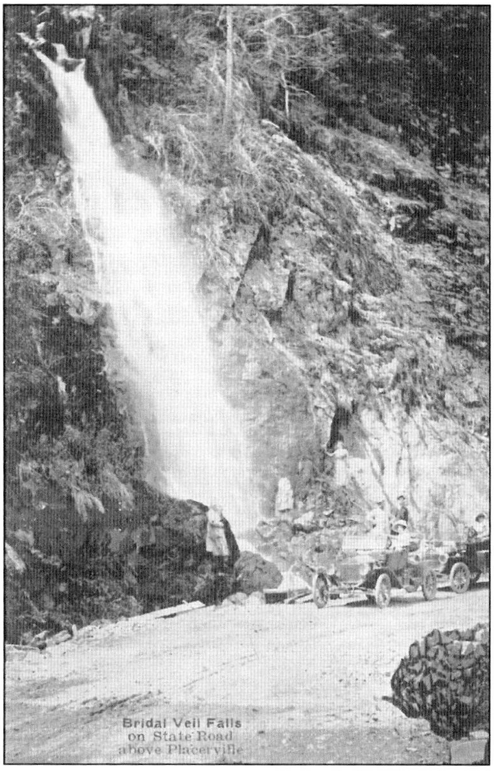

Built in 1849 and called 18-Mile House, Pacific House was a stage and freight stop along the Placerville-Genoa road. Among guests who traveled this road were Mark Twain, Horace Greeley, and Thomas Starr King. Pacific House was a Pony Express relay station from April 1860 until October 1861 when the Overland Telegraph was completed. The Pacific post office operated from March 10, 1880, until November 15, 1893, resuming on September 15, 1894, as Pacific House until June 1, 1958. By 1940, little remained of the original stone inn. (Courtesy of Dorothy De Mare.)

Bridal Veil Falls was originally known as Esmeralda Falls. It has always been a place of beauty with clear water cascading down the mountainside and under the roadway. In the old days, the falls served as a thirst-quenching stop for stagecoach drivers, teamsters, livestock, and steaming automobiles. Even today, people stop to explore the serenity of the falls, as they have for over 150 years. (Courtesy of Paul DeWitt.)

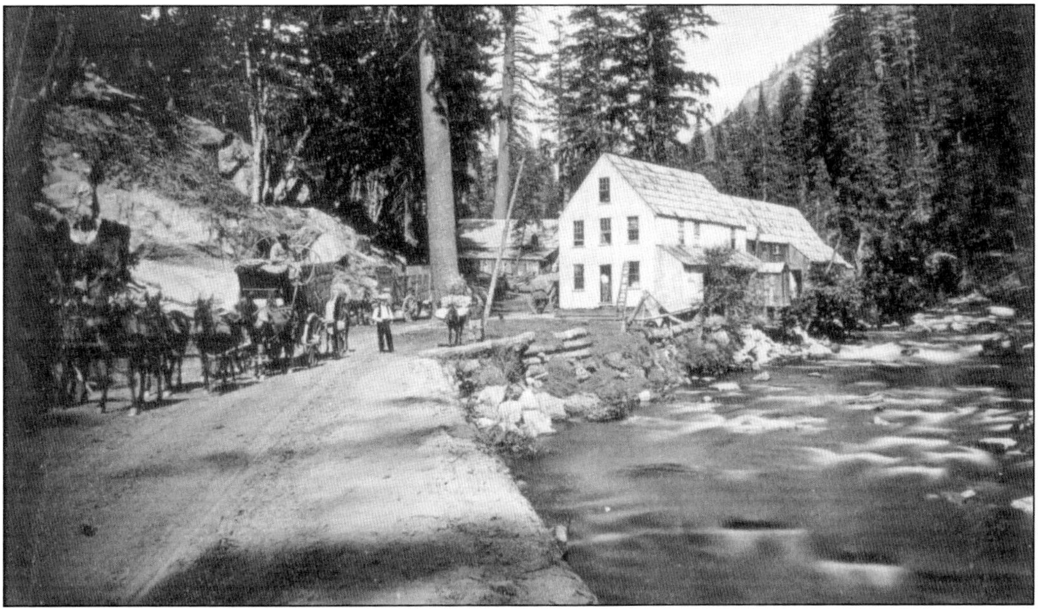

In the early 1850s, Riverton, pictured here, was known as Moore's Station, located on the American River. It became the main crossing point on the American River on the Placerville-Genoa road after floods and fire destroyed two other bridges downriver in the early 1850s. The Pioneer Stage Company operated a saw mill and stables at Moore's Station. Riverton was the lowest point on the American River, with a steep grade going up to Pacific House and Pollock Pines to the west, and a long, 30-mile uphill climb with some steep grades going toward Echo Summit. (Courtesy of the Society of California Pioneers.)

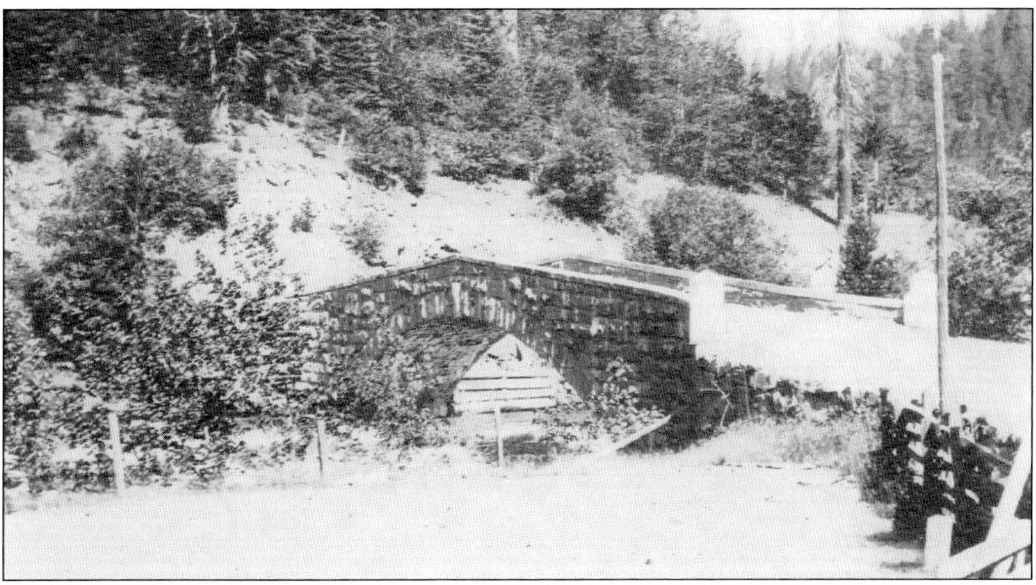

In 1895, the Placerville-Tahoe road became California's first official state road. It was named the Lake Tahoe State Wagon Road. Since the road had not been maintained for years, the state needed to make numerous repairs. The main feat was the construction of a stone arch bridge over the American River at Riverton in 1900. It replaced the original wooden bridge, built in the 1850s. (Courtesy of Dorothy De Mare.)

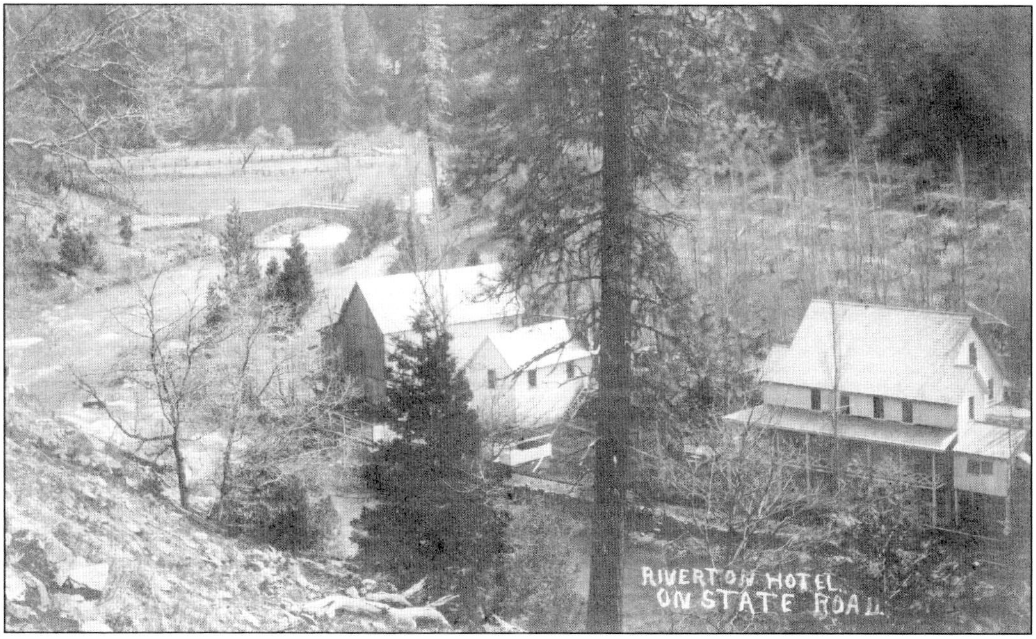

When the Sacramento-to-Reno railroad was built in 1868, the large numbers of teamsters, freight-wagons, peddlers, and stagecoaches going to Virginia City declined to almost nothing. Riverton had to change its identity. It became a resort and hotel for tourists traveling along the road. Hotel lodgings were built over the river, allowing the tourists to view the scenery downriver and to catch trout from their windows. The hotel burned down in the early 1960s. (Courtesy of Paul DeWitt.)

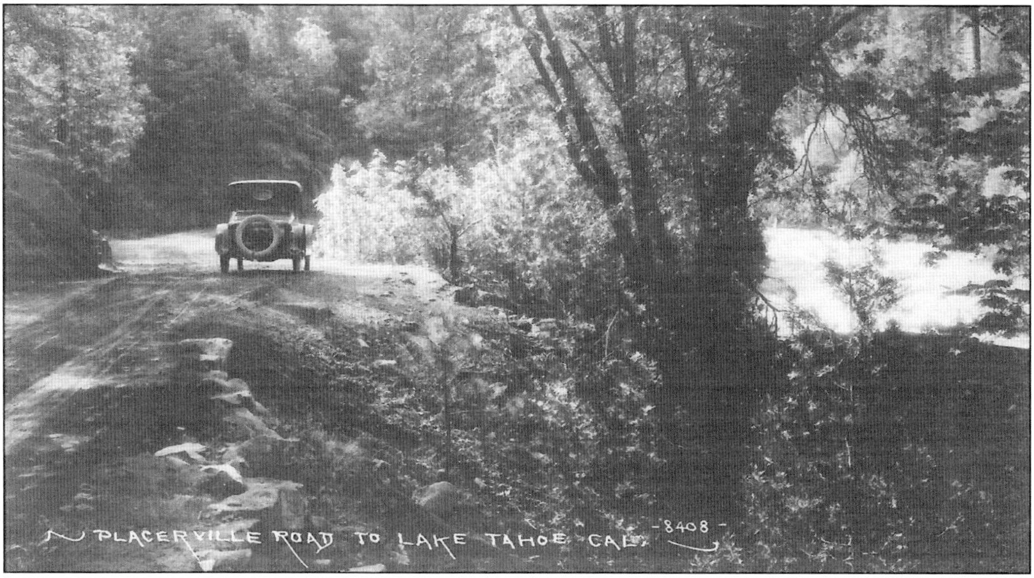

The Placerville-Tahoe road parallels the American River for about 22 miles. In the 1860s, when the road was a muddy track from the snows and rains, one teamster described it as being 50 miles long and five feet deep. The road was sand and dirt into the 1920s, when the State of California oiled it. The state began paving the road with asphalt and concrete in the 1930s. (Courtesy of Dorothy De Mare.)

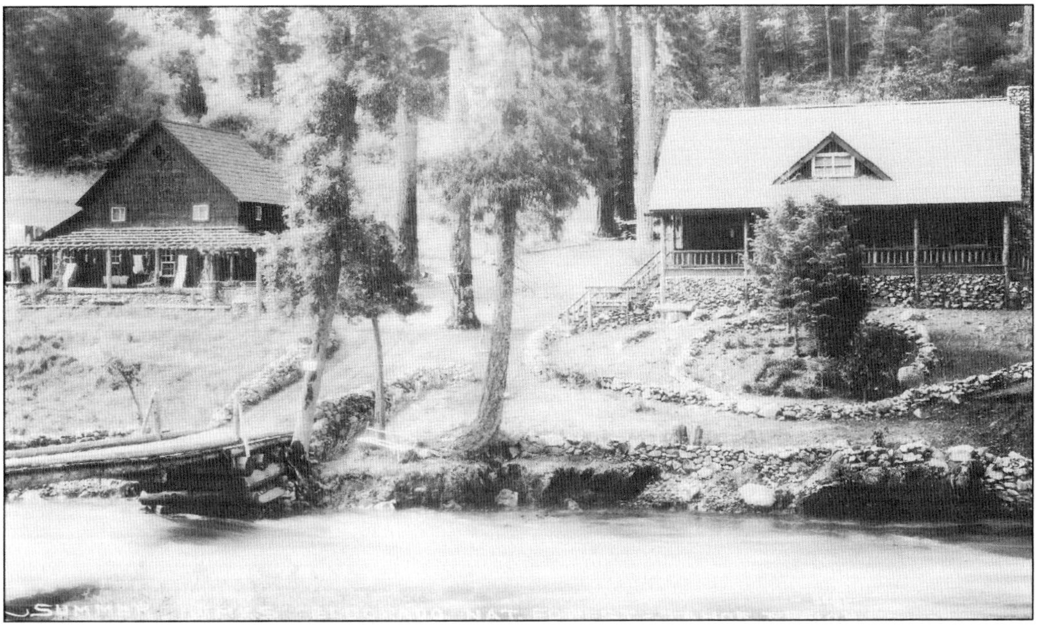

The riverfront cabin on the right was known as Schaffhirt's Lodge. It dated to about 1915. Located across the American River from Whitehall, covered wagons circled along the Schaffhirt's big riverfront bend. A US flag and cannon could be seen on the hillside nearby. Picnics, barbecues, and fellowship brought many of the family's friends and neighbors together, where they enjoyed the symbols of pioneering, patriotism, and peace. (Courtesy of Dorothy De Mare.)

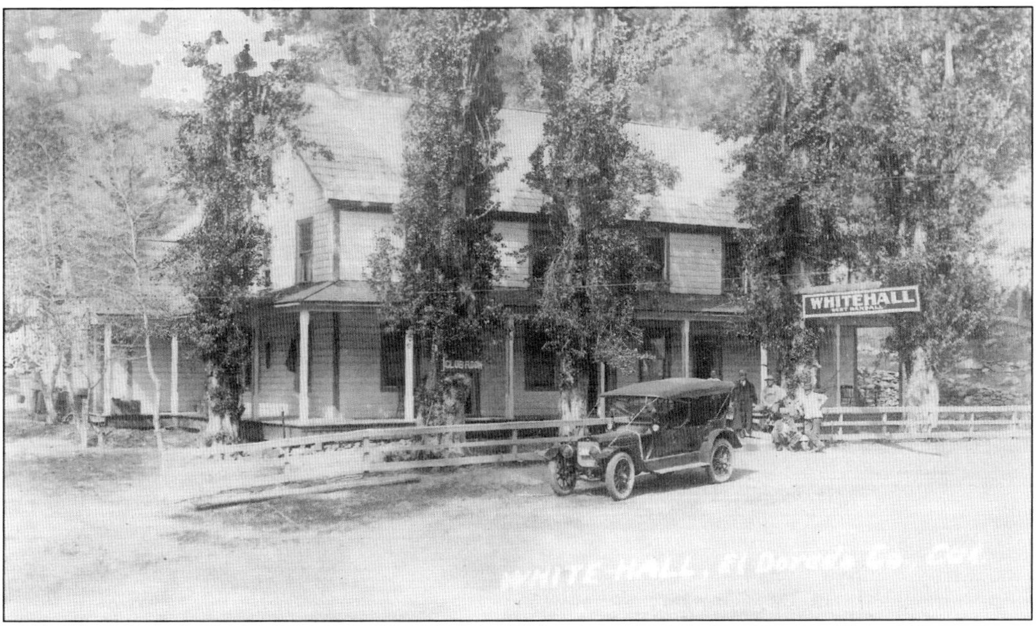

Whitehall was a roadhouse built in the early 1850s, a mile east of its present location. After it was destroyed by snow, a new Whitehall Hotel was built at the new site. This Whitehall Hotel had quite a social life from the early 1900s to the 1920s. For several years, it hired an orchestra from Sacramento to play on Saturday nights. Everyone from miles around came to dance until late in the evenings. (Courtesy of Paul DeWitt.)

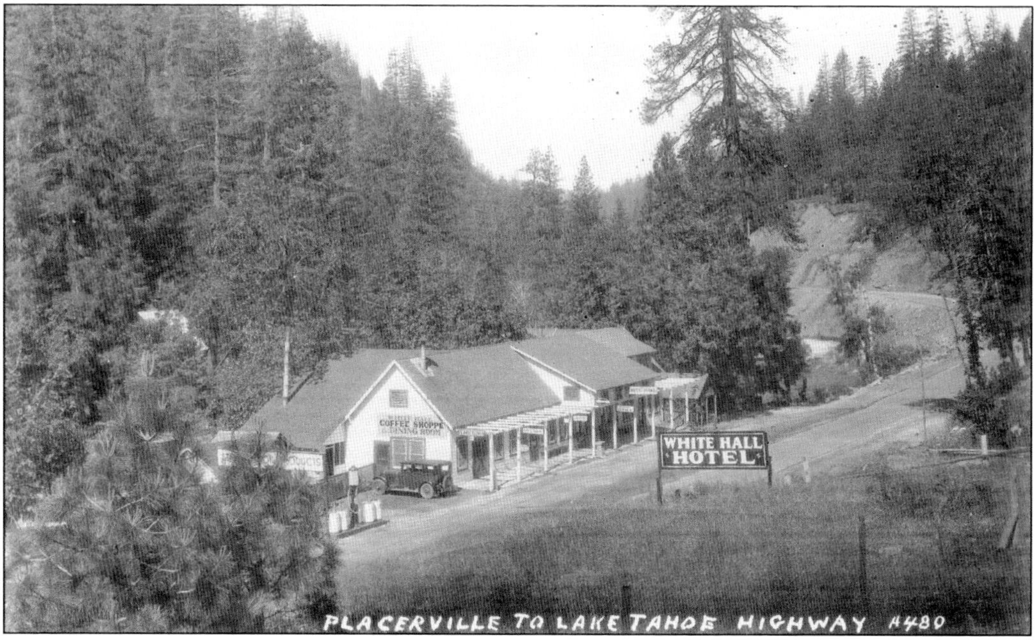

Whitehall Hotel was built at 25 milestone, one mile west of its original location. Albert Randall owned Whitehall in the early 1910s, becoming its postmaster. Tragedy struck in 1927 when fire destroyed Whitehall, and it was rebuilt in 1928. Whitehall was later owned by L.H. Christianson and in 1935 by the Virgil Jones's. Prior to Whitehall's existence, the Phelps family operated nearby Phelps Station where Alder Creek met Oglebee's cutoff. (Courtesy of Dorothy De Mare.)

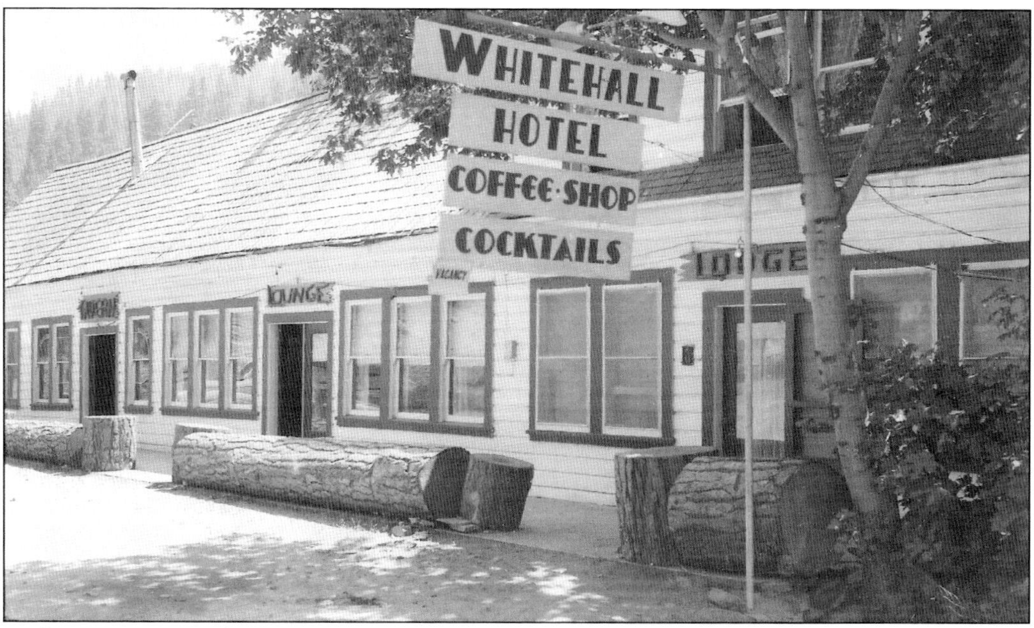

In the 1950s, Jim and Betty Gratterole were the proprietors of the Whitehall Hotel. There was a restaurant and bar and hotel rooms for 10 guests. Spaghetti sauce was the restaurant's specialty. The Whitehall Hotel has been closed for more than 30 years, but on the eastern end of the building, the name "Whitehall" still appears in large bold letters (Courtesy of Paul DeWitt.)

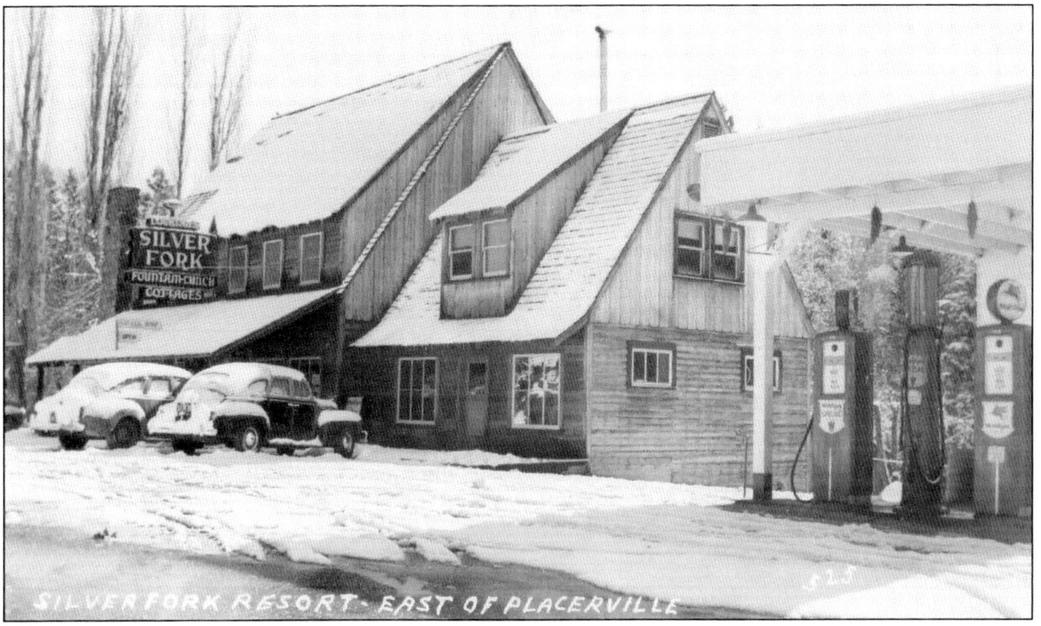

Saul Perrin built Silver Fork as a roadhouse in the mid-1850s. It served as a watering station for livestock pulling freight wagons and stagecoaches. The bar served the needs of the teamsters and passengers. In the 1950s, Earl and Frances Snavely operated the Silver Fork Lodge, serving fine foods and cocktails. The lodge also had a gas station. Today, the gas station is the only one between Fresh Pond and Meyers. (Courtesy of Paul DeWitt.)

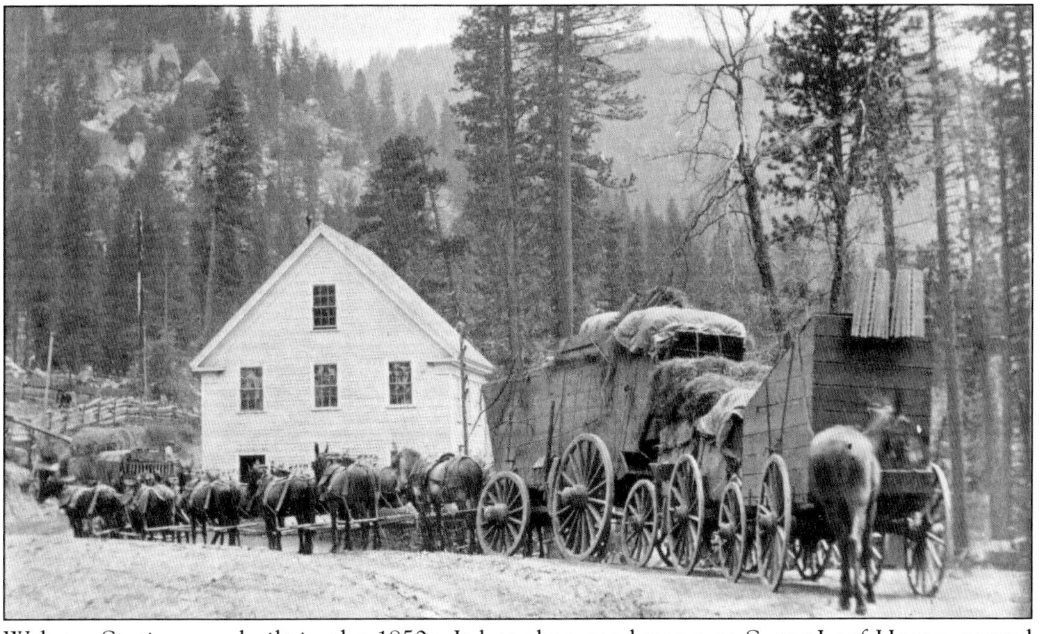

Webster Station was built in the 1850s. It later became known as Sugar Loaf House, named after Sugar Loaf Peak on the left behind the station in this 1864 photograph. Until 1868, the establishment was a popular stagecoach and teamster stop. In the foreground is a typical 12-mule team, hauling a large freight wagon, a second wagon with hay to feed the mules, and a third wagon with other supplies heading for Virginia City. (Courtesy of the Society of California Pioneers.)

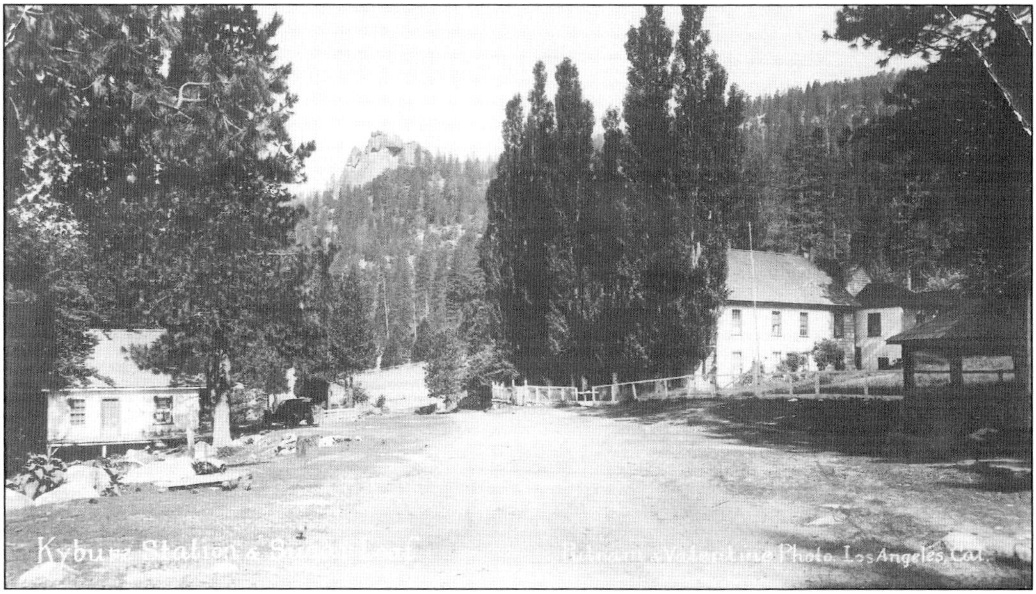

The community of Kyburz had its beginning around 1858, when a cabin was built in an area known as Slippery Ford. Dick Yarnold expanded the cabin, built a large fireplace, and turned it into an inn. He operated the River Toll Road, 11 miles between Sugarloaf Station and Strawberry Flat in the late 1850s and the 1860s. In the mid-1870s, Dennis Johnson turned Yarnold's inn into a resort. (Courtesy of Paul DeWitt.)

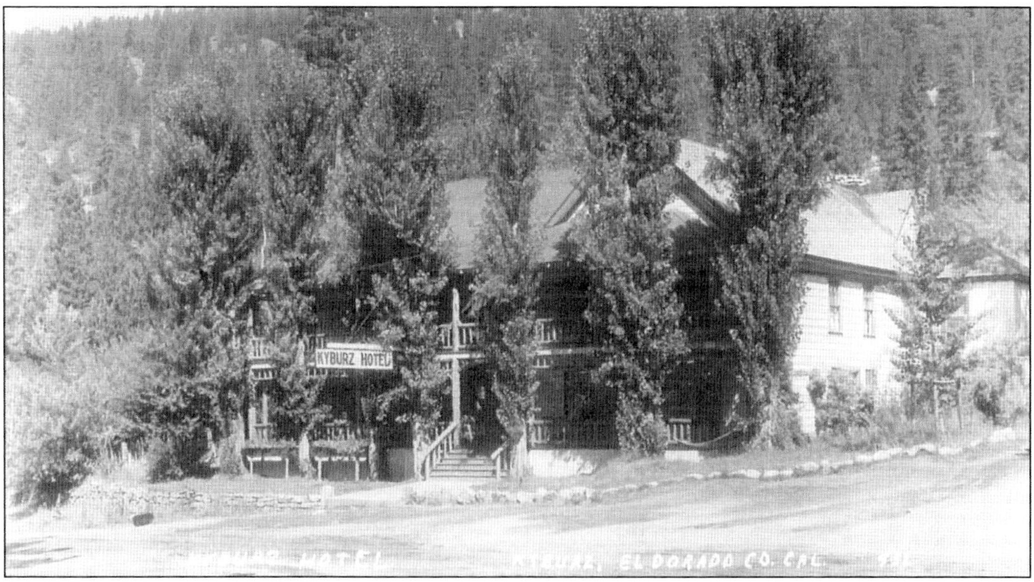

Albert Kyburz took over Dennis Johnson's resort in 1901 and changed the name to "Kyburz" in honor of his father, Samuel Kyburz. Samuel Kyburz immigrated to America in 1833 and became Capt. John Sutter's advisor, living at Sutter's Fort from 1846 to 1848. When Albert sold his resort to Charlie and Dorothy Witcher in 1944, there was a well-maintained campground, 64 buildings, including 40 rental cabins, and tennis courts. In 1951, the Kyburz Hotel burned down. The Witcher family continued renting cabins until 1957. Today, Kyburz Resort properties are subdivided into private lots for permanent residences and summer vacation homes. (Courtesy of Paul DeWitt.)

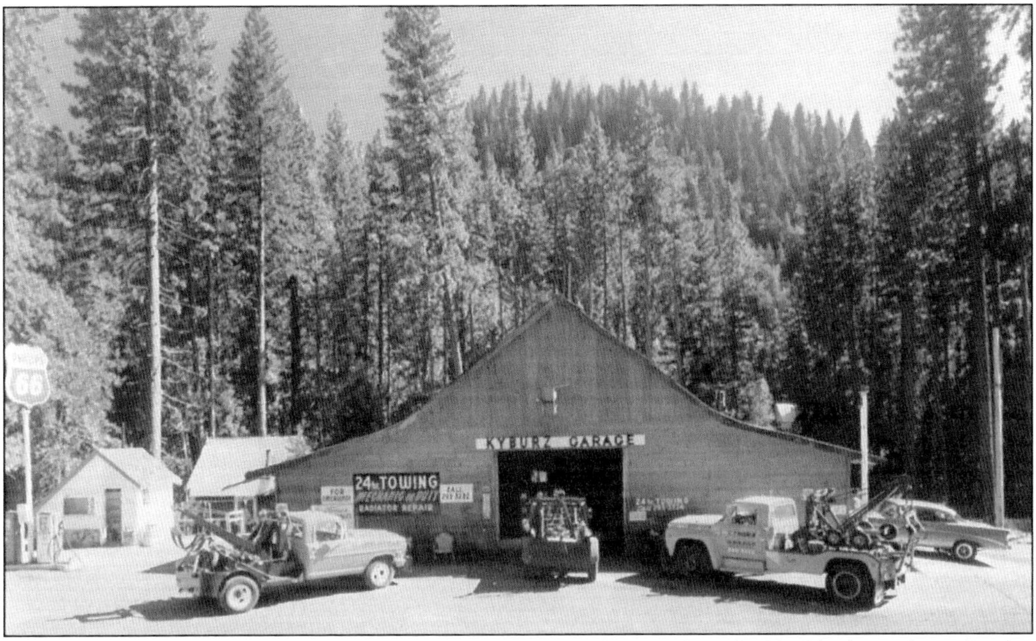

Kyburz's garage was built in the 1860s as a barn to serve livestock and offer blacksmithing for the freight wagons and stagecoaches heading for the Comstock Lode. As automobiles were introduced to the road, the barn became a gas station and garage to service and repair cars. When business for the station declined, the building was converted again, to a grocery and convenience store for travelers on their way to Lake Tahoe. (Courtesy of Paul DeWitt.)

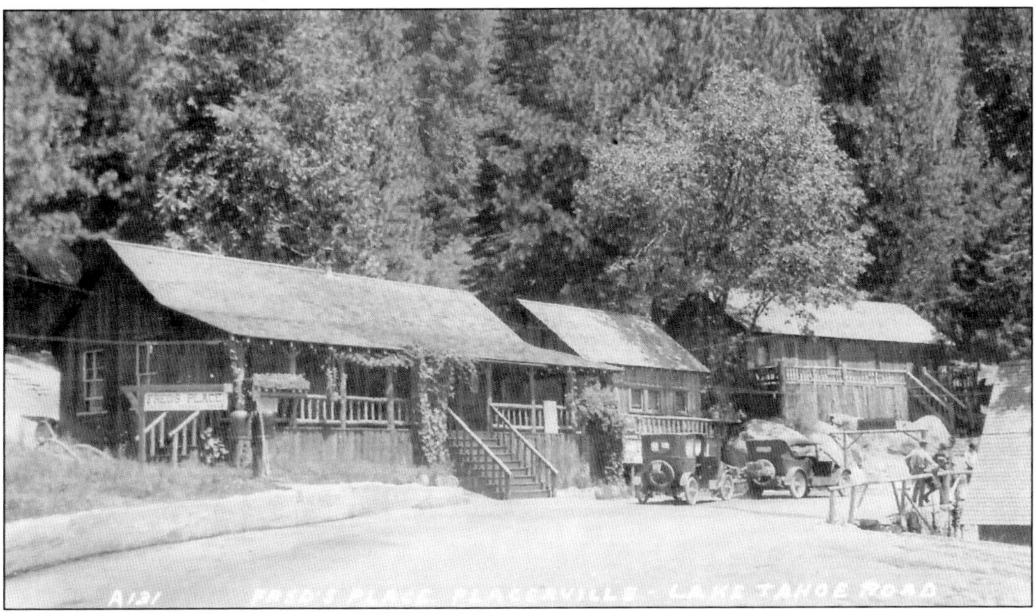

Fred's Place was built in 1918 by Anna and Fred Spriggs at the site of the historic Champlain House above the 36 milestone. Their newly built store, inn, restaurant, and gas station also offered swimming in the cool waters of the pond near an early bridge over the creek. Severely damaged by the creek's flooding in 1964, Fred's Place was dismantled. It is now a California Department of Transportation (Caltrans) storage area for sand and gravel. (Courtesy of Dorothy De Mare.)

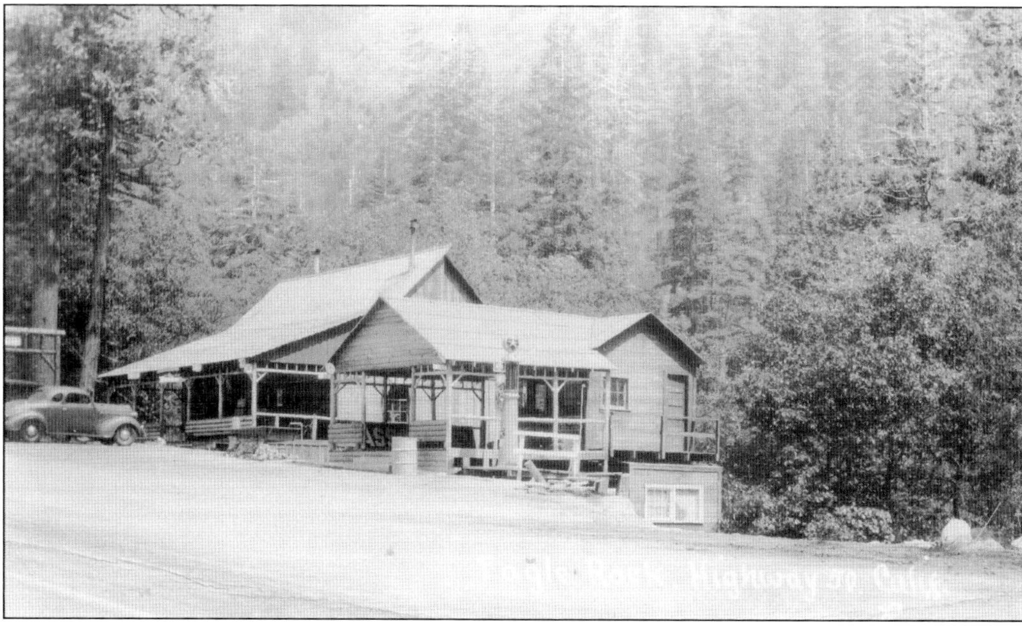

The name of the Eagle Rock Resort comes from a large dome of granite higher up the hill on the south side of the American River. The original name for the rock outcropping, Cottage Rock, is mentioned as early as 1855. Beginning in the early 1930s, the Eagle Rock Resort was first known as White House, later as Brown House. The Eagle Rock Resort burned down in the early 1960s. (Courtesy of Paul DeWitt.)

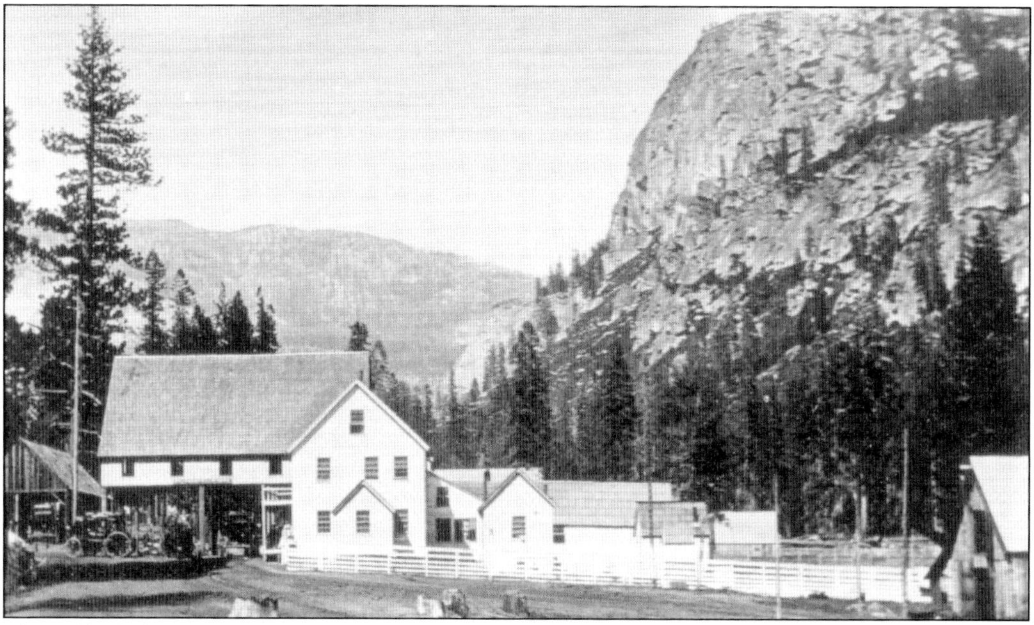

The valley below Lovers Leap acquired its name when young ladies from Placerville and their beaus traveled to the valley for an afternoon picnic in the very early 1850s. They noticed wild strawberries growing in the meadows and gave the valley its name, Strawberry Valley. The name "Strawberry" appeared in William Bartlett's *Guide to California* in 1853. Lovers Leap is the peak at right in this photograph of Strawberry Valley House. (Courtesy of the Society of California Pioneers.)

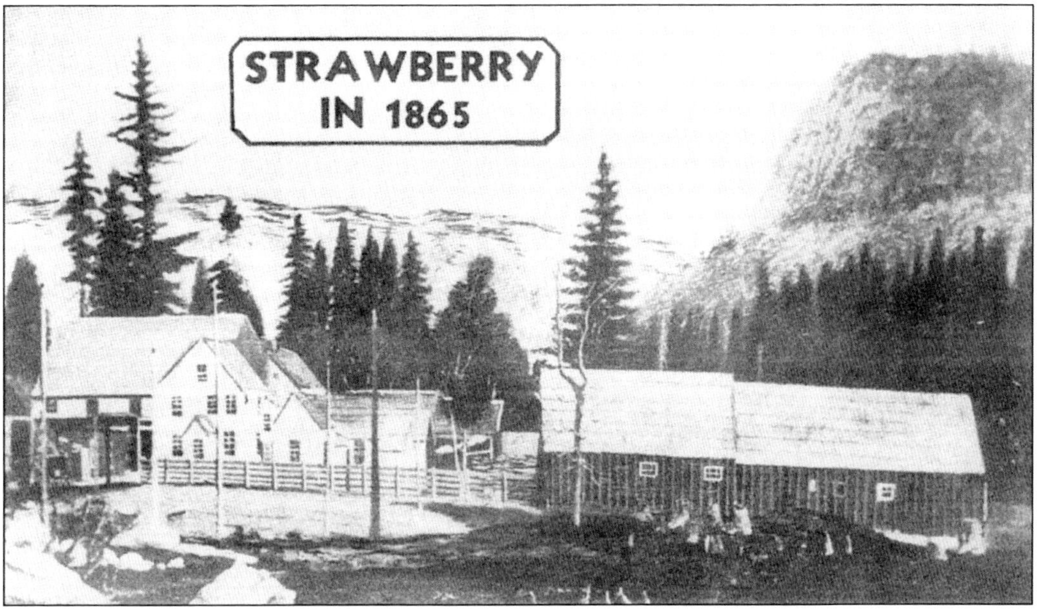

Strawberry Valley House was built in 1856. Irad Berry, who became the owner in 1858, was a wretched innkeeper. He stuffed straw into the guests' mattresses and pillows instead of goose down. He mixed cheap straw into the expensive feed for the teamsters' livestock. The teamsters eventually brought their own feed in a wagon towed behind their freight wagons. Berry became known as "Straw" Berry; he was not the most popular innkeeper on the road. (Courtesy of Paul DeWitt.)

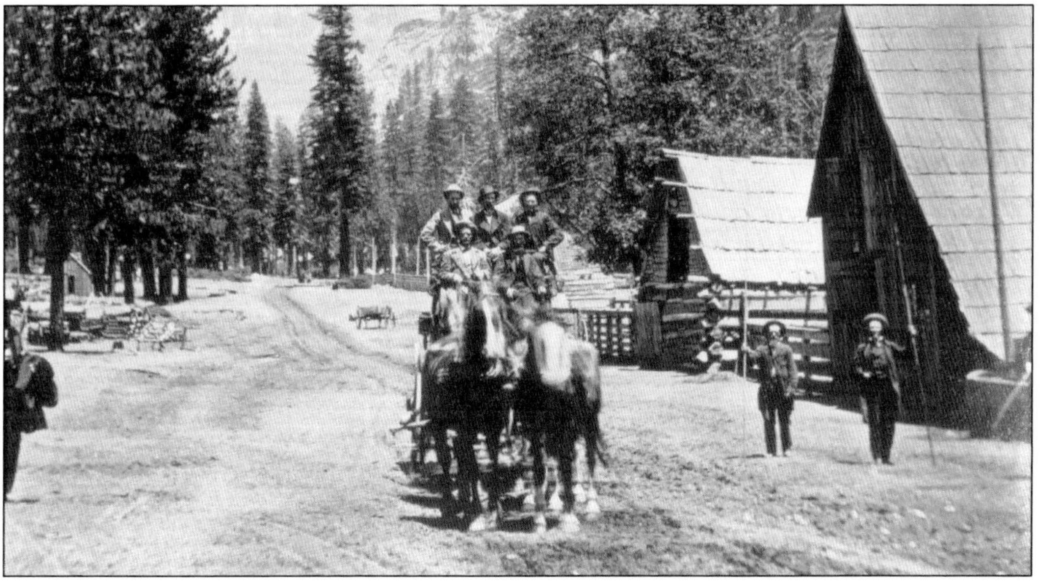

A stagecoach arrives at Strawberry Valley House from Carson City. Since Comstock freight wagons could travel only eight to ten miles a day, stagecoaches preferred to travel at a faster pace during the nights and early mornings, while the freight wagons stopped overnight. More than 30 coaches carried passengers daily. Famous coachman Hank Monk set a record in 1859, driving a coach 109 miles from Carson City to Placerville in 10 hours, with Horace Greeley as the passenger. (Courtesy of the Society of California Pioneers.)

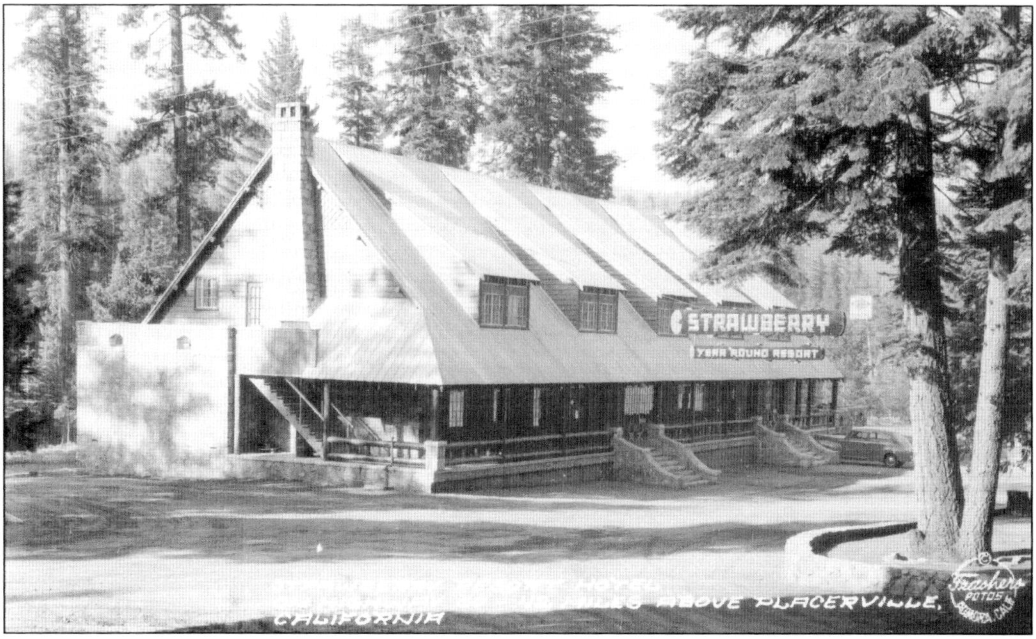

In the mid-1930s, a new highway was built west of the Strawberry Hotel, bypassing Slippery Ford. In 1939, Fred Baumhoff built the new Strawberry Lodge and hotel annex next to the highway. It still stands today. With few tourists on the road during the Depression and World War II, the lodge struggled financially. Today, Strawberry Lodge is the only resort from Placerville to Lake Tahoe. (Courtesy of Paul DeWitt.)

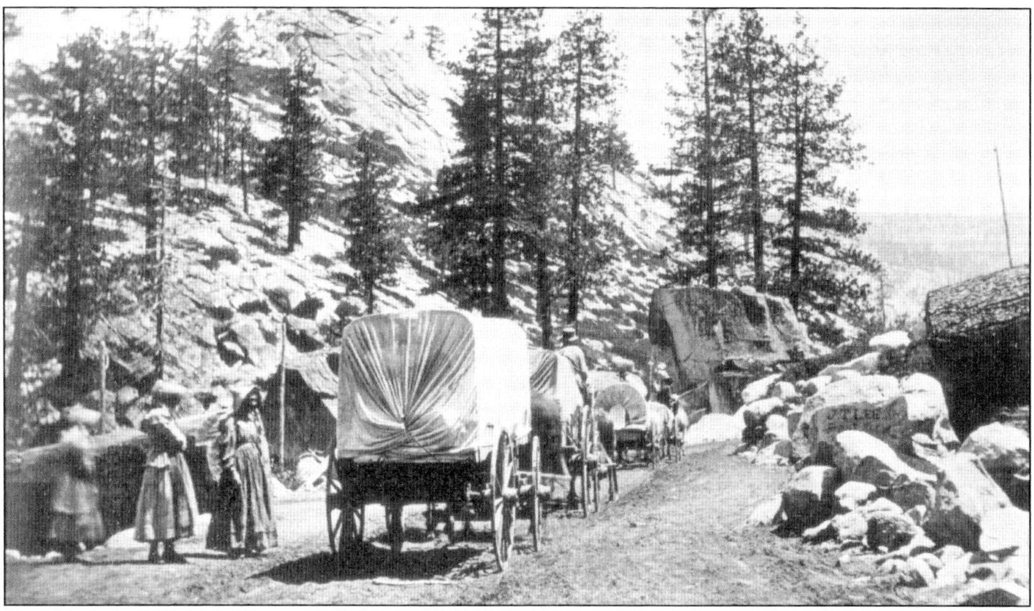

Besides the many freight wagons and stagecoaches heading for the Comstock Lode, there were many families headed in the same direction with their covered wagons. These women are walking with their covered wagon on the steep grade up Devil's Gap from Strawberry to Slippery Ford House. They are passing between Lovers Leap and Strawberry Butte, seen above the wagons. (Courtesy of the Society of California Pioneers.)

Slippery Ford House was located between Lovers Leap and Strawberry Butte. There was a steep rocky grade from Strawberry to Slippery Ford House. A small trading post operated in the early 1850s. In the early 1860s, a larger Slippery Ford House was built for the many teamsters and stagecoaches heading for the Comstock Lode. In August 1863, surveyor William H. Brewer hiked from Slippery Ford House to Pyramid Peak's summit and back in four hours, returning in time for dinner. Like other stations, business for Slippery Ford House declined after 1868. (Courtesy of the Society of California Pioneers.)

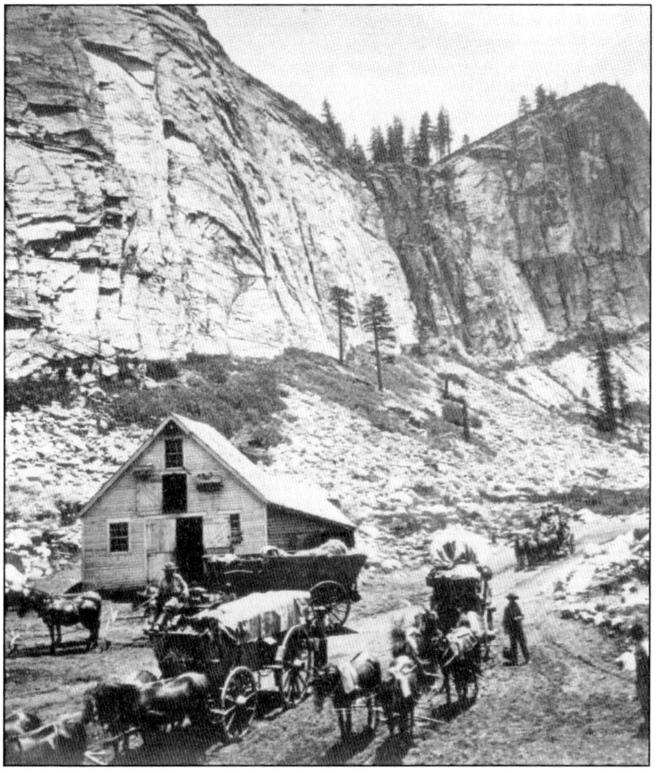

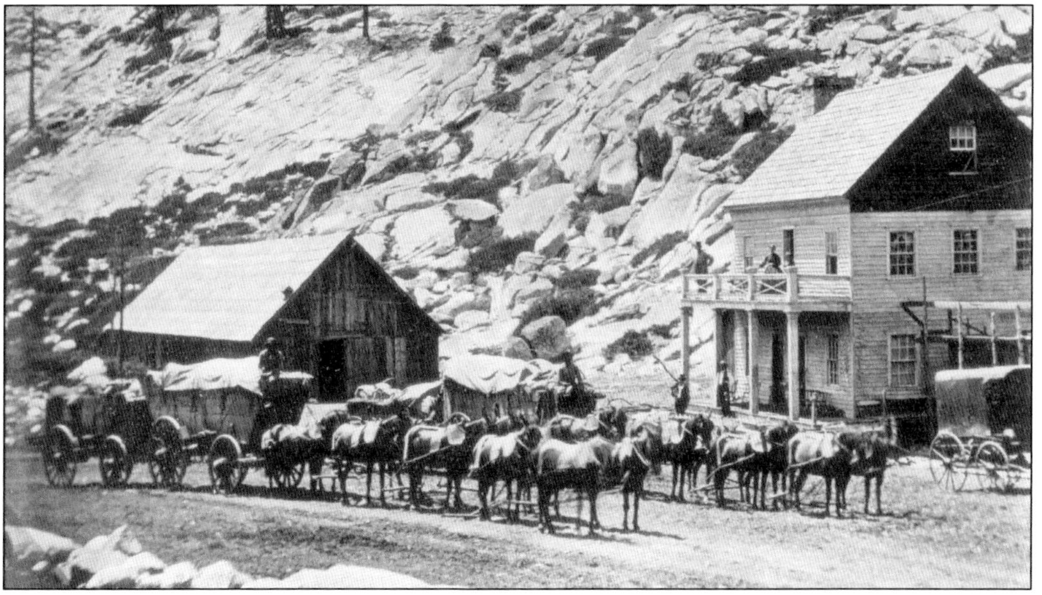

George Swan was the owner of Slippery Ford House in the early 1860s. He estimated that at least 250 tons of freight, 200 stagecoach passengers, and 1,000 mules, horses, and oxen passed through his toll station every day. Swan was assessed at $14,000 in taxes by El Dorado County in 1862. He collected more than $75,000 in tolls during the same period. As seen here, Slippery Ford House was built with the popular "6 up and 6 down" style of glass window panes. (Courtesy of the Society of California Pioneers.)

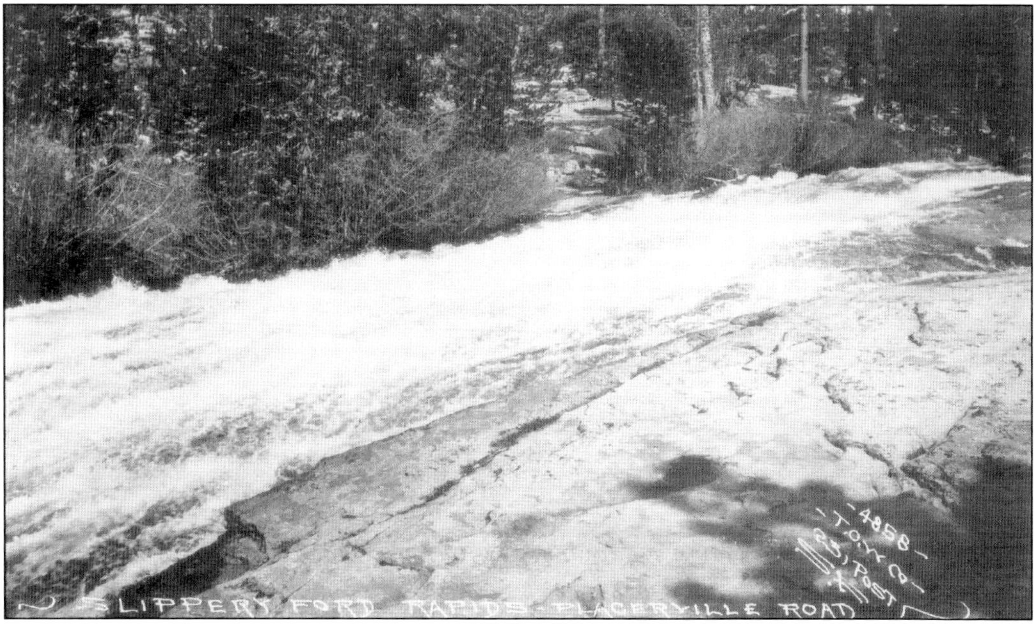

Slippery Ford was a treacherous crossing on the American River in the 1850s. In the spring and early summer, the danger was the rapids, as seen here. In the midsummer and fall, wet algae made the ford slippery. Occasionally, a pack animal would slip in the rapids or on the algae and slide with its load to its death over a waterfall. A bridge was built to bypass the ford in 1858. (Courtesy of Paul DeWitt.)

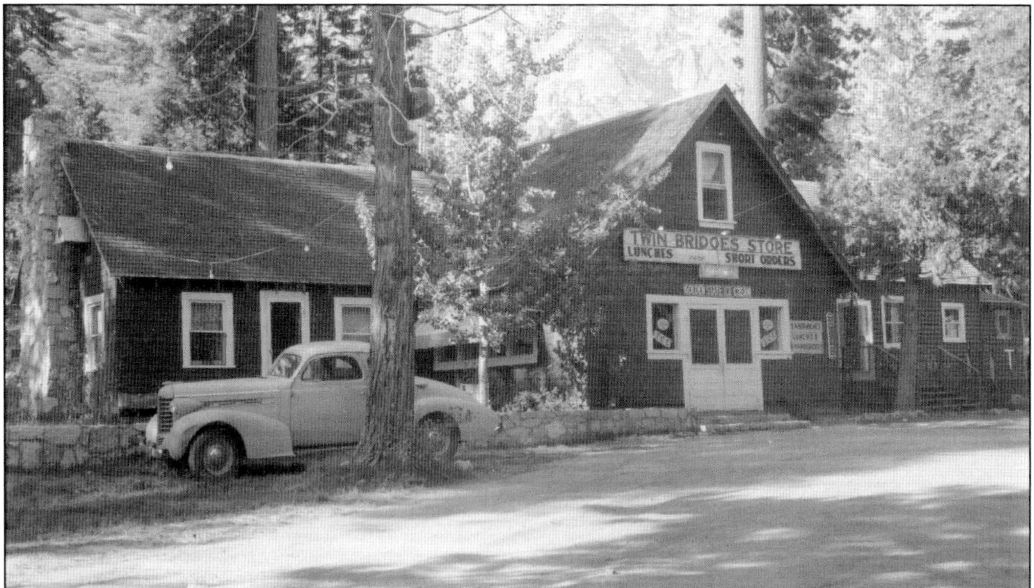

In the late 1850s, a way station called Twin Bridges was built just above Slippery Ford House, at a point where two bridges crossed the American River and bypassed Slippery Ford. This original Twin Bridges existed until the 1920s. In the 1930s, the Twin Bridges shown here was built where the new Highway 50 crossed Pyramid Creek. The establishment served the Pyramid Creek community with a grocery store, café, post office, and gas station. (Courtesy of Paul DeWitt.)

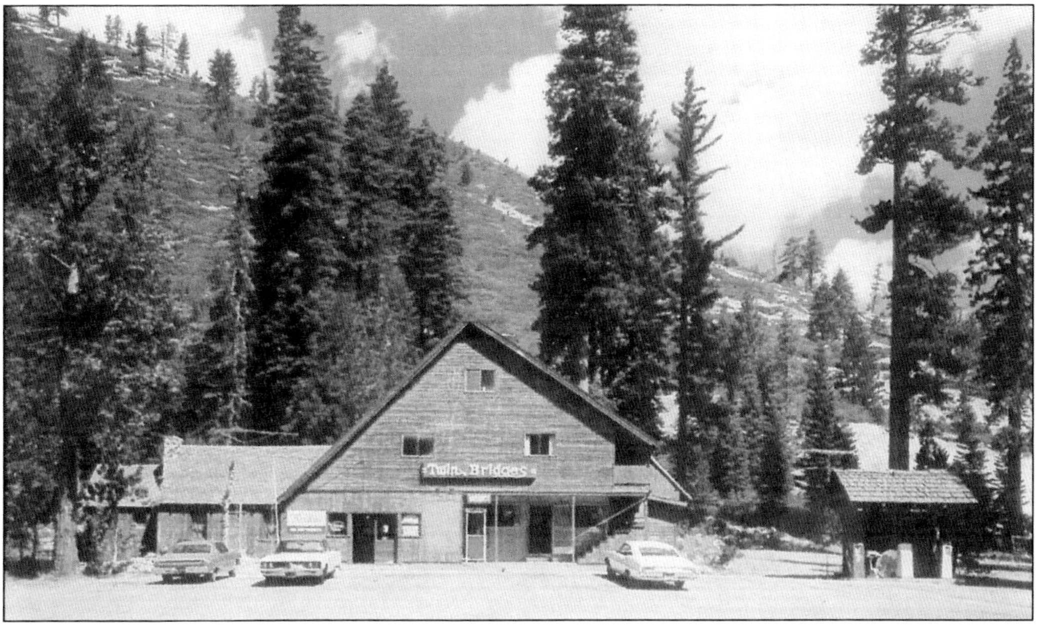

The new Twin Bridges Resort was rebuilt in 1931 near Pyramid Creek at the base of Horsetail Falls. A post office was established on June 10, 1947. Postmaster Lesta King and coworker Marie DePaepe were killed on January 14, 1952 when a snowslide from heavy winter storms tragically demolished the east section of the resort. That summer, Twin Bridges was operated by Alice and Elmer Butts. This 1960s image shows the bar, store, and gas station. (Courtesy of Dorothy De Mare.)

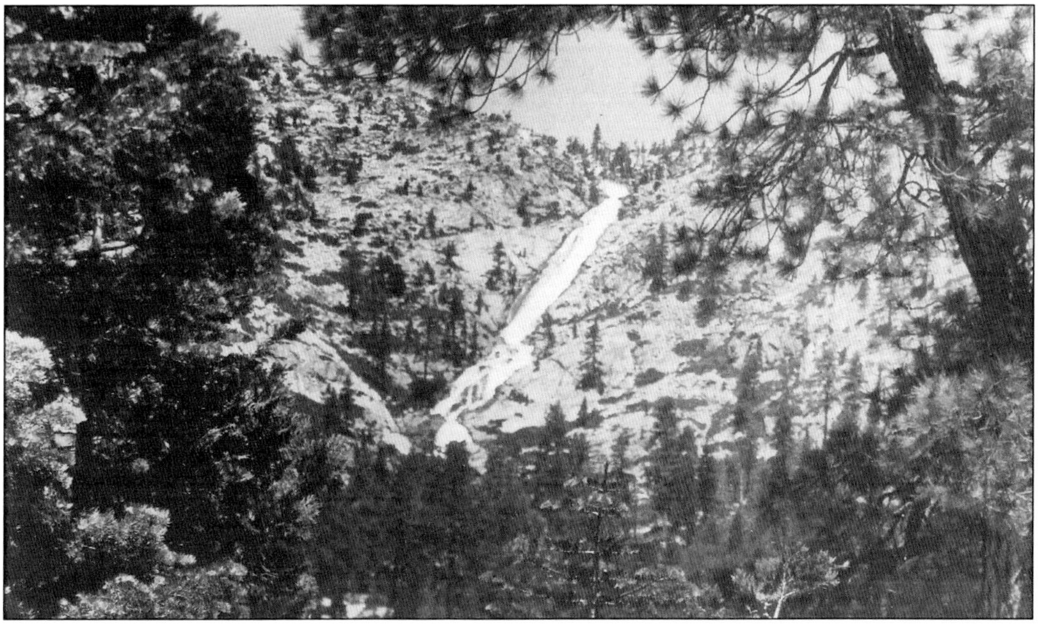

Horsetail Falls is the largest and tallest falls in the Lake Tahoe region. The Pyramid Creek Trail Head is used to hike up to Horsetail Falls and beyond to Aloha Lake and the Desolation Wilderness Area. The hike to the top is about two miles, with the last half-mile a steep climb without a clear trail. The main falls is about 800 feet, with smooth granite surfaces that are very slippery from the spray of the falls. (Courtesy of Paul DeWitt.)

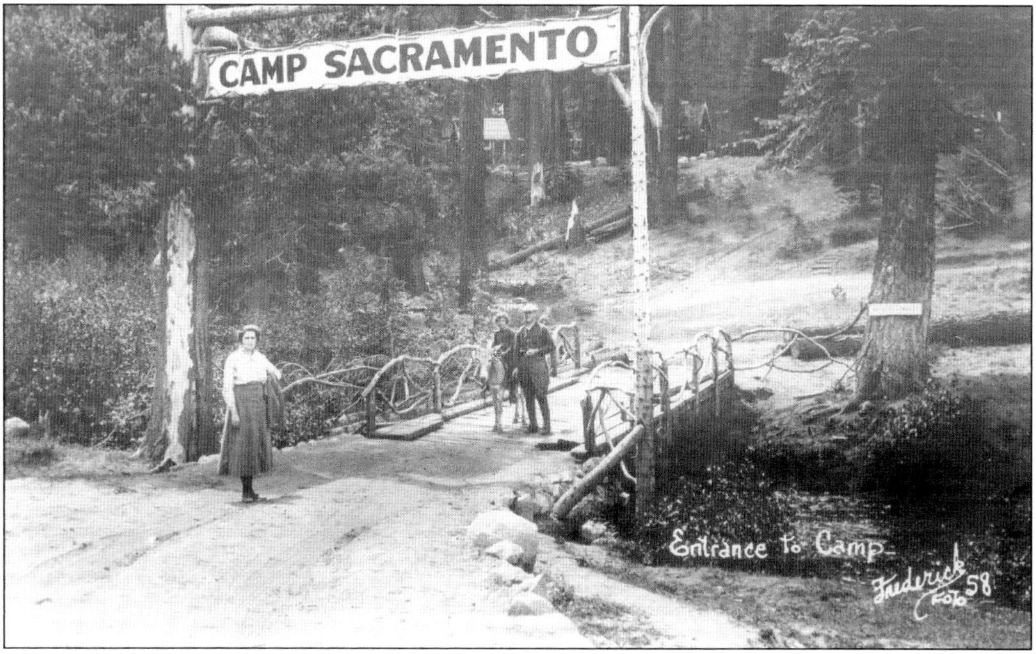

Camp Sacramento's entrance crosses the American River at Sayles Flat near the 45 milestone marker. The City of Sacramento has leased this government land since the early 1920s when many of its cabins and its lodge and dining hall were built. A 1924 brochure advertised a store and branch library on site. Open June through August, families still enjoy its mesa overlooking the American River and a broad meadow for abundant recreation. (Courtesy of Dorothy De Mare.)

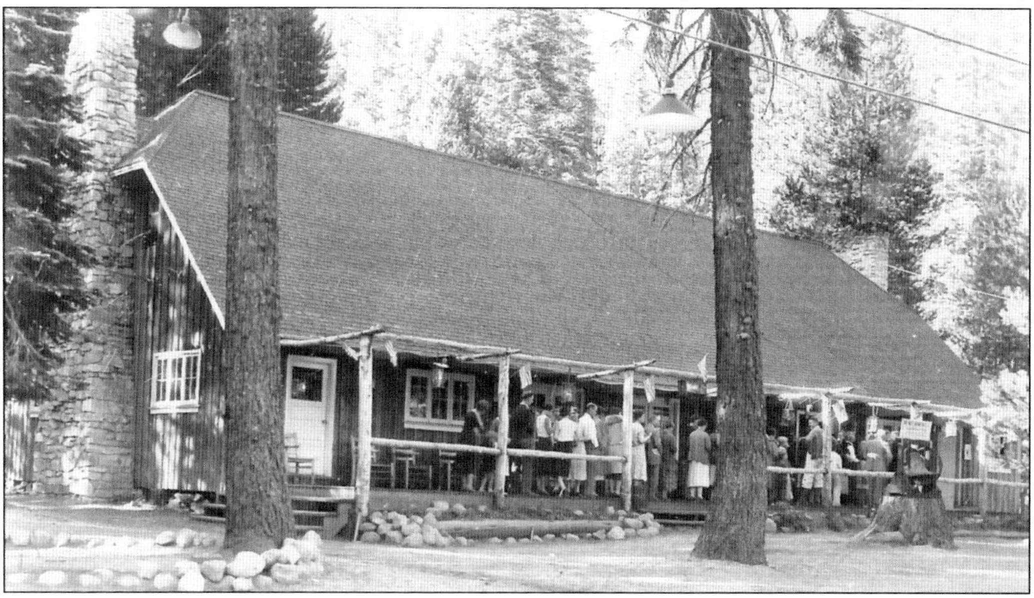

A 1940s view of Camp Sacramento's dining hall shows people waiting in line to enter where guests were served by the cafeteria plan. The Liberty Bell's sign asks guests not to ring it. During the winter of 1982–1983, heavy snow severely damaged the dining hall, about 15 cabins and vandals later caused further destruction. The camp remained closed in 1983 while a larger recreational and dining hall was constructed. (Courtesy of Dorothy De Mare.)

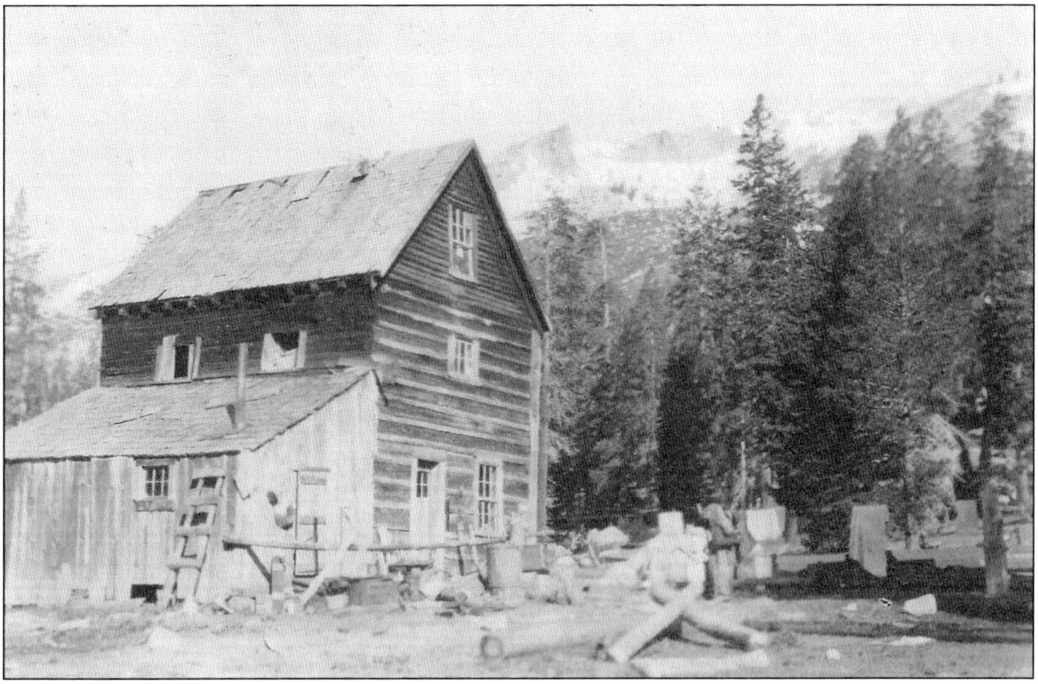

Joseph Phillips homesteaded 160 acres along the Johnson Cutoff in 1859 to establish a cattle ranch. When he saw the large numbers of freight wagons and stagecoaches headed for the Comstock Lode, he built a way station to provide meals and a place to sleep for the weary travelers. He also built large barns to provide shelter for their livestock. For a short time, Phillips' Station also served as a stop for the Pony Express. (Courtesy of Paul DeWitt.)

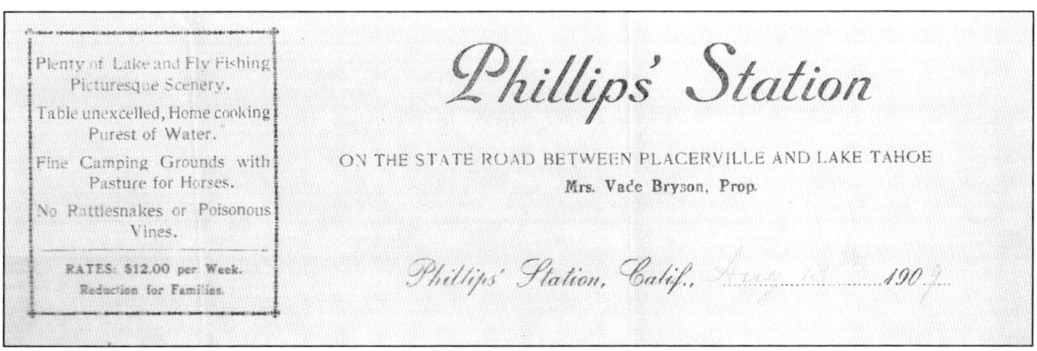

Plenty of Lake and Fly Fishing
Picturesque Scenery.
Table unexcelled, Home cooking
Purest of Water.
Fine Camping Grounds with
Pasture for Horses.
No Rattlesnakes or Poisonous
Vines.

RATES: $12.00 per Week.
Reduction for Families.

Phillips' Station

ON THE STATE ROAD BETWEEN PLACERVILLE AND LAKE TAHOE
Mrs. Vade Bryson, Prop.

Phillips' Station, Calif., ...190...

Sierra Nevada "Vade" Phillips Clark Bryson, Joseph Phillips's daughter, was successful managing resorts at Lake Tahoe and Rubicon Spring's Hotel. Vade added a store, bar, and campground after inheriting Phillips' Station in 1909. The above letter head lists the establishment's amenities. Her family almost perished when the hotel burned in 1911. Rebuilt the following spring, Vade established Vade Post Office on September 3, 1912, and became postmaster. Phillips's Station closed during the Depression, then reopened until it was crushed by the great snows that fell during the winter of 1951–1952. (Courtesy of Dorothy De Mare.)

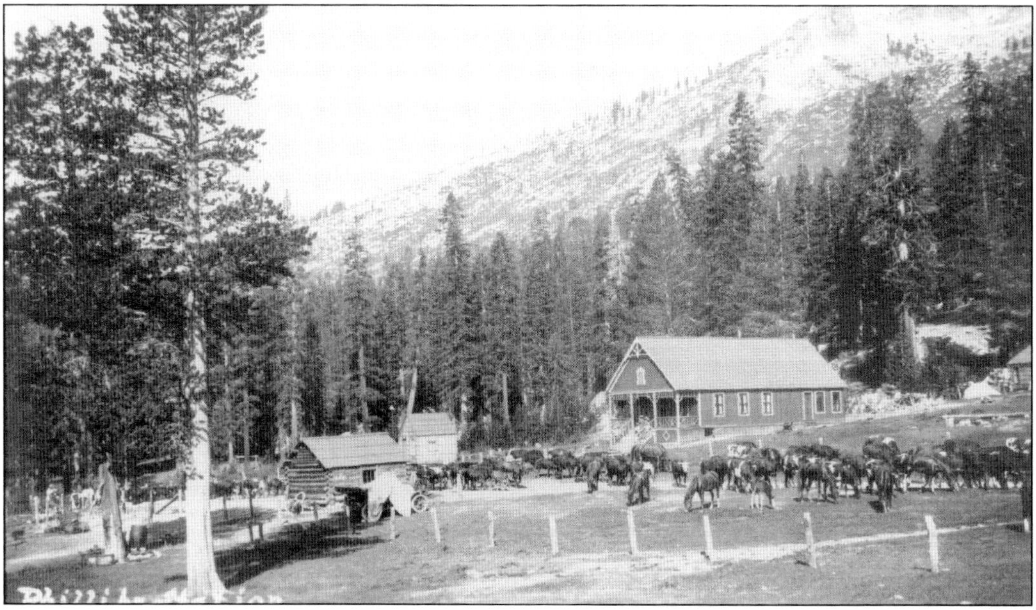

Pictured around 1920, horses graze among cattle at Phillips's Station. Beginning in the late 1880s and continuing for decades, Joseph Phillips leased land annually to many well-known El Dorado County ranchers. In the summer and fall, livestock were herded along the dirt Placerville-Tahoe Road to graze in the lush meadows of Echo Summit and Lake Valley. The twice-annual and extremely dusty drives each took about five days. (Courtesy of Dorothy De Mare.)

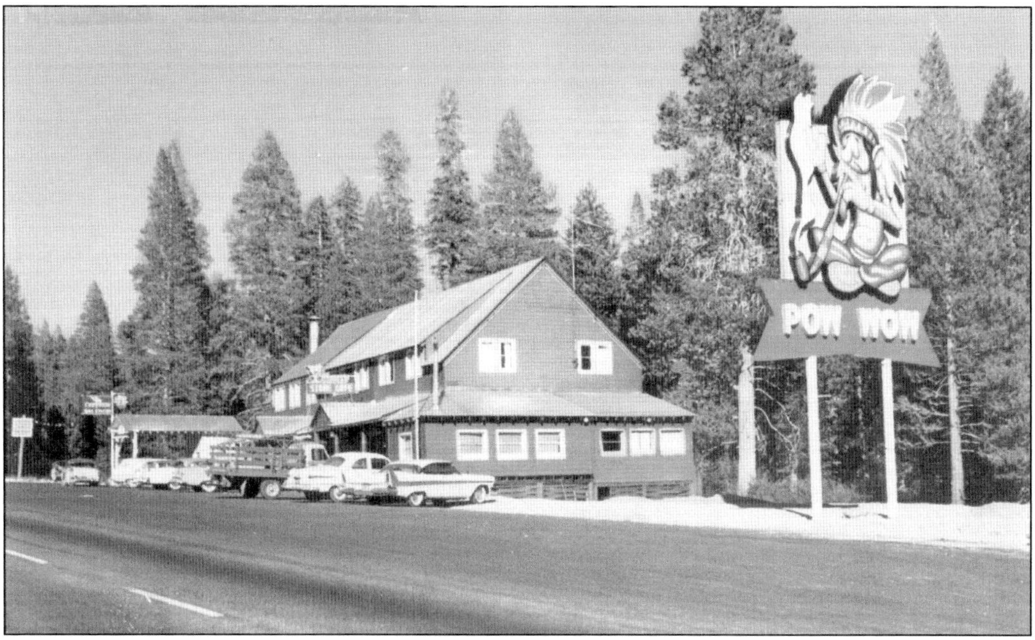

In 1961, at the site of the original Phillips' Station and present Highway 50 turnoff to Sierra-at-Tahoe, Mildred and Rolla Carter built Pow Wow Lodge. They operated a gift shop, café, cocktail lounge, and gas station. Rolla, a professional sign painter, intentionally and humorously crafted their roadway sign to read "Eat at Pow Wow and get gas." Destroyed by fire in about 1980, no commercial establishment was ever rebuilt there. (Courtesy of Dorothy De Mare.)

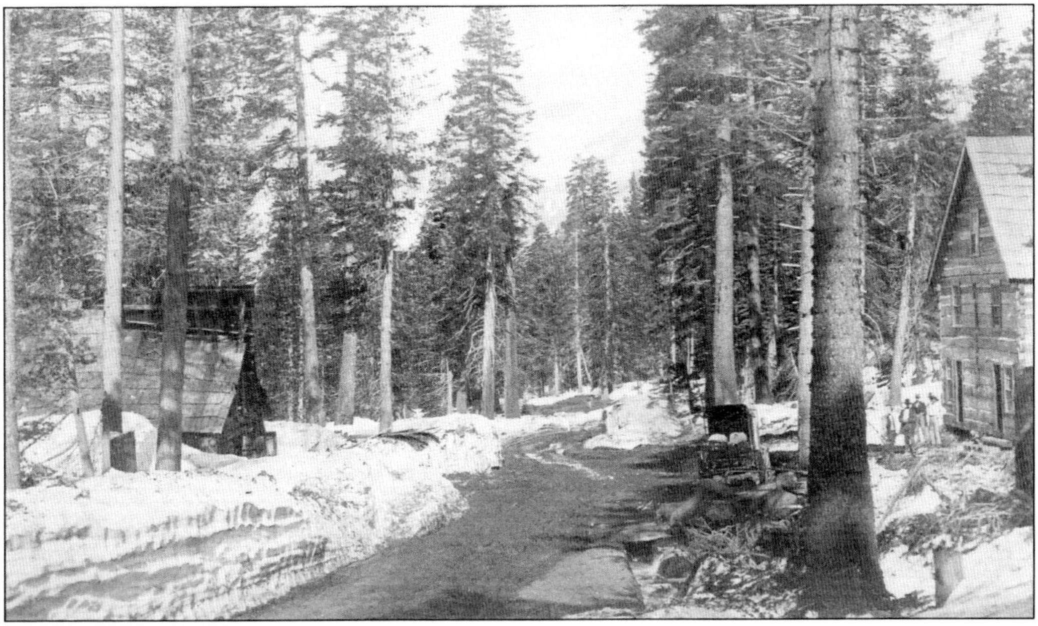

North America House was built and operated by Thomas and Elizabeth Coates in 1859 on the Kingsbury-McDonald toll road. It was a half mile west of Johnson Pass, at the junction with a trail heading toward Echo Lake. This site is where Echo Portals stood from the 1920s to the late 1990s. The Coateses sold North America House to Kingsbury and McDonald on November 18, 1862, for $2,000. (Courtesy of Dorothy De Mare.)

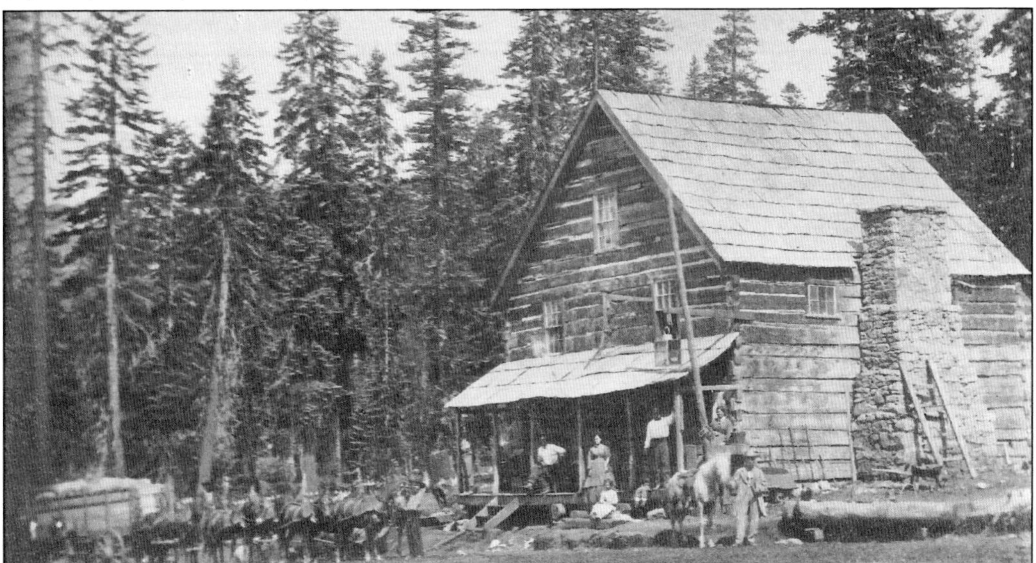

This c. 1865 photograph of North America House shows a weathered building from harsh summit winters. When news of President Lincoln's assassination reached Audrain Station on the road to Johnson Pass, Southern-sympathizer Thomas Audrain celebrated Lincoln's death by providing free food and drinks to his patrons. The guests, enraged, set Audrain's establishment on fire. They celebrated its burning, then moved to the North America House 1.5 miles east and mourned Lincoln's passing. (Courtesy of Dorothy De Mare.)

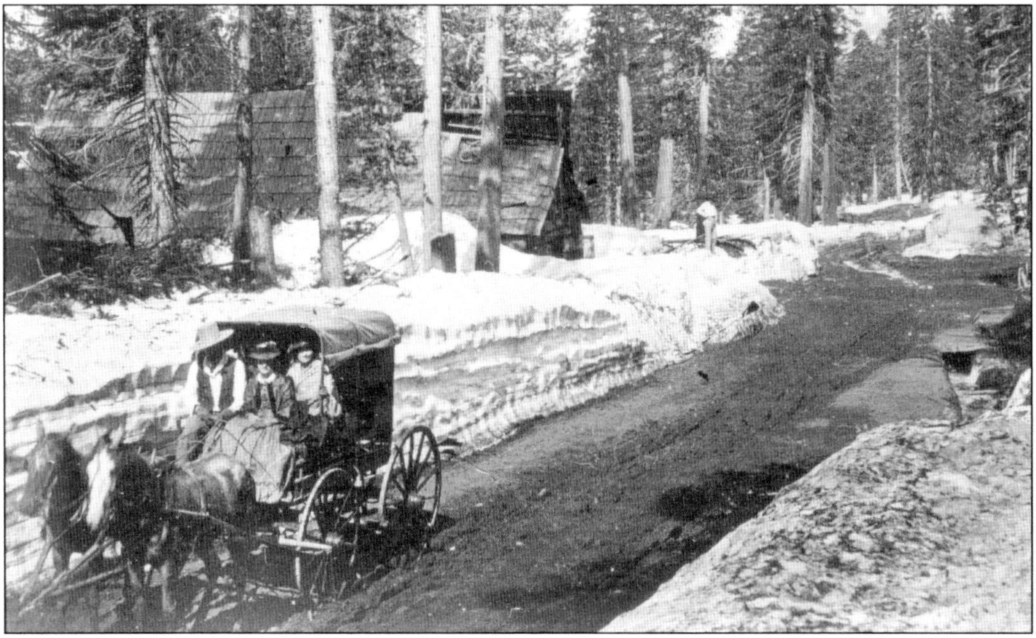

From 1864 to 1865, Eli Clark was the proprietor of North America House. Like other roadhouses, it offered a bar, dining room, and overnight accommodations. Its stable across the road provided hay and grain for livestock. It is not known what happened to North America House; however, a US Forest Service letter dated 1918 states that a depression was still discernible where the old well was located. This same well later provided water for Echo Portals. (Courtesy of Society of California Pioneers.)

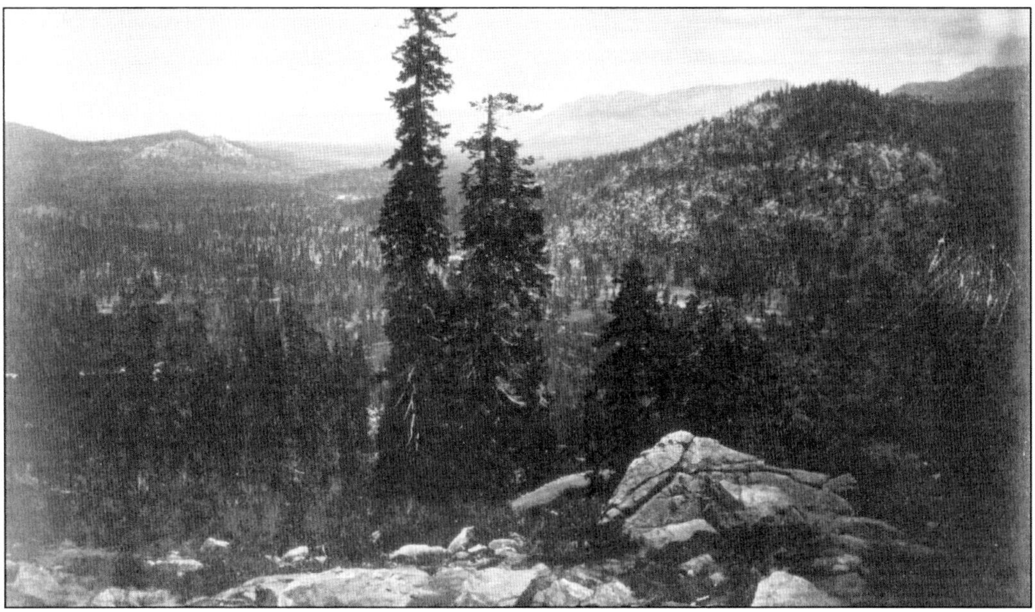

As stagecoaches and freight wagons traveled east of North America House and over Johnson Pass, they came, 100 yards on, to the edge of the summit ridge. Travelers could look down into southern Lake Tahoe and Lake Valley. On a clear day, the gorgeous view included the whole Tahoe Basin. (Courtesy of the Society of California Pioneers.)

Three

ECHO SUMMIT AND THE NEW MEYERS GRADE

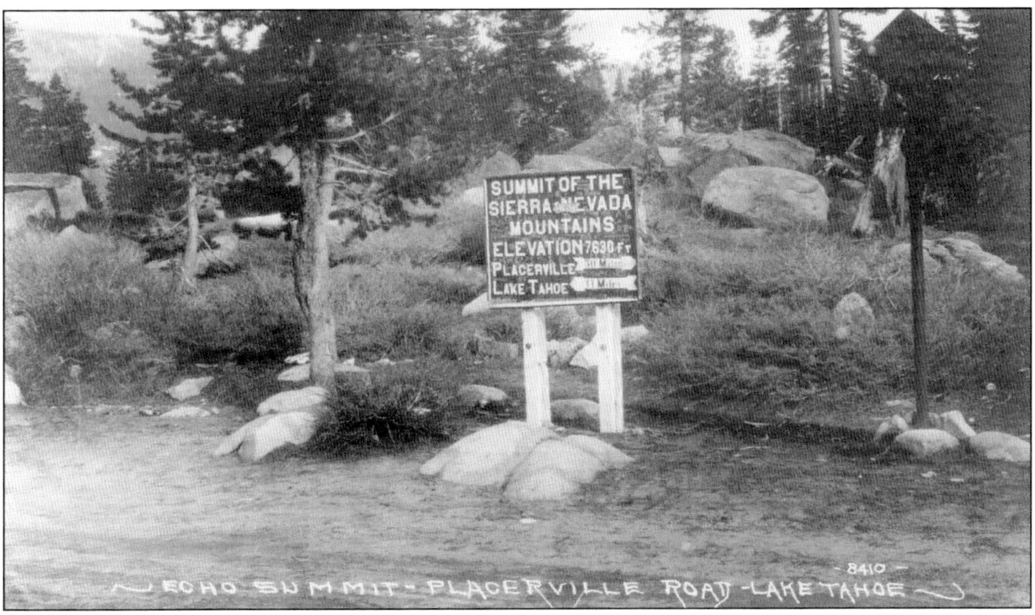

When riding wagons or driving vehicles, it was always an accomplishment for travelers to reach the top of Echo Summit, regardless of which direction they came. This sign, posted about 1915, declared improperly that the travelers had reached the end of their climb at an elevation of 7,630 feet. (The actual elevation was 7,394 feet.) A traveler wrote on this postcard, "Our car is parked in front of the sign. We can see Lake Tahoe. See how high we are! Alice." The card is postmarked July 1, 1924. (Courtesy of Paul DeWitt.)

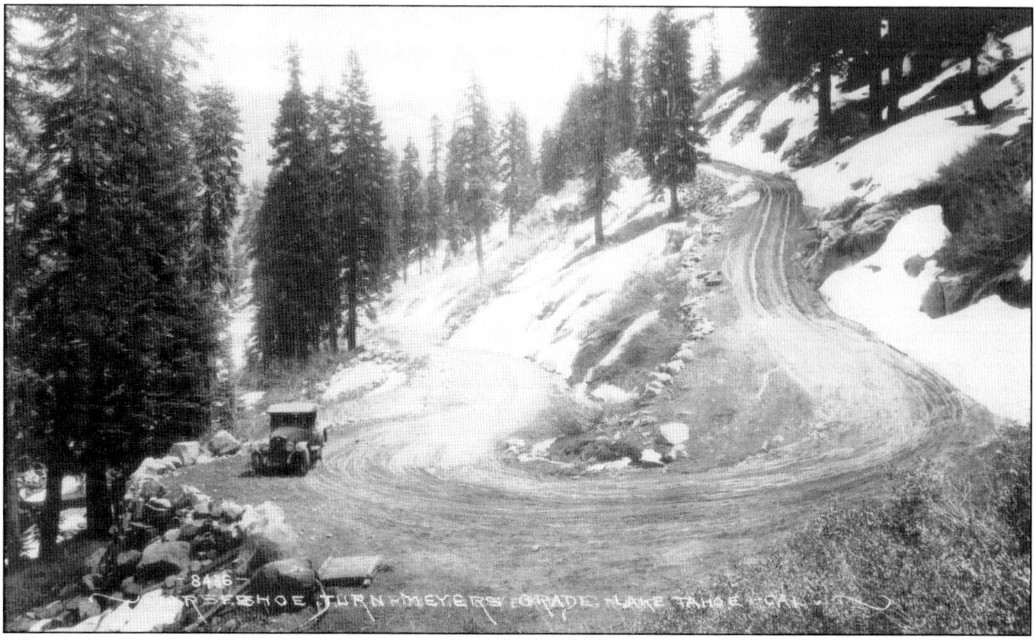

The twisting turns and 11- to 18-percent grades at the top of the old Osgood Grade made it very difficult to drive to the top. Some automobiles, low on gas, had to drive up backwards when they got near the top of the grade, as they did not have fuel pumps to get gas to the engine. In the 1890s, the old Osgood Grade became known as the Meyers Grade. (Courtesy of Paul DeWitt.)

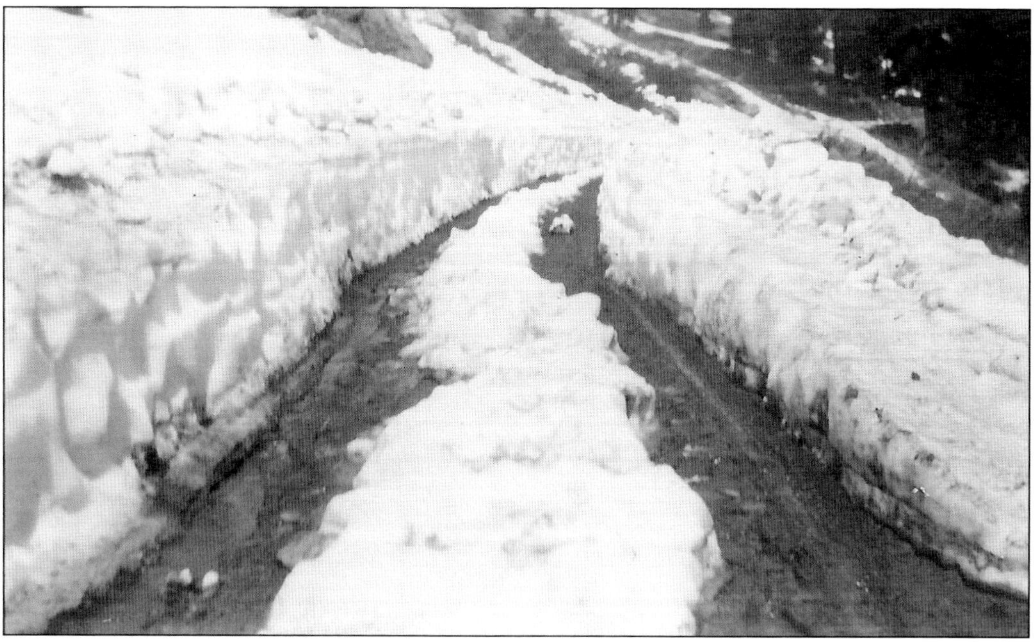

Until the 1940s, winter snow was always a major problem on the road going down Meyers Grade from Johnson Pass on Echo Summit. It took many men long hours to clear the road, hand-shoveling the snow. There were no snowplows in those days. During most winters, the road and summit were closed due to snow. (Courtesy of Miles Celio.)

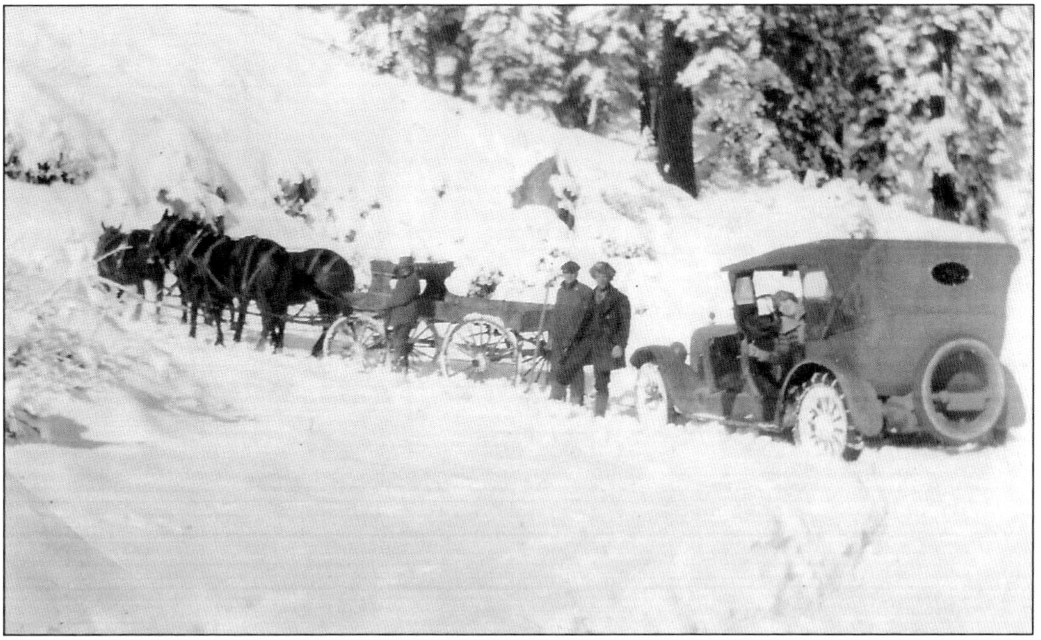

Sometimes, in the early winter, there was more snow at the top of Meyers Grade than the driver anticipated. He would get stuck and have to hike down the grade to get help. The nearest assistance was the Celio Ranch in Upper Lake Valley. The Celio Ranch hands would send out a wagon with four horses to tow the car to the summit or bring it back down to the valley. (Courtesy of Miles Celio.)

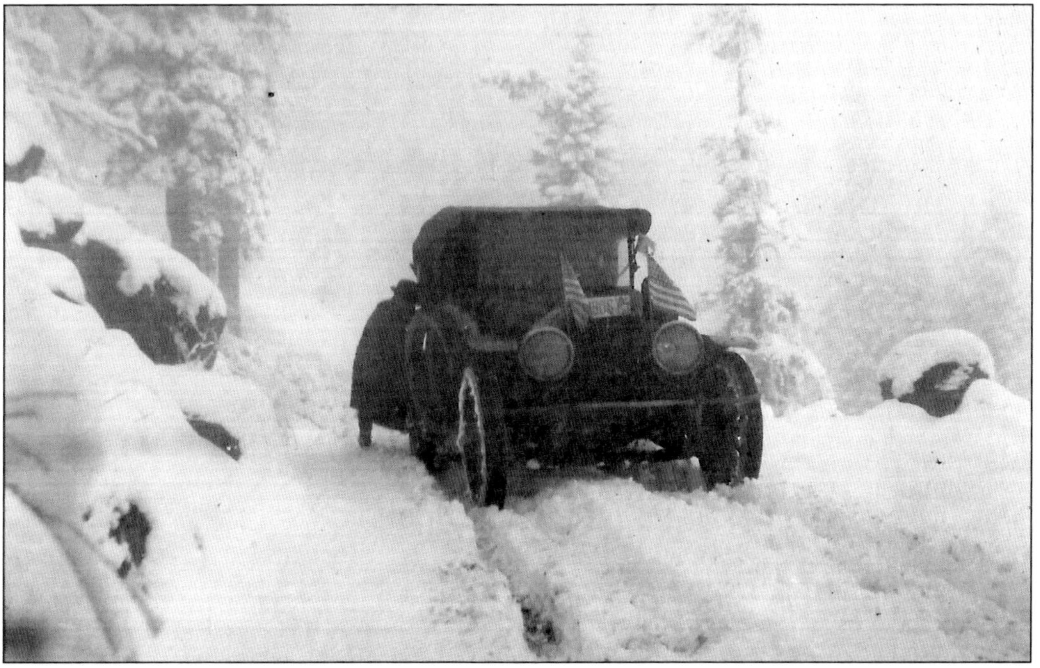

Even though Meyers Grade had been shoveled of snow and other vehicles had used the road, this car became stuck during a fresh snowfall just below the summit. Passengers in their heavy coats had to climb out and push the car up the grade to the summit. (Courtesy of Miles Celio.)

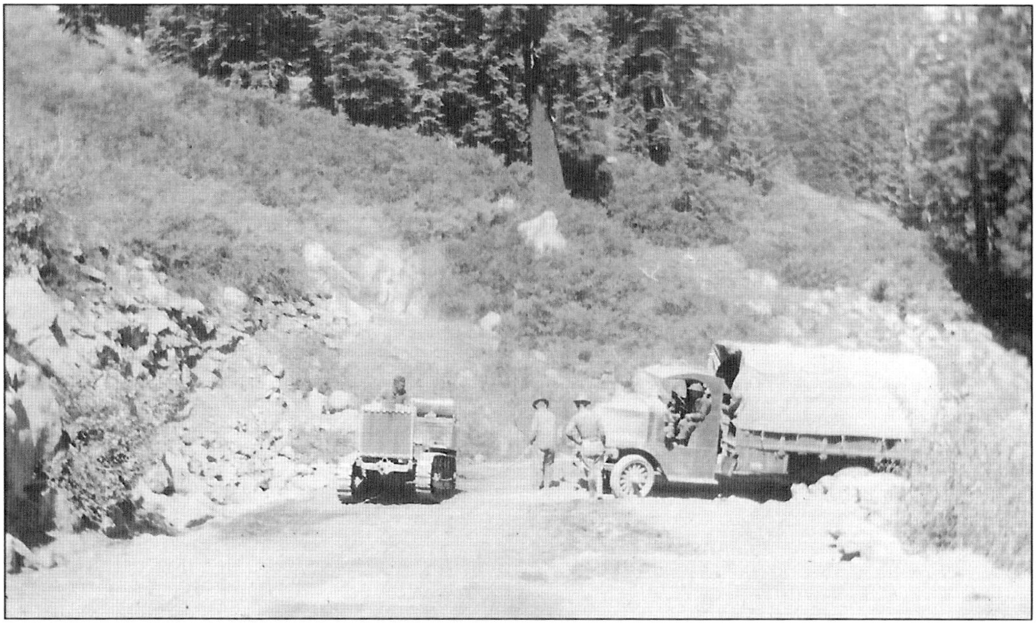

In the summer of 1919, the US Army Transcontinental Motor Convoy made a trip across the United States on the Lincoln Highway. When one of the trucks could not make it up the last hairpin turn of Meyers Grade, an Army caterpillar had to tow the truck over the turn and up to the summit. It was an embarrassment for the Army, but everyone else enjoyed the action. (Courtesy of Miles Celio.)

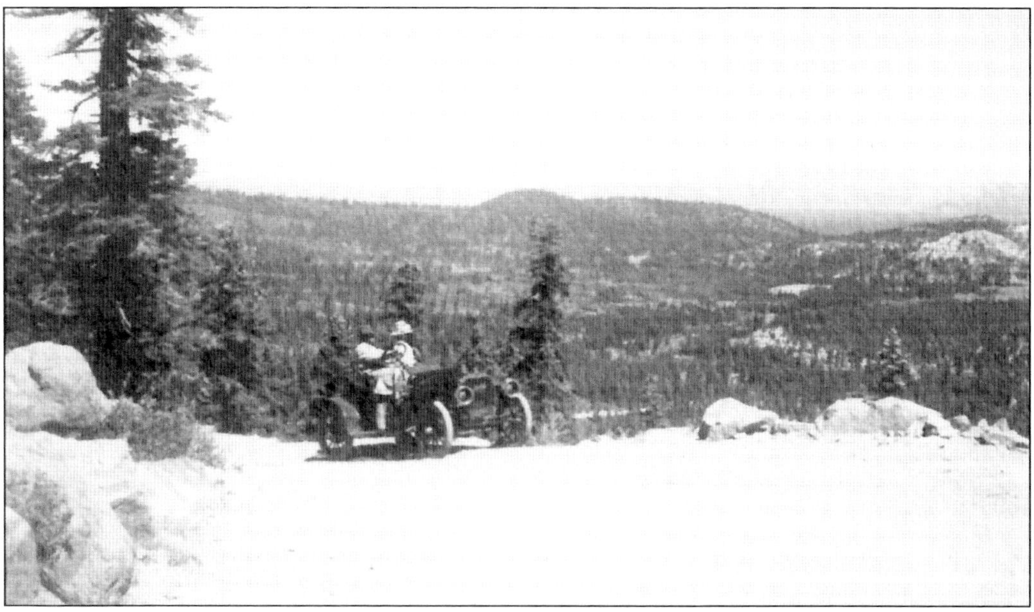

A couple driving up Meyers Grade in their open-air automobile stops for a breathtaking view of Lake Valley and the Lake Tahoe Basin below. The vehicle then needed to make a right turn and still had a mild climb of about 150 yards to get to the summit. In about 1908, a sign appeared marking the summit. (Courtesy of Dorothy De Mare.)

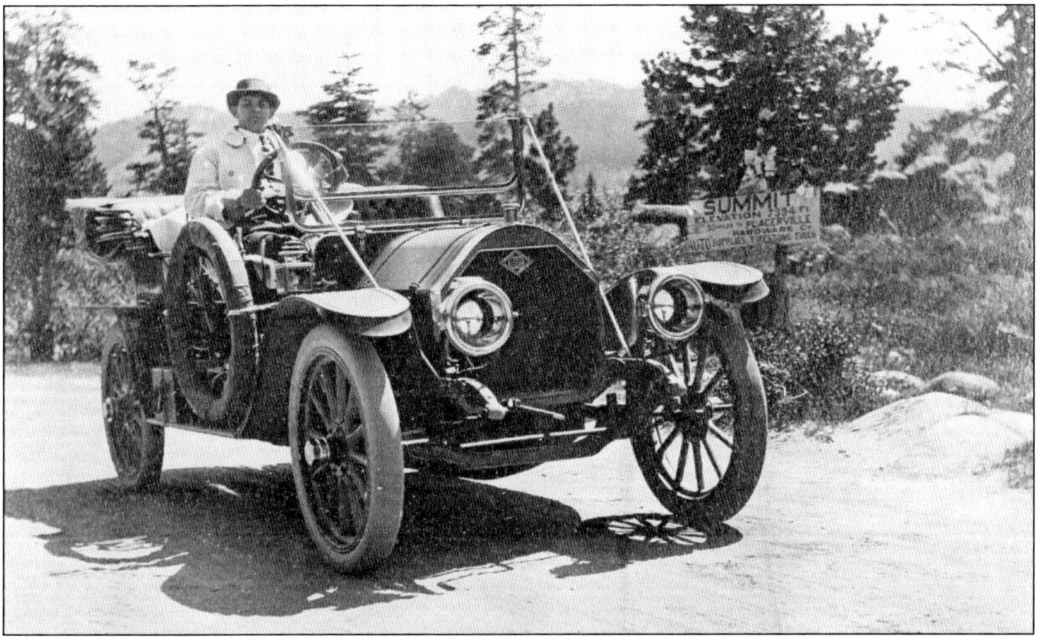

This automobile reached the summit from Tahoe at about 10:00 a.m. The car stopped, and a passenger got out to take this photograph. The summit sign, nailed to a tree, is in reality a roadside advertisement. It reads as follows: "Summit, Elevation 7394 Ft, 50 miles to Placerville Hardware Co., Auto Supplies Firestone Tires." (Courtesy of the El Dorado County Historical Museum.)

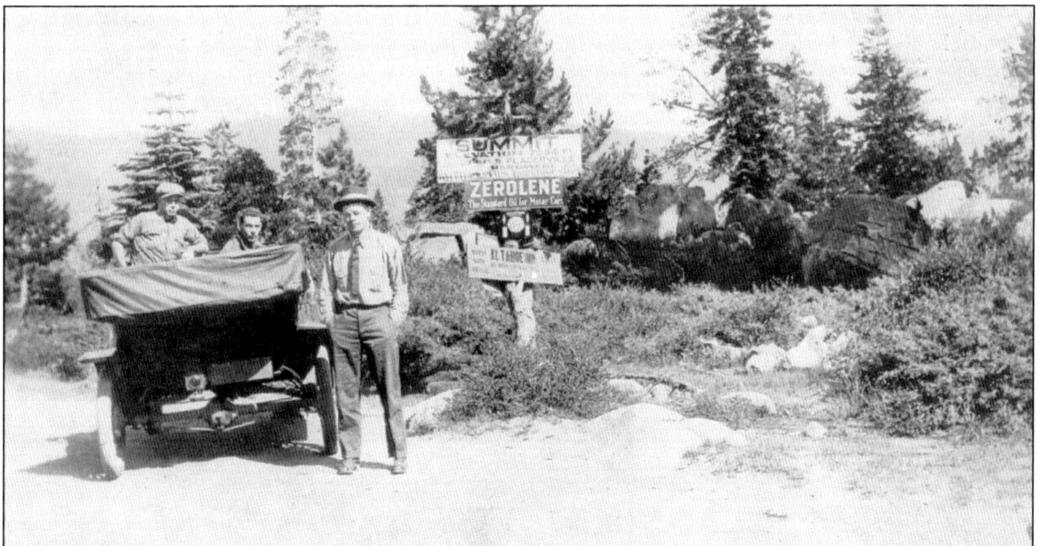

This vehicle arrived at the summit from Placerville. The summit sign appears to be nailed higher up on the tree, and three more advertisements have been added. The first reads, "Zerolene, the Standard Oil for Motor Cars." The second sign is for Champion Spark Plugs. The last is for the "Al Tahoe Inn Modern Hotel and Cottages" at Lake Tahoe. (Courtesy of the Lake Tahoe Historical Society.)

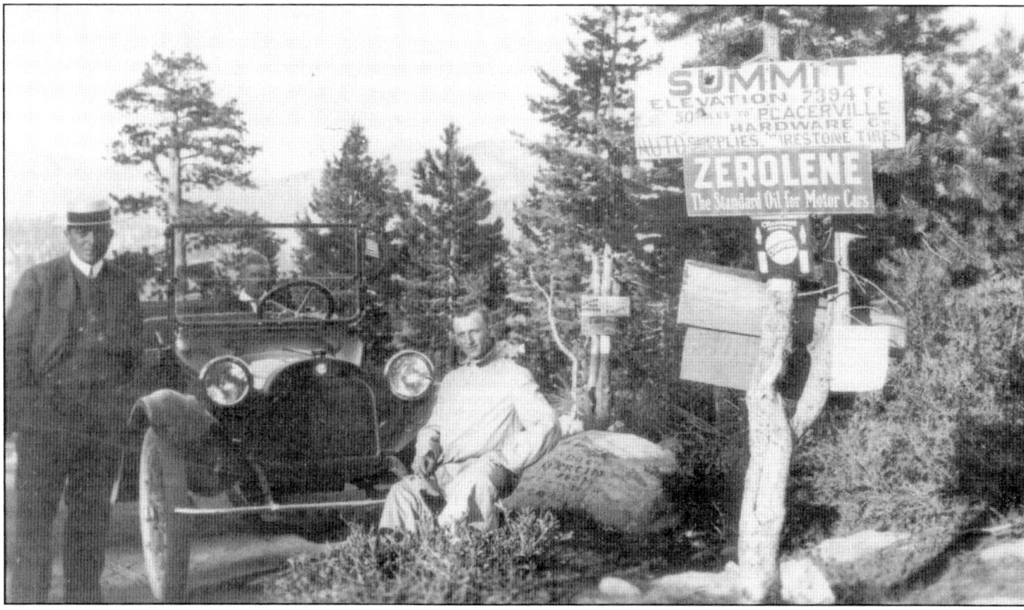

This automobile arrived from Tahoe. Among those seen here are William Kohn and Dick Hooker. The summit, Zerolene, and Champion advertisements remain on the tree. But the Al Tahoe Inn sign has been removed. There is a paper sign facing the camera, and two new advertisements facing Tahoe. On the tree in the background, there are two other advertisements. The man at center is leaning on a rock that reads, in part, "'Doc' Martin from. . . ." (Courtesy of the El Dorado County Historical Museum.)

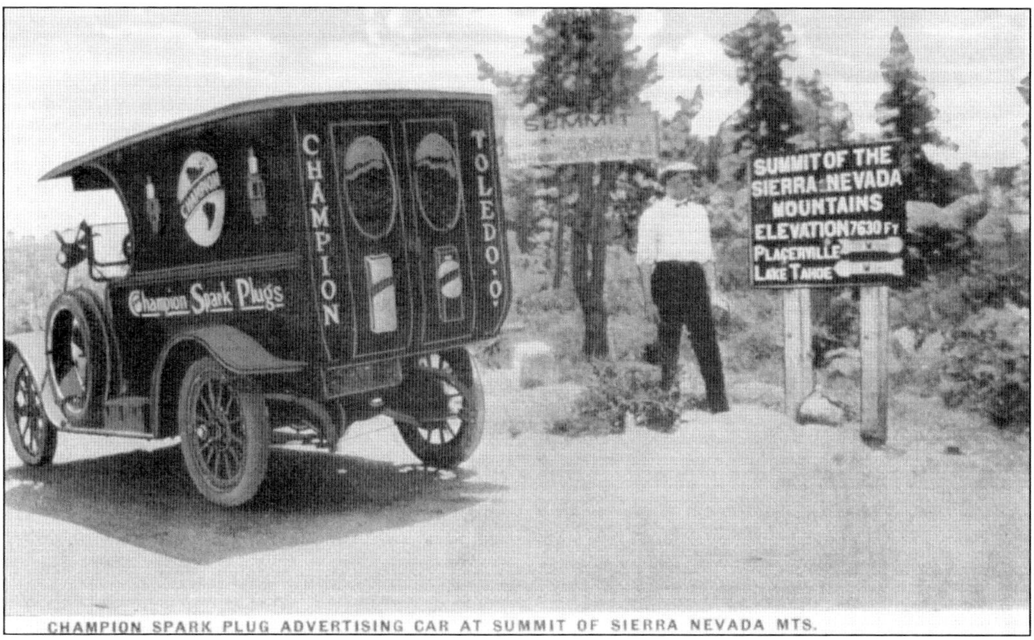

A Champion Spark Plugs advertising truck arrives at the summit, probably to check out the Champion advertisement. The driver finds only the old summit advertisement and a new sign, installed by the state, reading, "Summit of the Sierra Nevada Mountains, Elevation 7630 Ft." This sign, put up in 1915, listed an overly inaccurate elevation. (Courtesy of Paul DeWitt.)

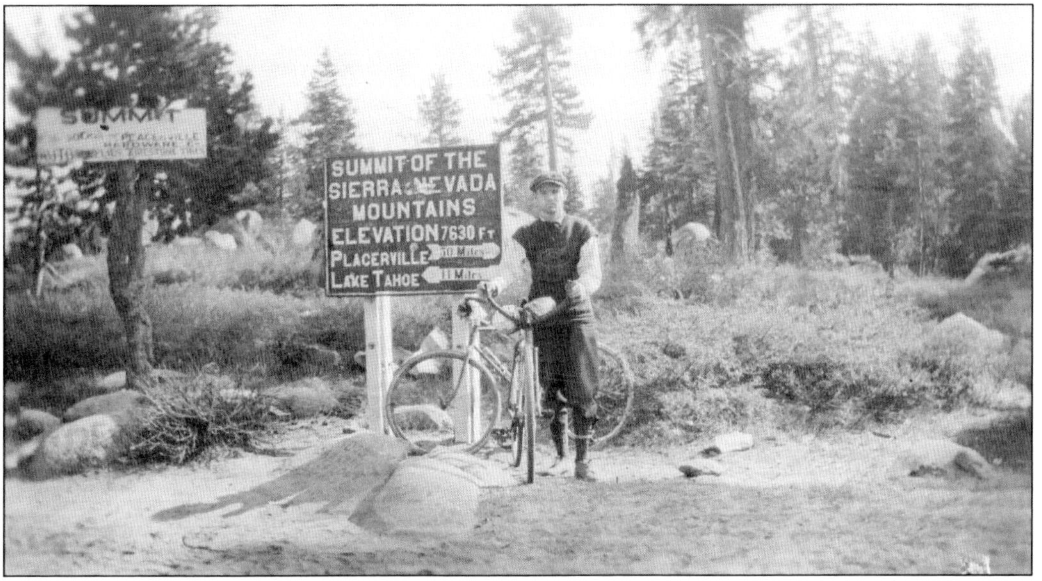

Gene Hepting took this photograph of his friend Abbie Budd as they road their bicycles from Sacramento to Lake Tahoe on October 19, 1917. They made it to Tahoe in 17 hours and 29 minutes and returned the next day. The road was sandy from Riverton to Tahoe. The grade was so steep from Strawberry to Slippery Ford and almost to Phillips that they had to walk their bicycles. (Courtesy of the Center for Sacramento History, Eugene Hepting Collection, 1985/024/2572.)

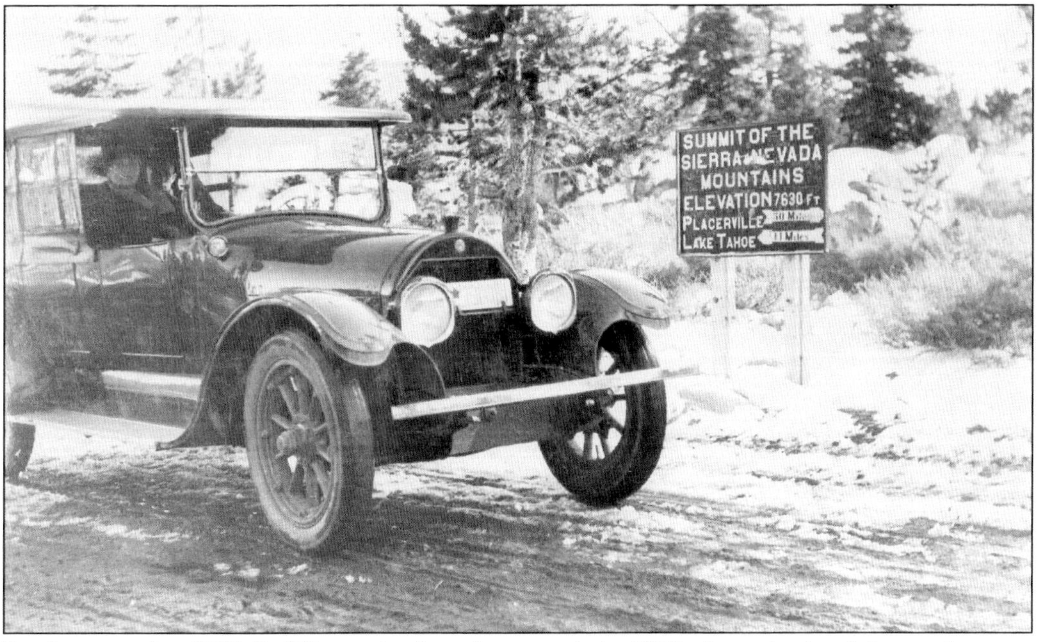

By the time this 1919 Cadillac arrived at the summit in 1920, the only sign left was the state summit sign with the incorrect elevation. In the five years since the sign was installed, about 100 people had carved or scratched their names or initials onto its surface. From a distance, as shown in these photographs, the sign looks pristine. But up close, the sign would show its ugly defacing. (Courtesy of the Lake Tahoe Historical Society.)

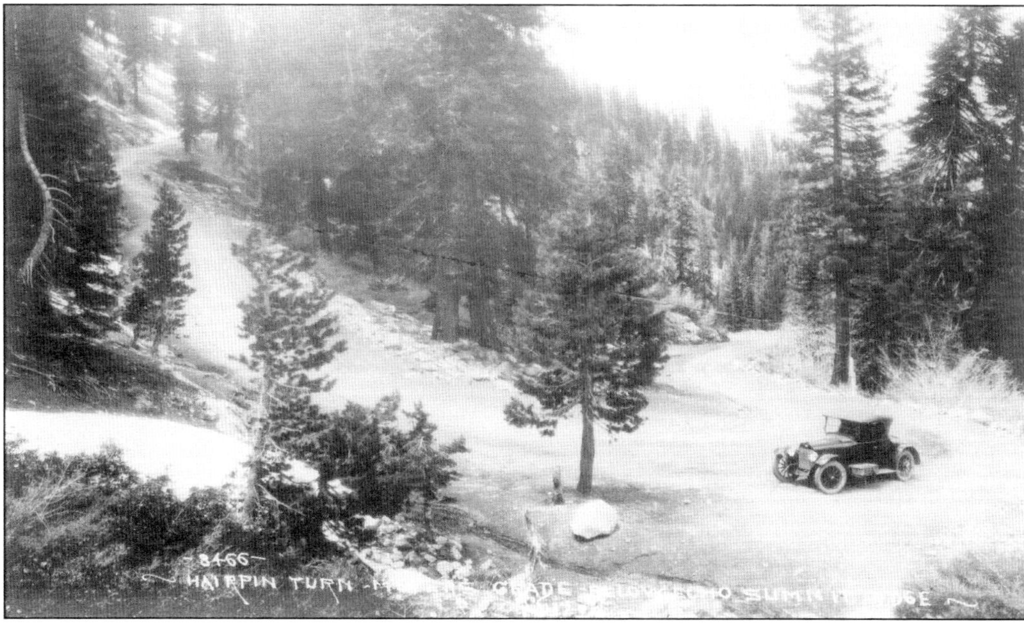

For 80 years, the shape and overall character of the road from Placerville to Meyers remained the same, whether as toll road, county road, or state highway. Several revisions improved it, like the highway from Strawberry to Pyramid Creek and up to Sayles Flat. But the worst part of the road was still from Echo Summit down the steep grade and hairpin turns at the top of the Meyers Grade. (Courtesy of Paul DeWitt.)

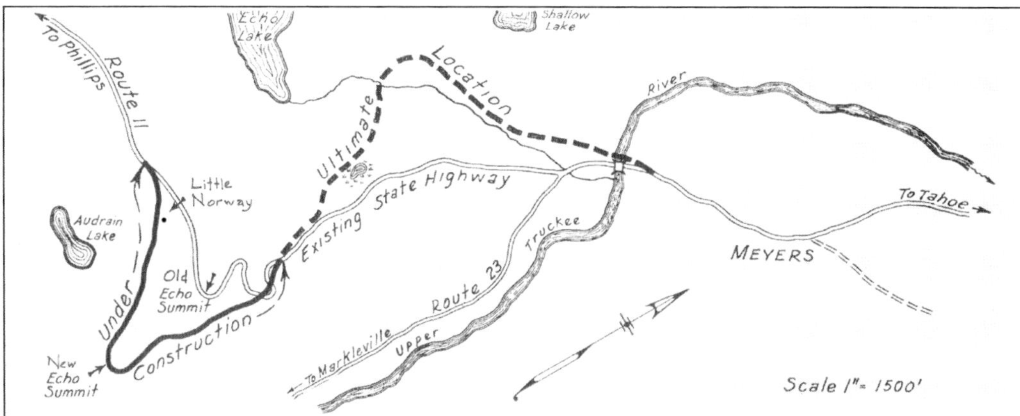

Map shows how relocated route will eliminate switchbacks below Echo Summit on existing Meyers Grade of Tahoe Highway.

(August 1938) *California Highways and Public Works*

In the mid-1930s, the state decided to change the route of Highway 50 to avoid the 11-percent grade and horseshoe turns at the top of Meyers Grade. This reconfiguration would create a much safer highway with at most a five-percent grade, no sharp turns, and a 24-foot-wide road surface. The new highway departed from the existing road two miles east of Phillips Station. It was easy to construct on a flat, mildly sloping, forested landscape to the new summit. (Courtesy of the California Department of Transportation; modified by Al DeWitt.)

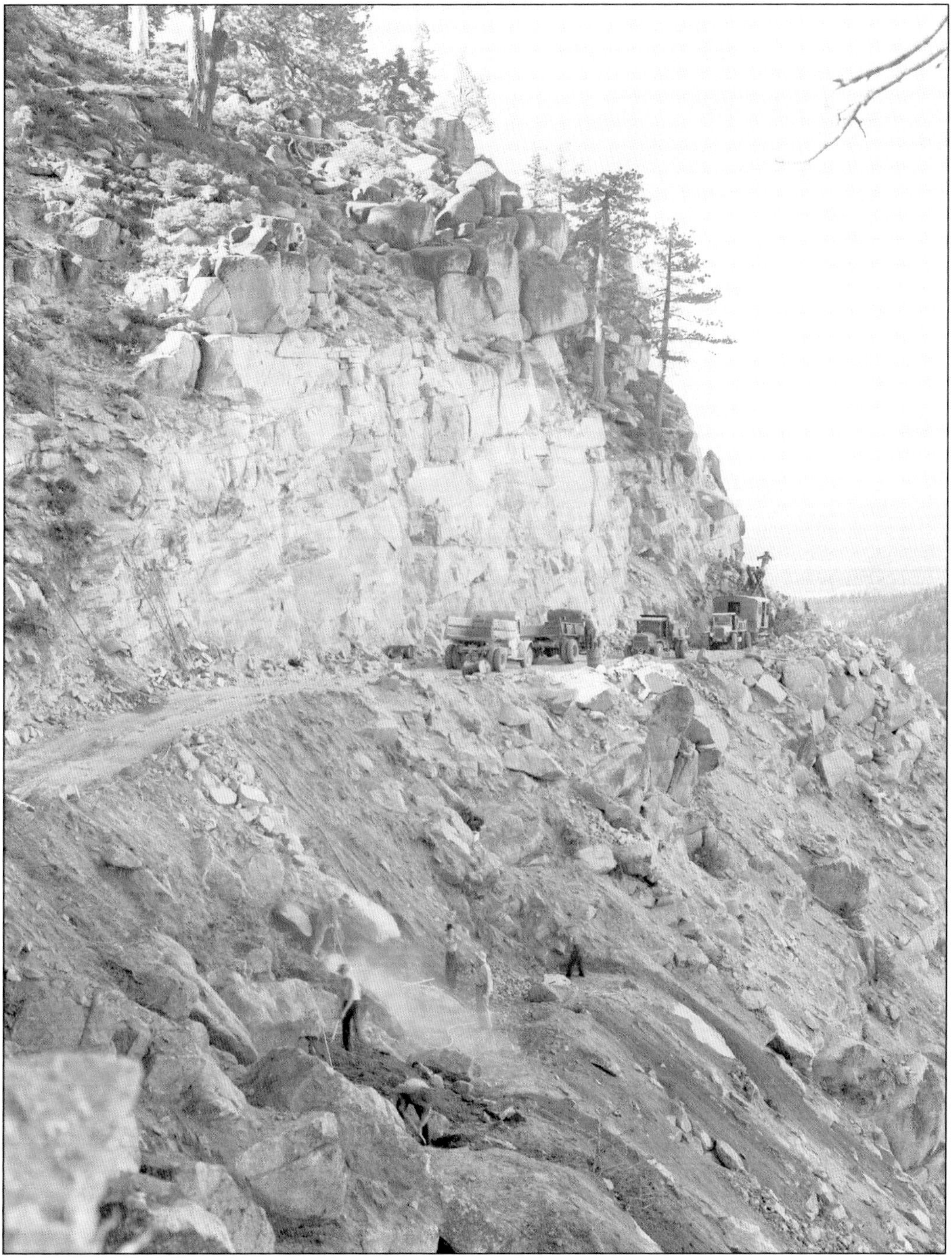

At the new summit, construction work made a left turn and was to go down the sheer rocky cliffs of the mountain ridge heading toward Meyers. At the top, construction obliterated the upper end of the old Hawley Grade. Continual blasting with dynamite was necessary to cut an almost vertical wall into the rocky cliffs. Some of the cliffs were dynamited 80 feet above the planned roadway. This photograph shows the magnitude and scope of the work being done. (Courtesy of the California Department of Transportation.)

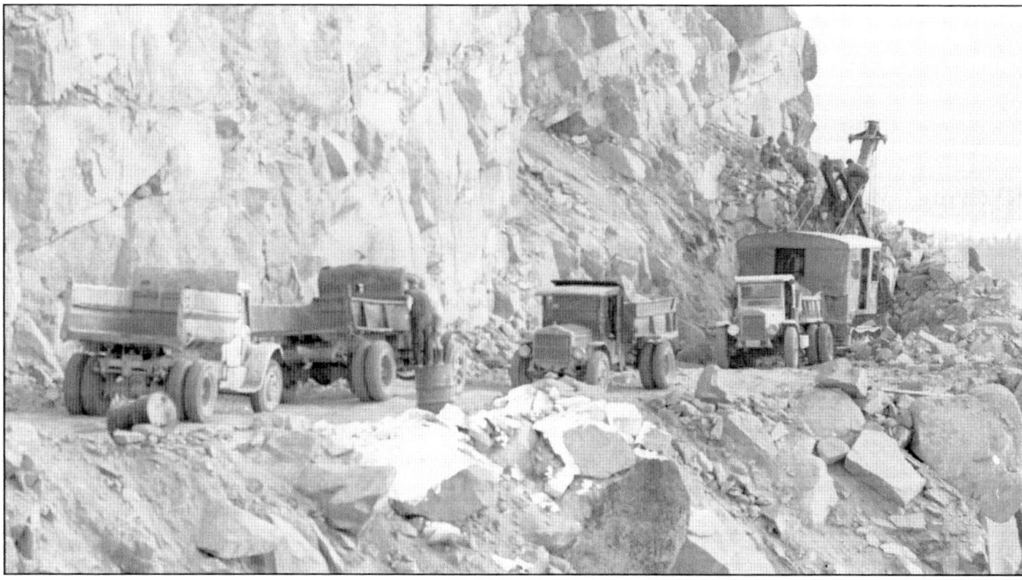

A steam shovel and large trucks worked to clear much of the blasted rubble from the roadway. The trucks could turn around on what later became a turnout on the finished highway. The work was very dangerous. (Courtesy of the California Department of Transportation.)

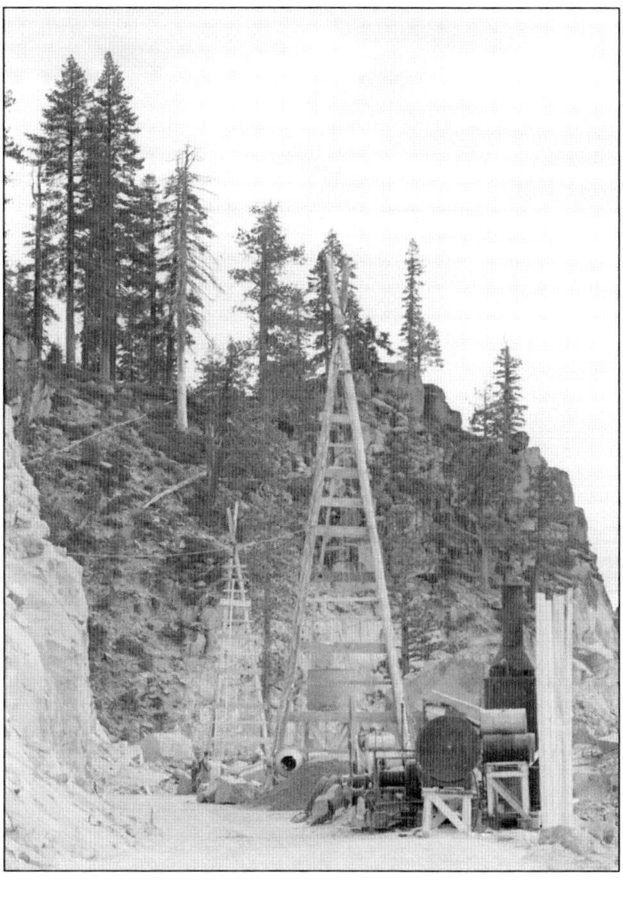

These power poles held electrical cables high above the roadway, allowing heavy equipment, like the steam shovel, trucks, and graders, to move under the wires without disturbing them. The electrical power was used to operate large rock drills, which made holes for dynamite, and possibly for electronic chisels, used to shape rock for retaining walls and roadside barriers. (Courtesy of the California Department of Transportation.)

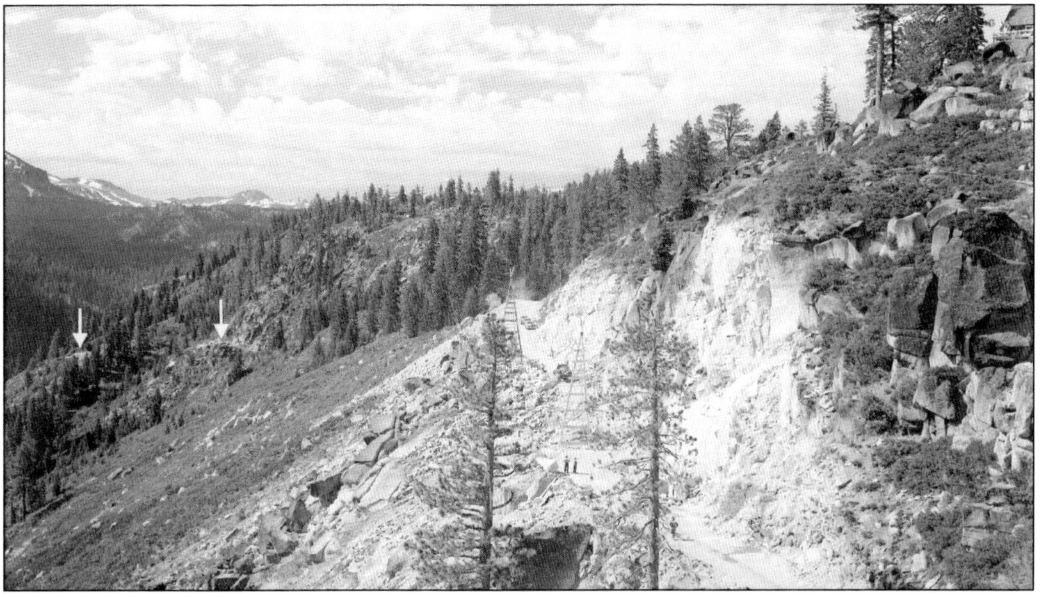

In this south-facing photograph of road construction, the arrows on the left indicate the old Hawley Grade, used from 1857 to the early 1860s. Numerous buildings, like the Echo Summit Lodge (top right), were just above the planned roadway and blasting areas. The highway department had to be careful in designing its dynamite blasts, to limit the damage to the landscape and to preserve the cabins. (Courtesy of the California Department of Transportation.)

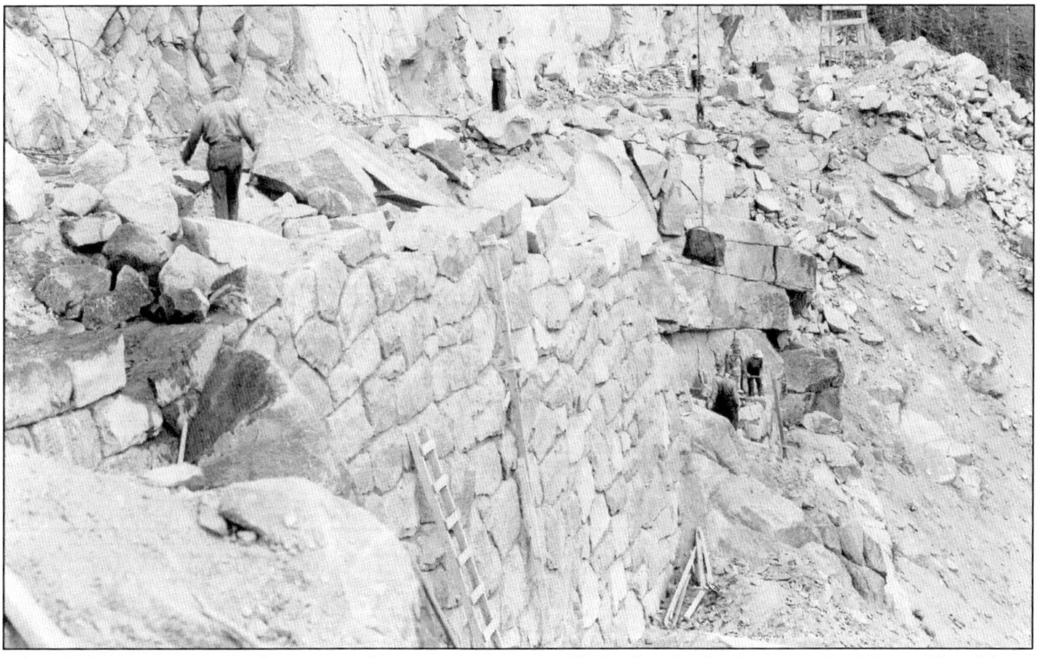

The cliffs were so steep that several large retaining walls had to be built from the blasted boulders. Some of the boulders weighed more than a ton, and all had to be chiseled and shaped to fit each other to make a strong and safe rock wall to support the roadbed. Cranes, wenches, tackle, and pulleys had to be used to lower the rocks into place to construct the walls. (Courtesy of the California Department of Transportation.)

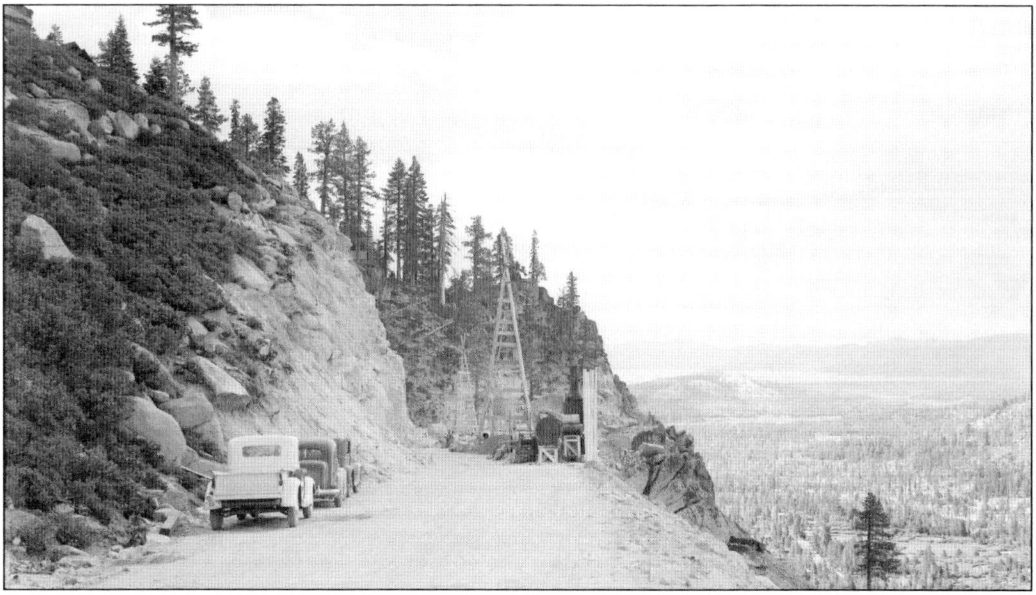

The building of the roadway at the top of the new Meyers Grade is almost complete at its 24-foot width. It is lacking the paved surface, the rock barrier walls, and guardrails. The cost of this whole project, from where it began two miles east of Phillips' Station to its junction with the old Meyers Grade, was only $320,000. The refurbishing of the road from Echo Summit to the old Meyers Grade in May 2011 cost about $3 million. (Courtesy of the California Department of Transportation.)

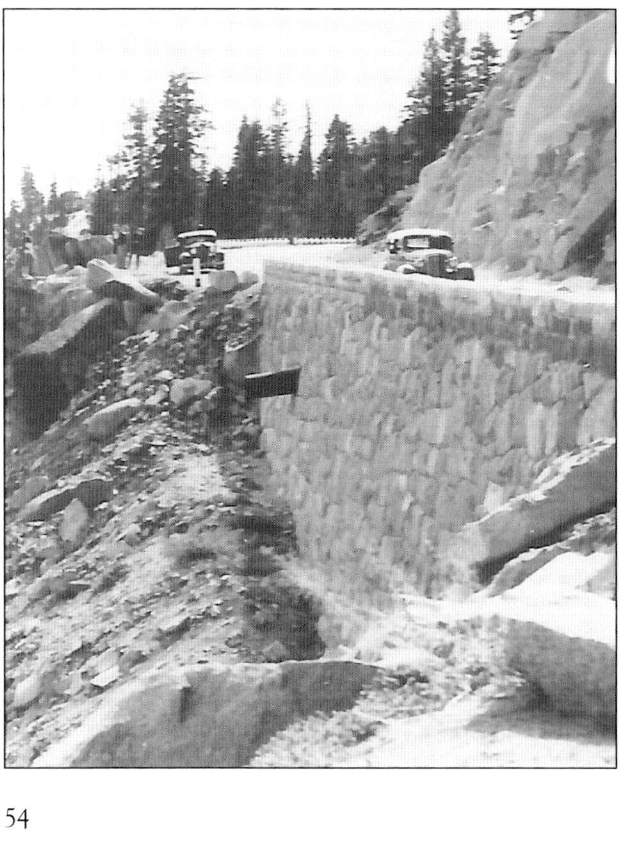

On the road from the summit, around the bend, there was a wooden guardrail, followed by a turnout where tourists could pull over and take photographs of the Tahoe Basin below. This was followed by retaining walls and rock-wall safety barriers. The retaining wall seen here is small compared to those 50 yards down the road. The pipe sticking out of the wall is for draining water from the cliffs on the other side of the highway. (Courtesy of Paul DeWitt.)

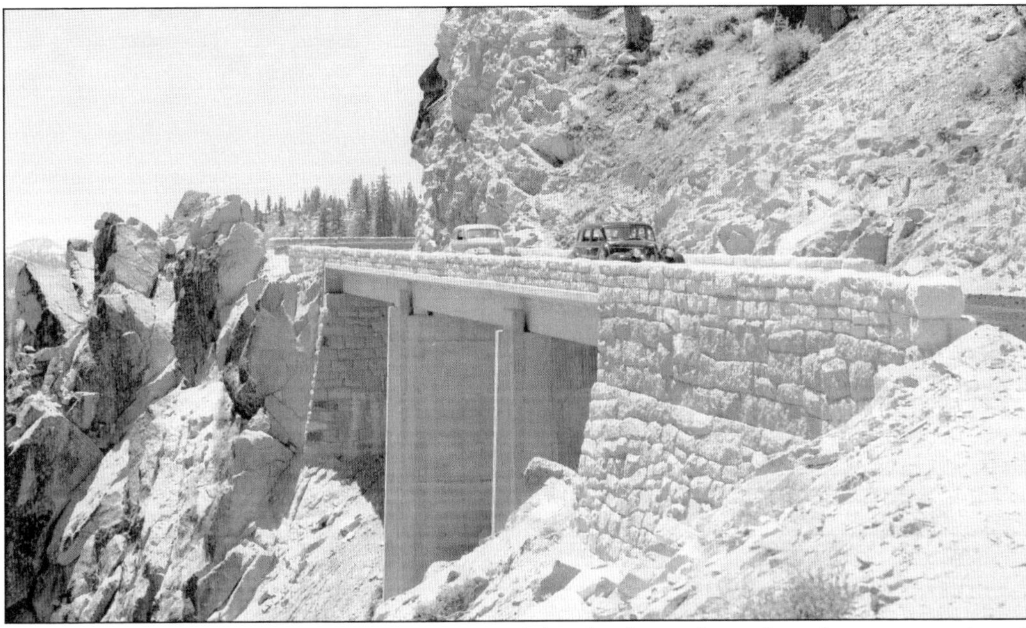

At one point, it was necessary to construct a 113-foot bridge with reinforced concrete and steel. When this section of the Meyers Grade was rebuilt from the summit to the junction with the old Meyers Grade in May 2011, the old retaining walls and road next to the walls were replaced with a new paving material and a granite-looking concrete barrier. The only place where the original rock wall remains is on this bridge. (Courtesy of the California Department of Transportation.)

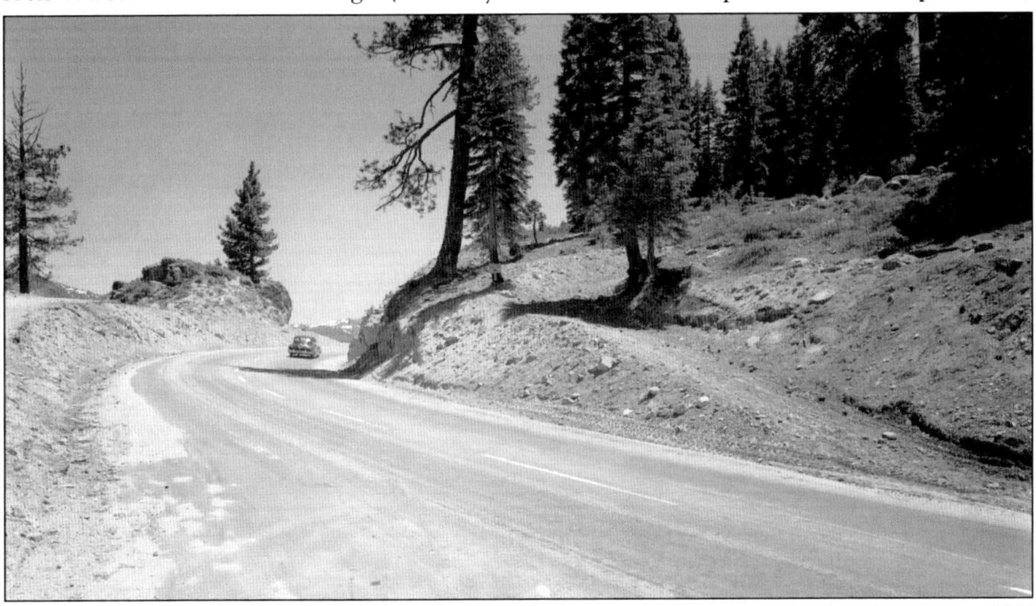

This is the end of the 1938–1940 highway project. The new highway crosses the old Johnson Hill trail at the second tree from the left. The old Osgood Grade (old Meyers Grade) is seen coming up on the left side and crossing over the new highway next to the large tree. There is a new road on the right going up from the highway and joining the Meyers Grade to the top at Johnson Pass road where Echo Summit Lodge is located. This road is still used today as a short cut to the ridge cabins. (Courtesy of the California Department of Transportation.)

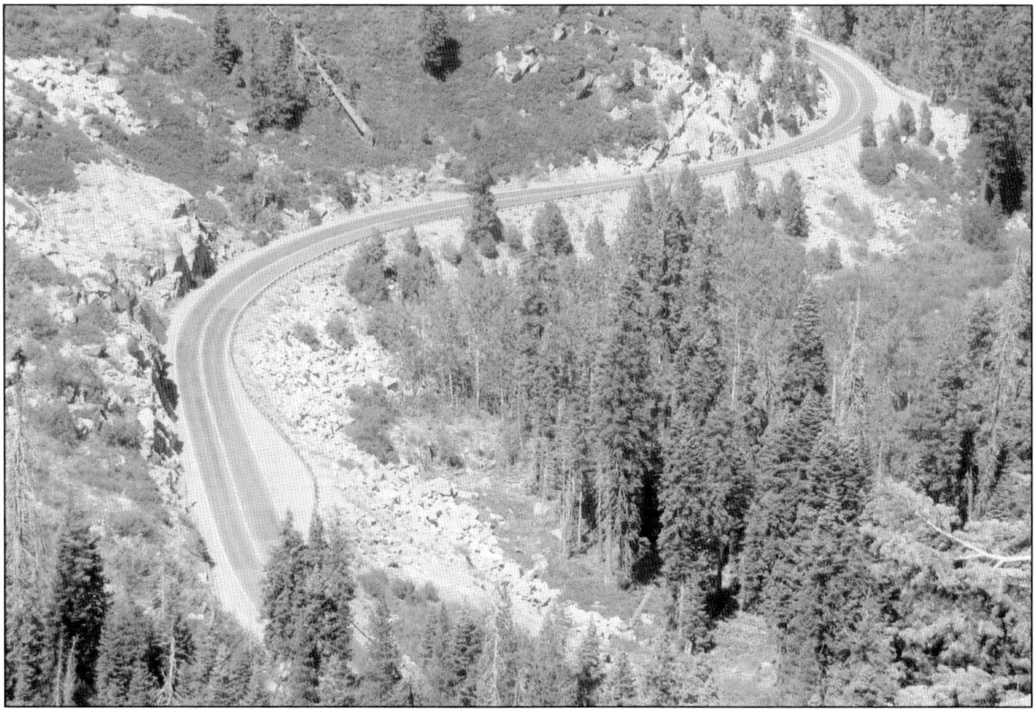

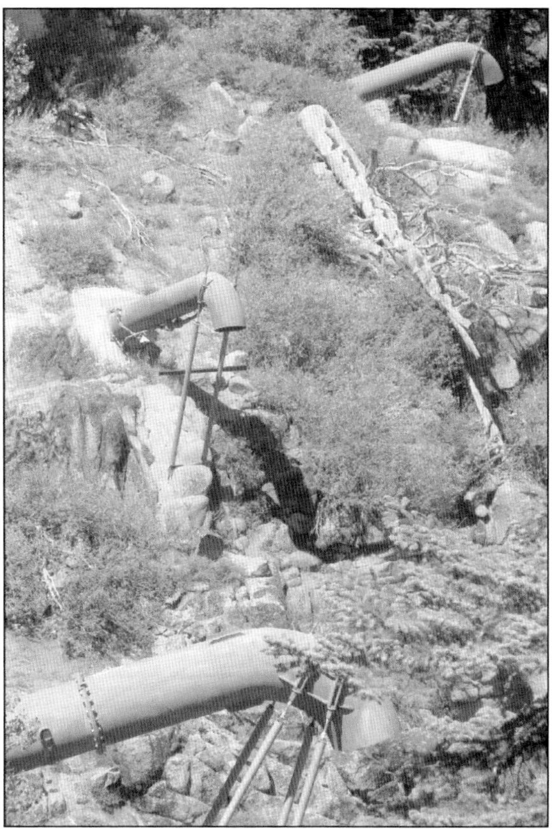

After World War II, the rest of the new Meyers Grade was completed, in 1946 and 1947. This section was easier to build, because there were no retaining walls and no granite barrier walls. Only steel guardrails were necessary. The old Meyers Grade is closed with a gate unless Caltrans opens it in winter when snow slides or avalanches block off the highway and tourists want to drive to South Lake Tahoe. (Courtesy of Paul DeWitt.)

In winter, snow slides and avalanches blocked the lower end of the new Meyers Grade. At first, Caltrans used a 75-millimeter recoilless rifle to fire shells into the packed snow. The exploding shells would loosen the snow, which would come down in a planned slide. In the 1990s, Caltrans constructed large snow cannons along the ridge, using propane and oxygen to create loud explosions. These explosions created the desired snow slides, and the road was cleared. (Courtesy of Paul DeWitt.)

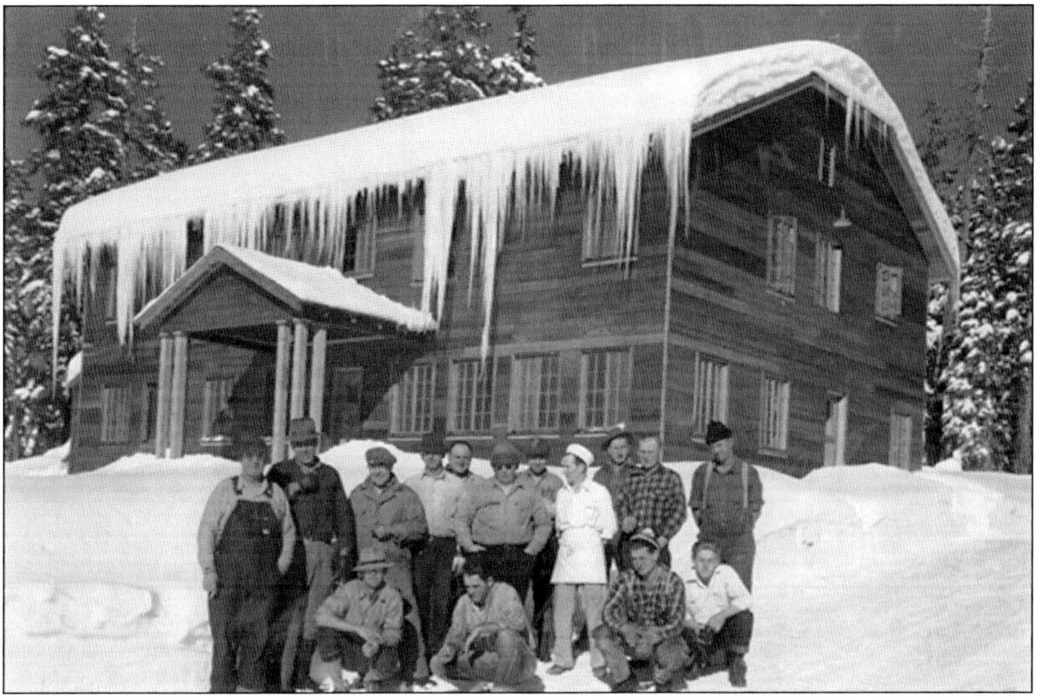

Seen here adorned with icicles, the California Division of Highway's maintenance station is located on Highway 50 at Echo Summit. Its courteous crew and snowplows are ready to keep Highway 50 open for automobile traffic from Kyburz to South Lake Tahoe. Everyone wants snow for the recreational winter season, and Echo Summit's maintenance station provides the best community and public services in the treacherous conditions. (Courtesy of the El Dorado County Historical Museum.)

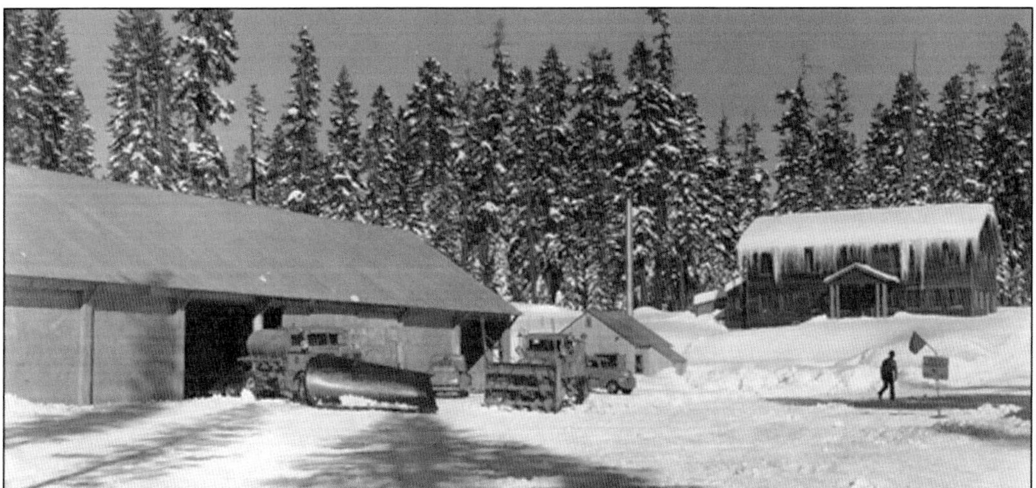

California Department of Transportation's Echo Summit maintenance station clears Highway 50 during winter storms. In January 1952, deadly snow slides stranded a bus of Mill Valley high school students here for a week. Foreman Mike Willet stated, "We aren't running a highway, we're running a nursery up here," quickly adding that the youngsters had been cheerful and cooperative. Pat Collins and Haven "Jorgy" Jorgensen skied from Echo Chalet bringing much needed food from Echo Chalet's Store. (Courtesy of the El Dorado County Historical Museum.)

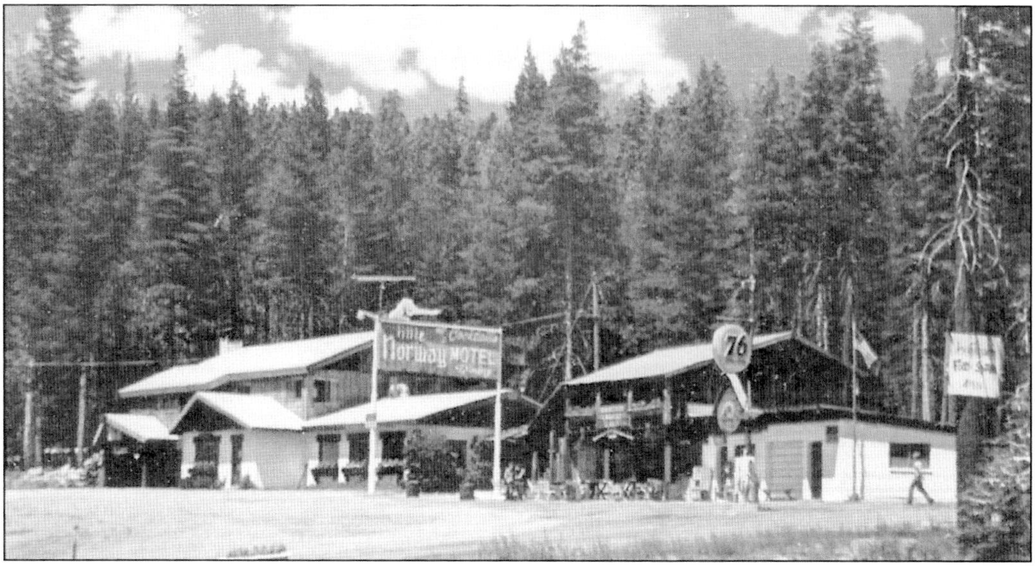

Don and Patricia "Winnie" Peterson opened Little Norway in 1956. Its name derived from neighbor Shirley King, who mentioned that the summit reminded her of Norway and Norwegian relatives. It was a popular Echo Summit resort, offering a year-round restaurant, bar, gas station, and lodging. A post office was established there on September 1, 1961, with Don Peterson as its postmaster. Damaged by fire, the post office was transferred to the Twin Bridges on March 14, 1986, which later relocated about a mile west, across from Strawberry Lodge. (Courtesy of Paul DeWitt.)

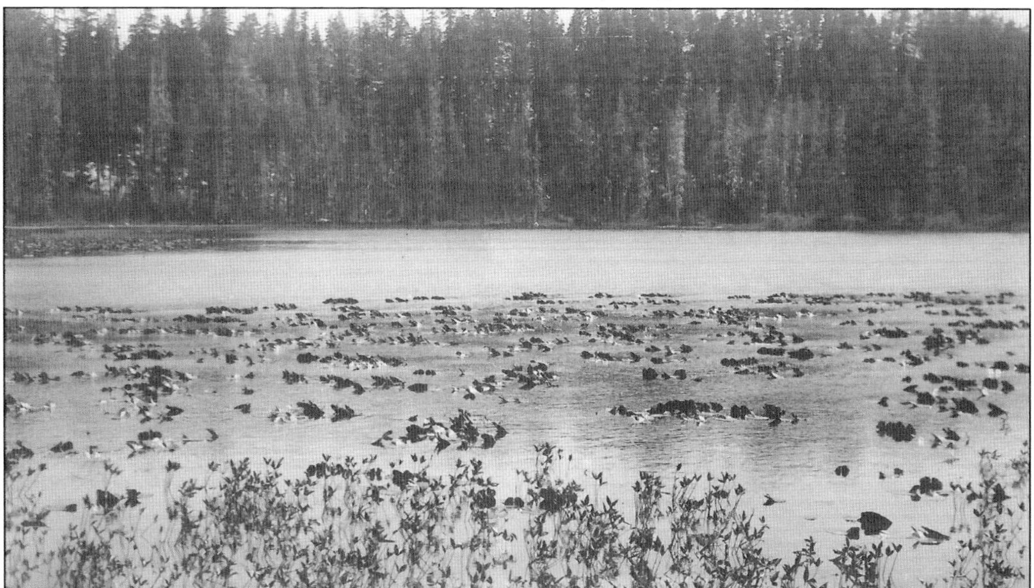

In this c. 1920 photograph, lily pads in Lake Audrain are abundant prior to Golden Empire Boy Scout Council's opening of Camp Audrain on US Forest Service land in 1940. The lake was named after Thomas Audrain, the Southern sympathizer who owned Audrain Station along the Placerville wagon road. Audrain-area springs are the source of the South Fork of the American River. Today, Lake Audrain draws visitors to swim, fish on its quiet shores, and gather abundant edible berries. (Courtesy of Dorothy De Mare.)

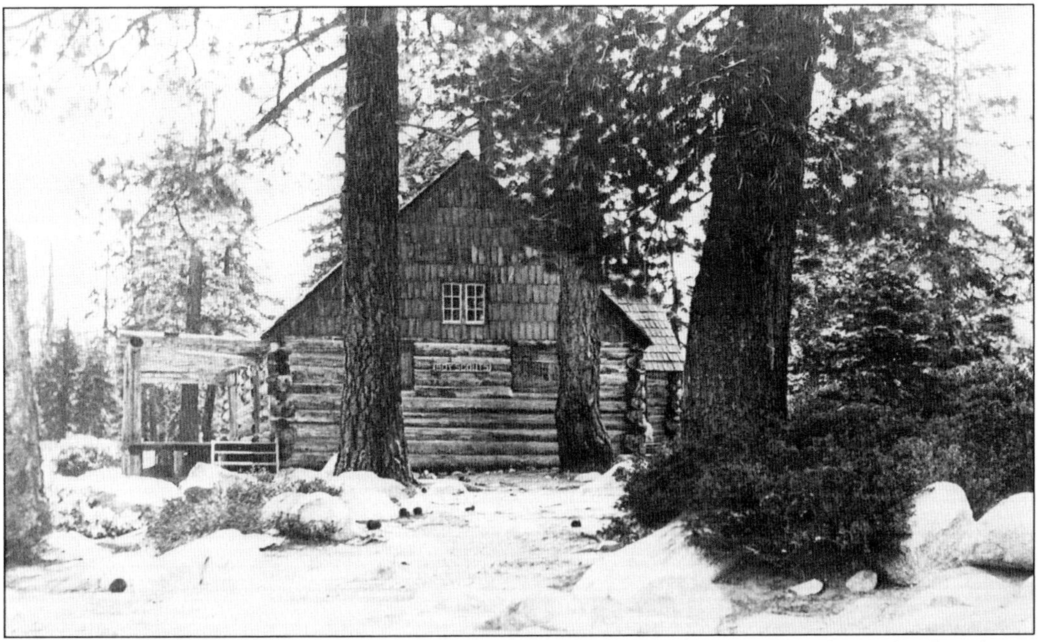

Access to Camp Audrain, located 48 miles east of Placerville and a quarter mile south of Highway 50 was made by driving on a dirt road and crossing over a small wooden bridge that no longer exists. Halfway into camp, on a plateau between the highway and Lake Audrain, was a large campfire area. The dining hall shown here was located on a low ridge above the plateau overlooking Lake Audrain's recreational area. (Courtesy of the El Dorado Historical Museum.)

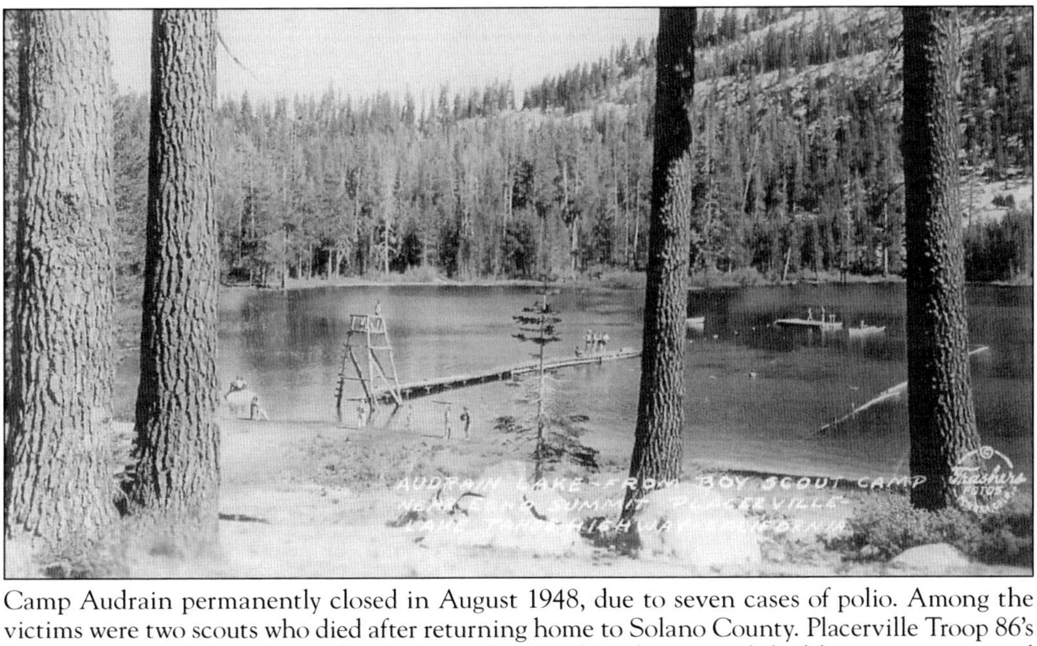

Camp Audrain permanently closed in August 1948, due to seven cases of polio. Among the victims were two scouts who died after returning home to Solano County. Placerville Troop 86's Robert Henson and Elwin Veerkamp acquired polio when their troop hiked from its campground in Phillips to swim at Audrain. Wesley Gray, son of Echo Lake concessionaires Euell and Nora Gray, recovered after being released in November 1948 from San Francisco Children's Hospital. (Courtesy of Dorothy De Mare.)

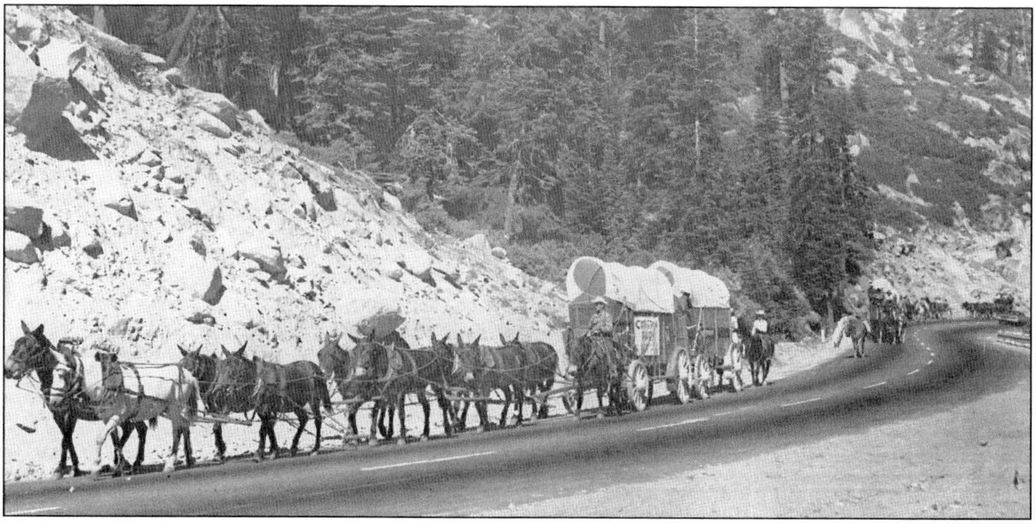

Highway 50's first wagon train began in 1949, commemorating the centennial of California's gold rush. During the annual event, participants dress in period clothing and ride in Conestoga wagons, stagecoaches, and on horseback. Beginning in Zephyr Cove, the journey westward to Placerville takes five days. Overnight stops varied yearly at Ralph King's property near Little Norway, Darrington Meadows, Phillips, Strawberry Lodge, Fred's Place, Kyburz, Pacific House, and Pollock Pines. Some of these places no longer exist. (Courtesy of the Highway 50 Association.)

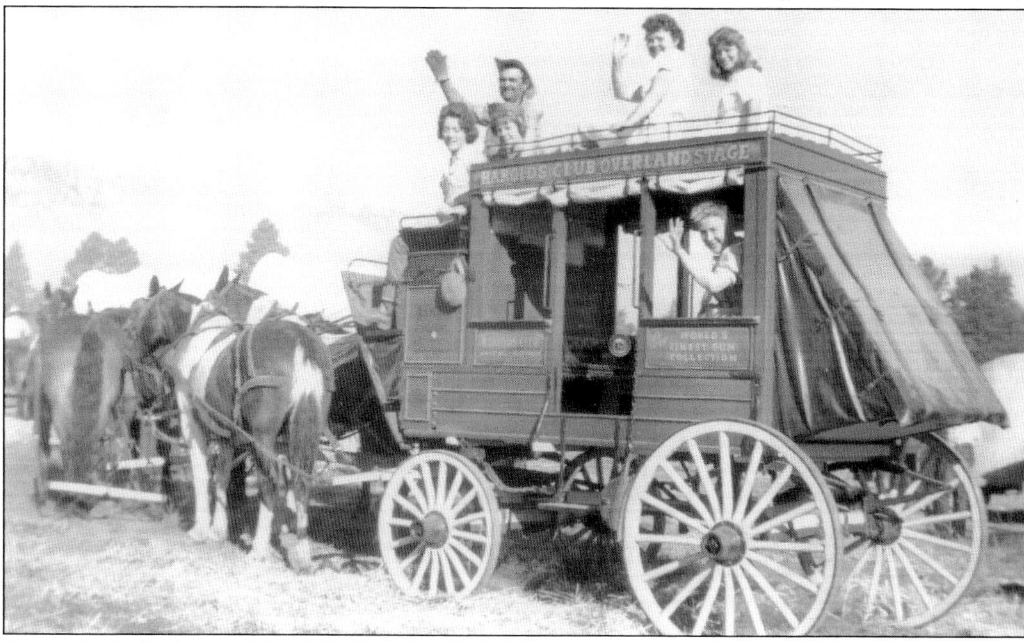

Chet Mitchell, driving Harold's Club Overland Stage, waves as the July 1961 wagon train leaves Meyers for passage up Echo Summit. Chet is sitting next to Dorothy King De Mare, also wearing a cowboy hat, and to the left of Dorothy is Kathy Ehrhorn. On the top right is Marylee King Larson and to Marylee's left is an unidentified woman. Inside is Florence Berry, the wife of Sen. Swift Berry, 1961's Highway 50 Association president. For years, Chet guided pack trains into Desolation Valley and operated Echo Summit and Alpine Stables with his wife, Carolyn. (Courtesy of Dorothy De Mare.)

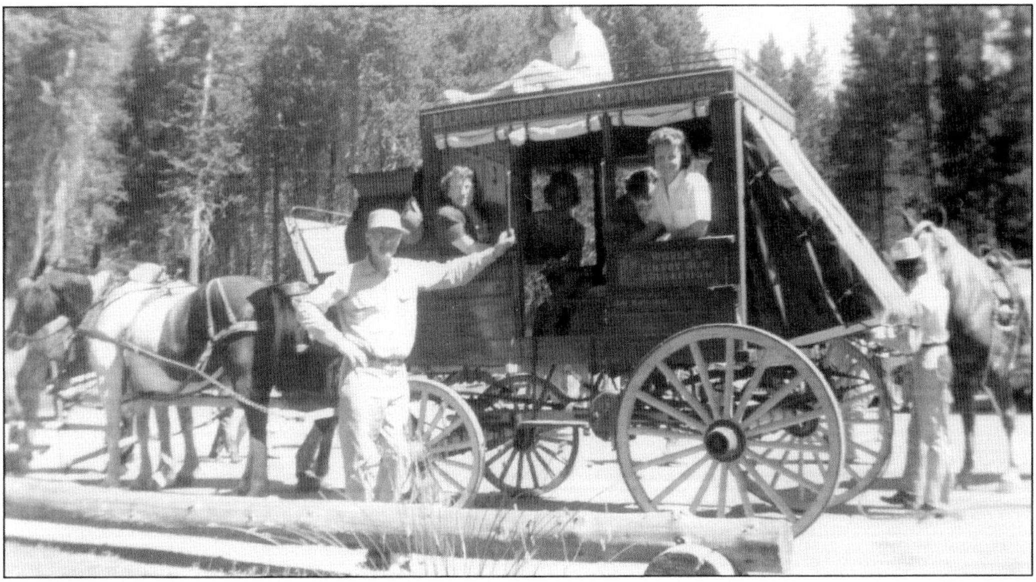

The Highway 50 Association, El Dorado County Chamber, and Sheriff's Posse's Annual Wagon Train reenactment from Stateline, Nevada, to Placerville briefly stopped at Little Norway before its overnight stay at Pow Wow. Highway travelers enjoy the slow-moving procession as they safely pass it. In July 1961, Echo Summit resident Adolph Ehrhorn greets stage riders Pearl King Shaw, Dorothy King De Mare, Helen Ehrhorn, and Shirley King inside the coach. Marylee King Larson is sitting on top. (Courtesy of Dorothy De Mare.)

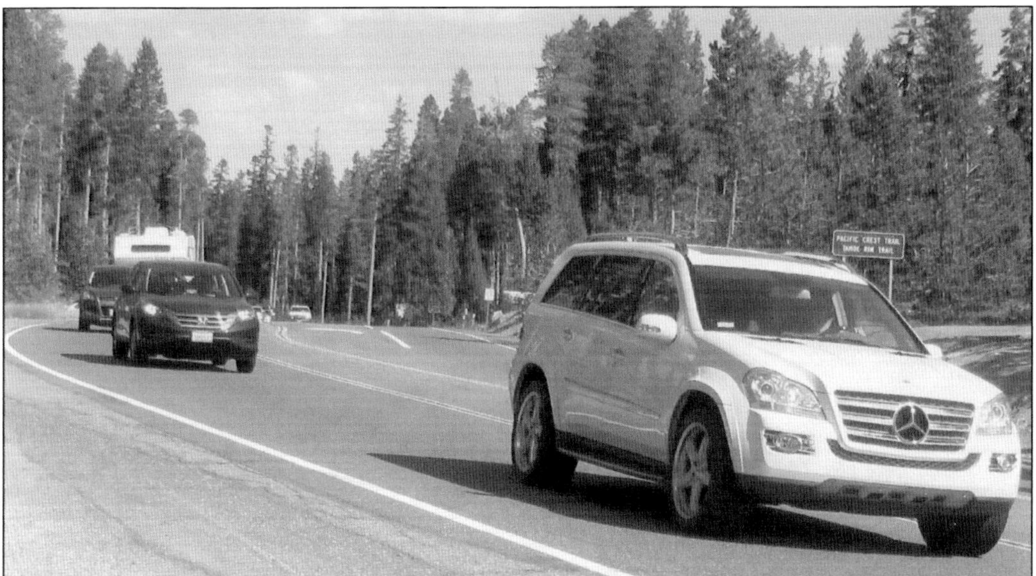

According to the South Lake Tahoe Chamber of Commerce, about one million vehicles visit the South Lake Tahoe Basin and Lake Valley every year. In the summer months, the heaviest travel occurs during the Memorial Day, Fourth of July, and Labor Day holidays. The heaviest travel periods during ski season are Thanksgiving, the two weeks of Christmas and New Years, and Easter. The most popular way of coming to South Lake Tahoe is over Echo Summit. (Courtesy of Paul DeWitt.)

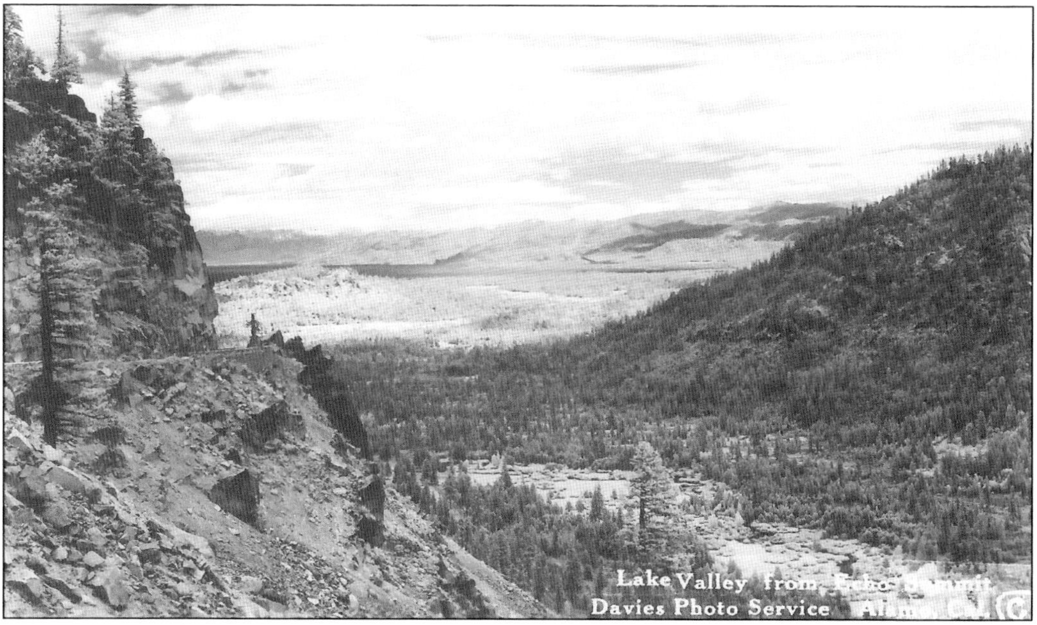

As tourists start down Meyers Grade, they often stop at the turnoffs to photograph the spectacular view of the Tahoe Basin or to pose with friends and relatives, using the view as a background. After climbing back into their vehicles, they proceed to the valley for gambling at casinos, lodging at resorts and motels, boating and water-skiing, staying at campgrounds, visiting beautiful beaches for swimming and sunbathing, and skiing and snowboarding in the winter months. (Courtesy of Paul DeWitt.)

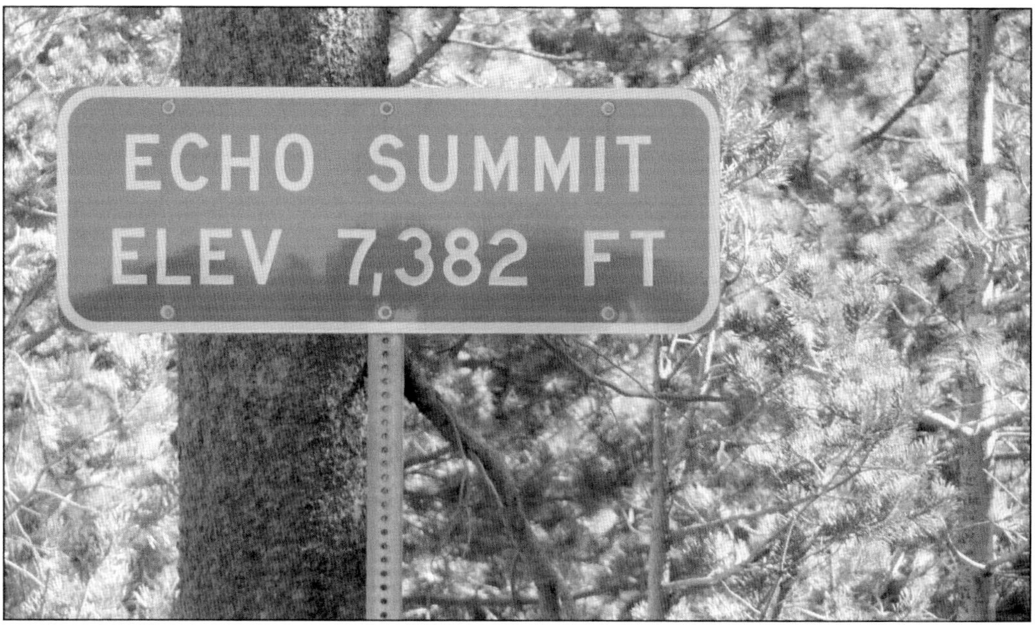

Unlike during the first few decades of the 20th century, no one today stops to have their photographs taken at the Echo Summit sign, which reflects the correct elevation, 7,382 feet. People are in such a hurry to get to the valley that many of them pass the sign without even paying attention to it, or they do not see it at all. (Courtesy of Paul DeWitt.)

Four

ECHO LAKE

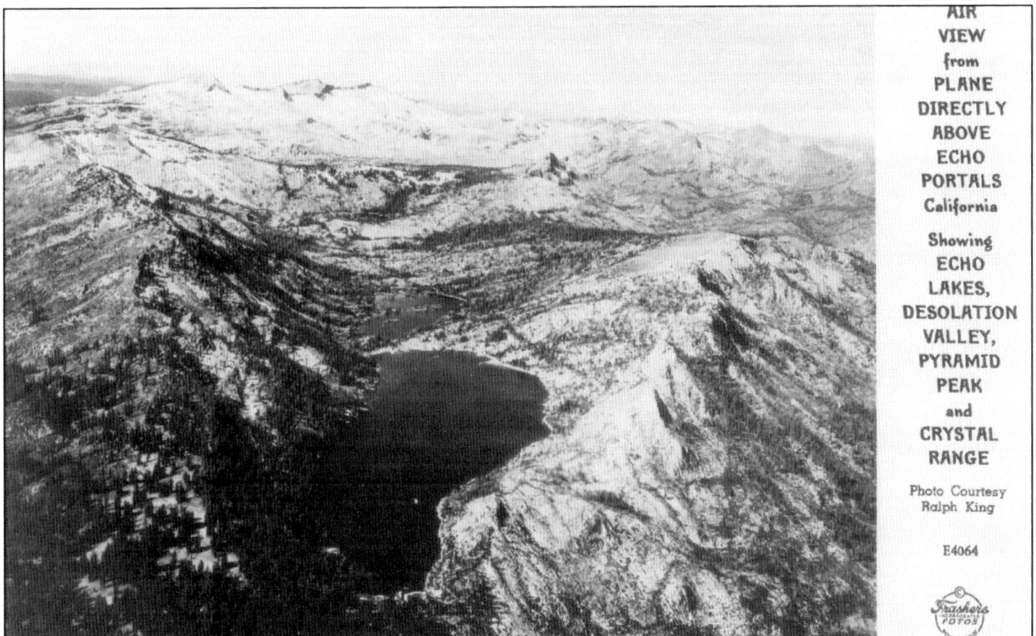

Shirley and Ralph King commissioned photographer friends Josephine and Burton Frasher Sr. to publish this 1936 aerial image of Echo Lakes and the Desolation Valley Wilderness Area. It advertised Echo Portals Store, which the Kings had recently opened a mile south of Echo Lake. Ralph King was Burton Frasher Sr.'s tour guide while hiking and skiing this pristine wilderness, so Burton's lens could capture its surrounding beauty. From the mid-1930s to the late 1940s, Frasher published views for King, Echo Chalet, and other resort owners on Highway 50, Echo Summit, and in the Lake Tahoe area. The Echo Lake Improvement Association published a 1939 directory map of Upper and Lower Echo. The tract names are Island Tract, Boys Camp, Public Landing, North Shore Tract, Hemlock Tract, Dartmouth Cove, The Channel, Public Camp, Channel Tract, Mermaid Cove Tract, South Shore Tract, Juniper Tract, Echo Chalet, Echo Road Tract, Berkeley Municipal Camp, the Portals, and Atwood Tract. (Courtesy of Dorothy De Mare.)

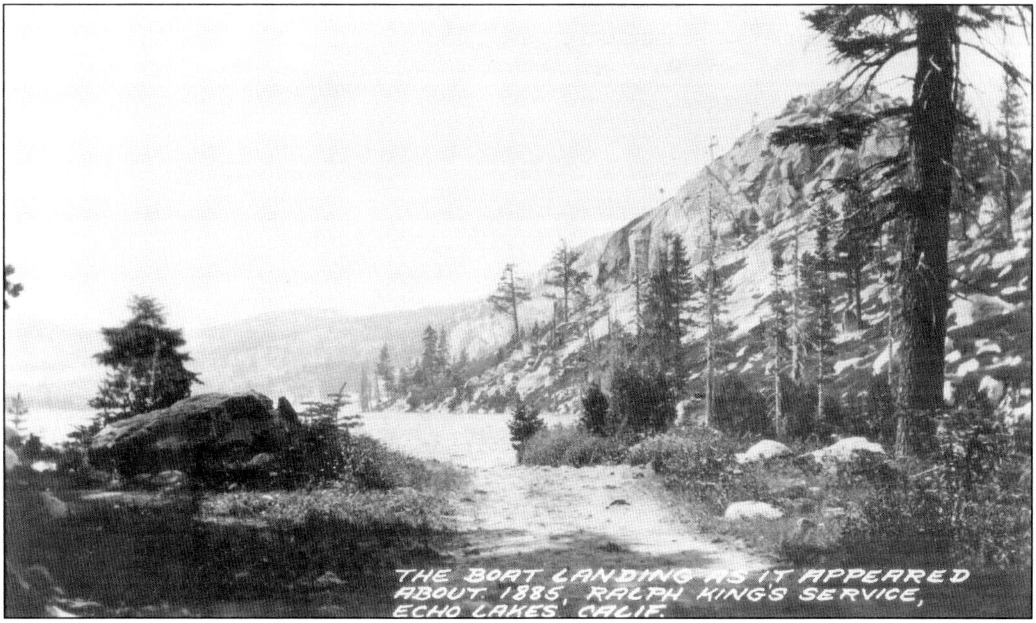

In 1860, Echo Lakes were called Lake McClelland and Osgood's Lake. Sources differ as to how Echo Lake was named. In May 1866, Ramsdale Buoy yelled, "Raise the dead!" His partying friends loudly repeated the cry, and echoes followed. Buoy replied, "If that's the best you can do, boys, I still give you Echo Lake." Others reported that a fishing party heard an echo after dropping an oar on the water. John Becker, who owned much of the land surrounding the boat landing, built his homestead cabin in about 1895 near the three rocks pictured on the left. In 1938, the Echo Chalet was built on the same site and continues to provide services for the Echo Lakes community. (Courtesy of Paul DeWitt.)

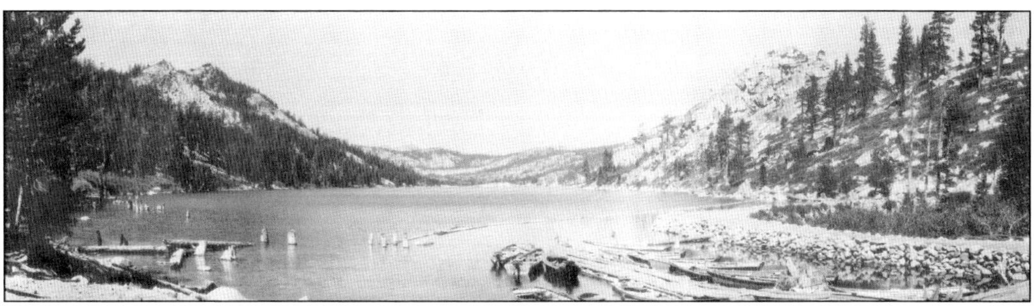

This c. 1906 photograph of Lower Echo's harbor looks west to Desolation Valley and the Crystal Range. Dumbo (formerly Flag Rock) and Flag Pole Peak (formerly Eagle Rock) are to the right (north) side, and Becker's Peak and Talking Mountain are on the south side. Stumps of trees that once grew are visible along the original shoreline. The trees died after the dam, built in 1876 of granite rock, raised the lake's level. (Courtesy of Dorothy De Mare.)

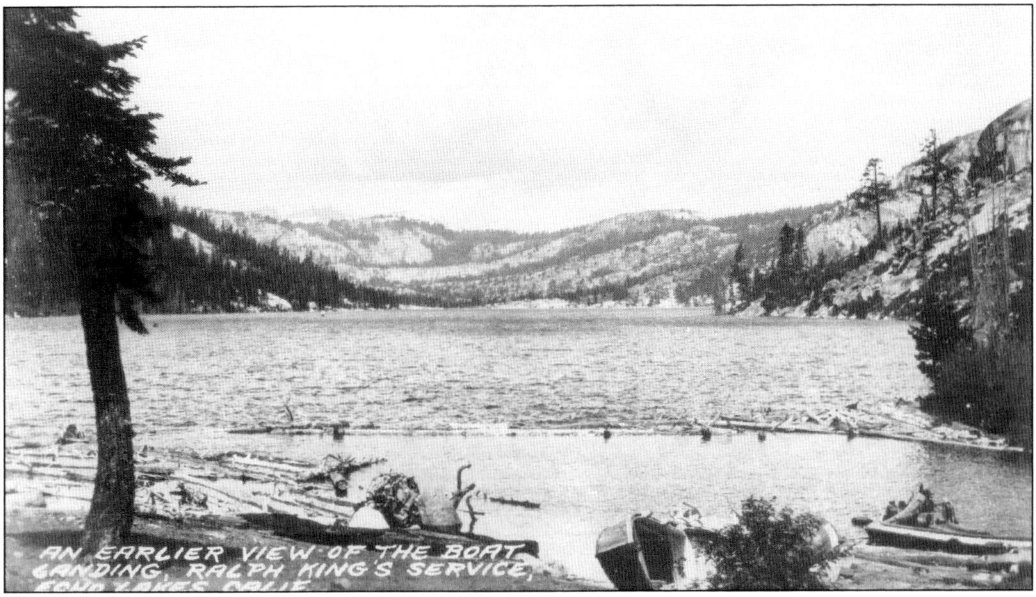

This 1890s photograph was used to advertise Ralph King's 1928 Echo Lake services. Boat operations were provided by the following: Hamden Cagwin (1897–1914); Captain Lenay and a few others provided some services during the World War I era (1915–1922); Uncle Tom Swansborough (1923–1927); Ralph King (1928–1942); Euell Gray (1927–1937); Curt Rocca (1939–1946); Haven Jorgensen (1946–1968); Kay and Roy Johnson (1968–1974); Haven Jorgensen (1974–1975); Mary Lou and Bruce Brown (1975–1982); Medshallah Group (1982–1984); and Kathleen and Tom Fashinell (1984–present). (Courtesy of Dorothy De Mare.)

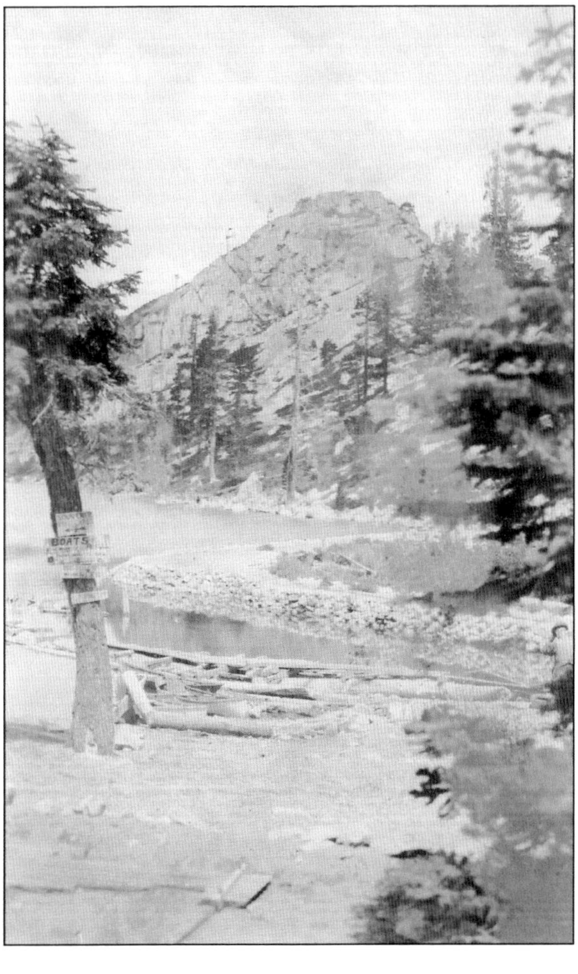

Ed Hawley, descendant of Asa Hershel Hawley and photographer friend of Ham Cagwin, kept a tent 100 yards east of Cagwin's Echo Lake cabin and a cabin below Old Meyers Grade, near Osgood's Toll House. Tree signs advertise Hawley's postcards. "Souvenir Post Cards, Boats for hire from hours 5 to let at 25 cents—rates made per day, Echo Lake—H Cagwin & Co., Ice Cold Beer, and Chewing Gum." This is all that could be read on the signs. (Courtesy of Dorothy De Mare.)

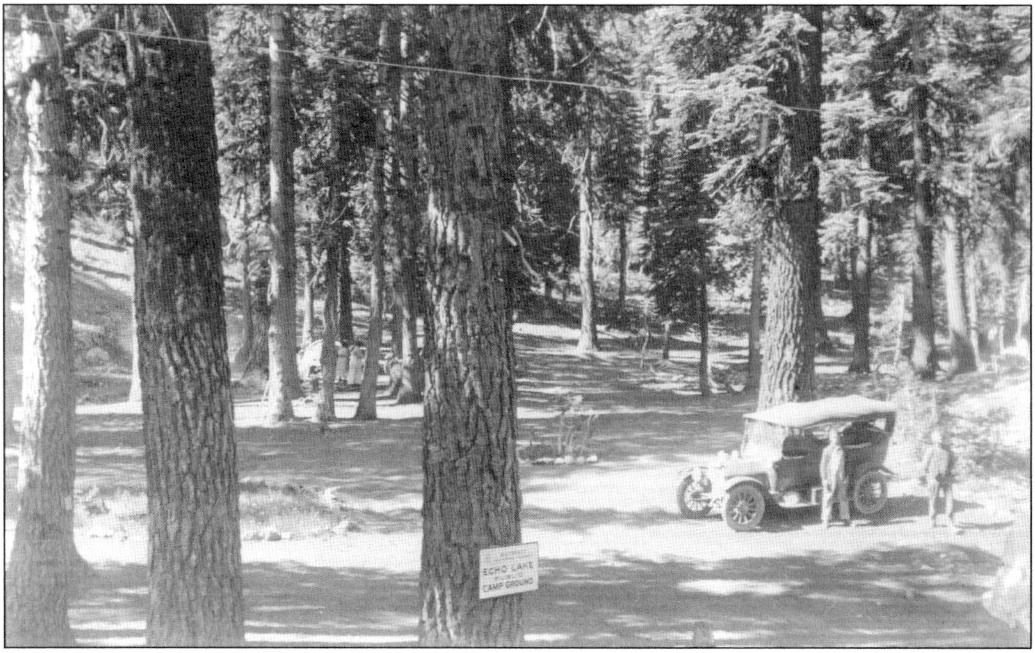

Campgrounds throughout the Sierras provided affordable family recreation that became popular with the expansion of automobile tourism. Future Echo Lake cabin owners fell in love with Echo when they first camped at Uncle Sam's Campground, known as Echo Lake Government Campground, now the upper parking area. Photographer T.C. Wohlbruck published this postcard around 1920. After people secured their US Forest Service lease sites, they built their cabins. Many cabins are still owned by descendants of original leaseholders. (Courtesy of Dorothy De Mare.)

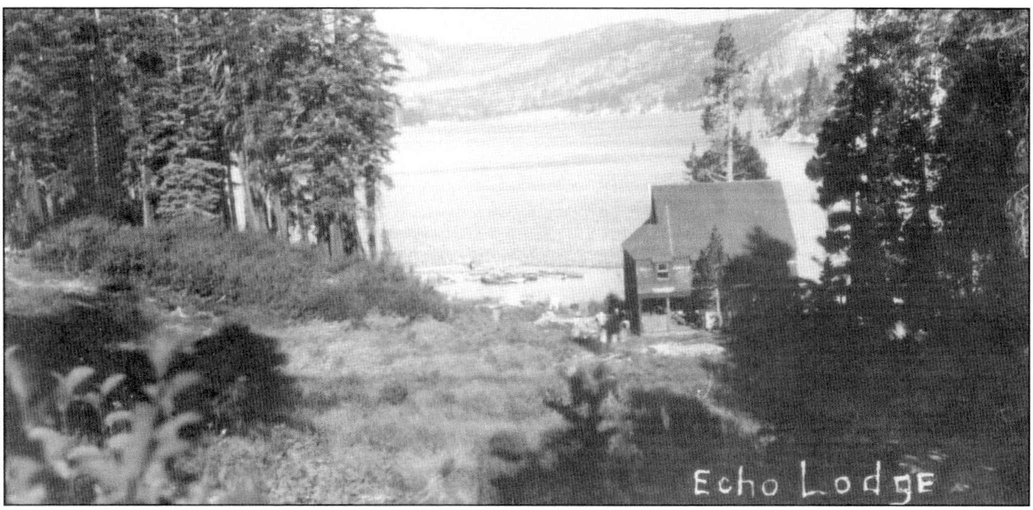

Nora and Euell Gray built a lodge and store around 1925 and purchased John Becker's Echo Lake land on July 27, 1927. Nora became postmaster on December 11, 1926, when the post office returned. Ralph King had a competing boating concession. The Depresssion and the loss of the Grays' lodge to fire prompted the transfer of their land to the US Forest Service on April 13, 1936. The Rocca family acquired the new lease and King's cabin overlooking Echo, due partially to King's lack of competing funds. The US Forest Service authorized King's continued boat operations until 1942, when the Roccas bought out King. (Courtesy of Dorothy De Mare.)

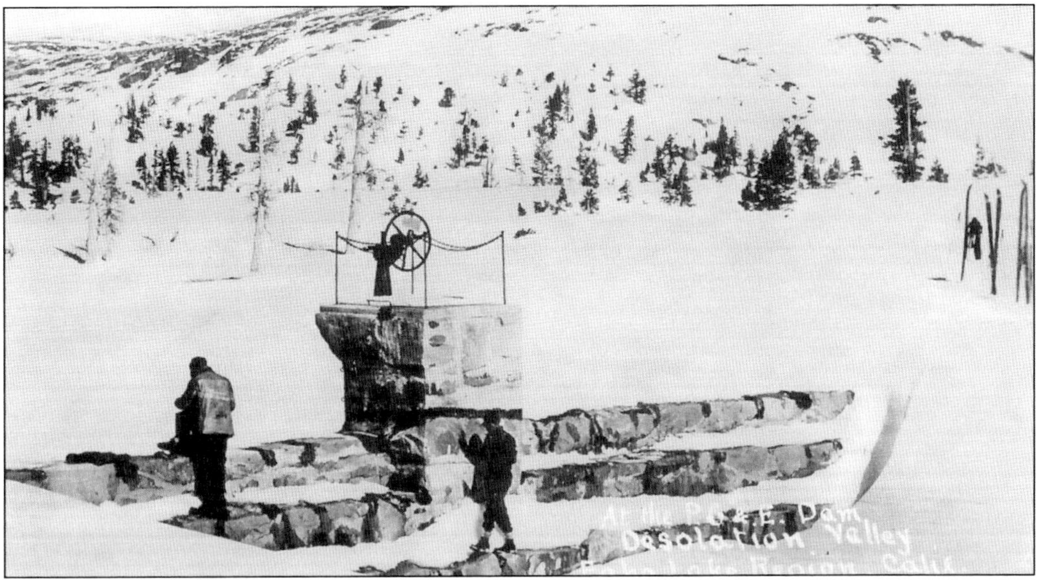

Prior to Pacific Gas & Electric Company's (PG&E) winter dam checks in Desolation Valley, from 1897 to 1914, Hamden Cagwin was the caretaker on Echo Summit for the El Dorado Water and Deep Gravel Mining Company. The dam and water system frequently transferred ownership to Sierra Water Supply, Placerville Gold Mining Company, and Western States Gas & Electric. From 1923 to 1927, Tom Swansborough, who was known as the best gravel miner in El Dorado County, was caretaker for Western States. In 1928, PG&E took over. (Courtesy of Dorothy De Mare.)

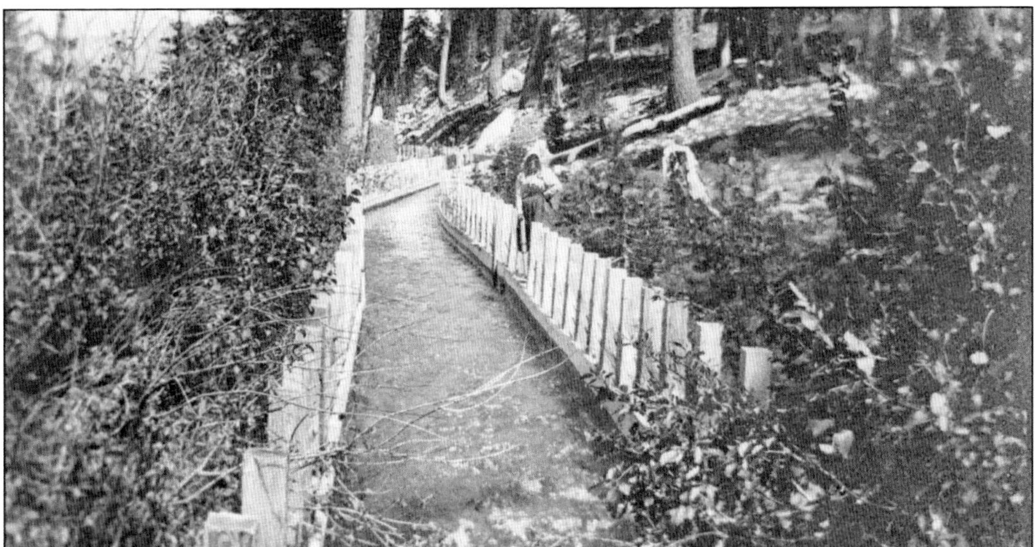

Amelia Celio stands beside Echo Lake's water system diversion canal. John Kirk, project owner with partner F.A. Bishop, constructed the canal to transport water to the American River. With uphill grade difficulties, they sold to the El Dorado Water and Deep Gravel Mining Company in 1873. The system was operational in 1876, after Chinese workers dug a 1,058-foot tunnel underneath Echo Summit and built a dam raising Lower Echo Lake. The system was expensive to operate, and the Placerville Gold Quartz Mining Company took over in the late 1890s. (Courtesy of Miles Celio.)

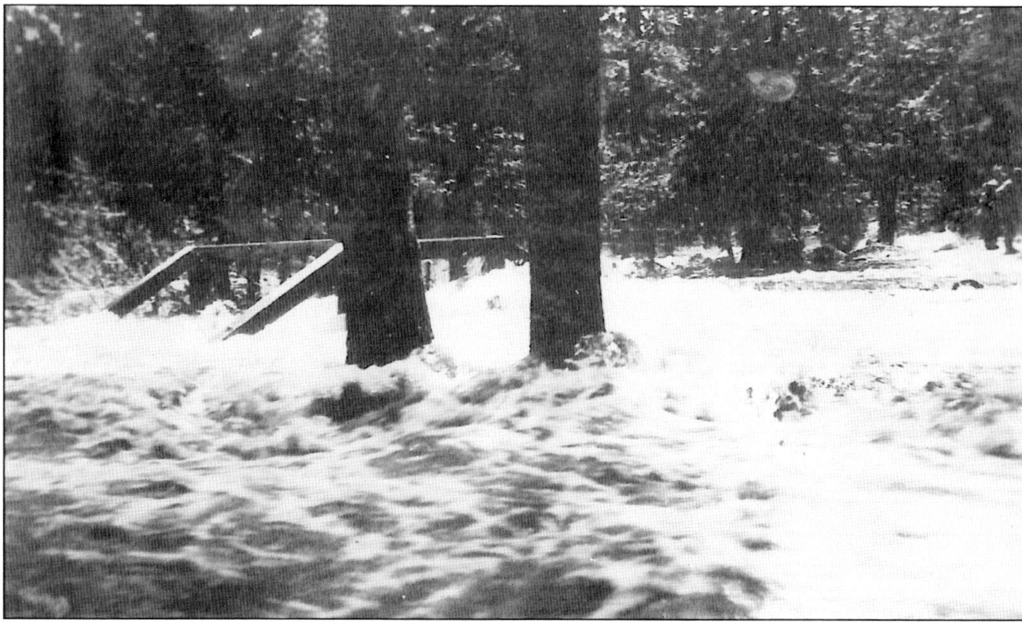

A fast-moving wall of water from a dam failure during Echo Lake's 1911 spring thaw unleashed 2,000 acre-feet of water into Echo Creek and down the mountainside to Meyers and Lake Valley. A large amount of debris traveling with the water added to the destruction. Buildings were washed off their foundations, including Osgood's Toll House, which was relocated to Meyers. High waters flooded Upper Lake Valley past the Celios' homestead ranch. (Courtesy of Miles Celio.)

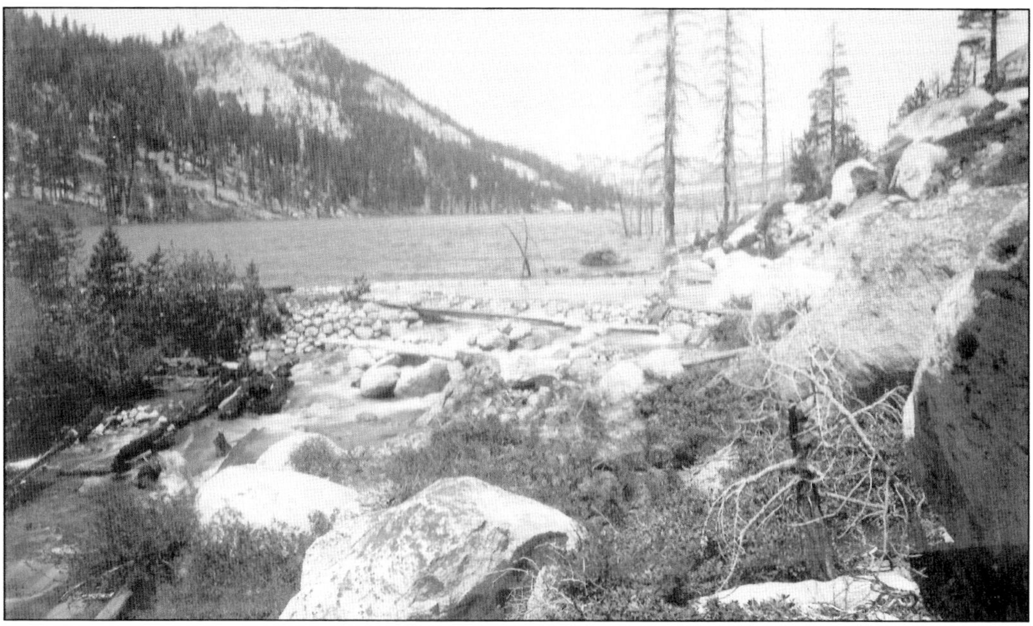

On June 9, 1911, people in Meyers and Upper Lake Valley heard a loud roar, looked up, and saw a wall of water 20 to 100 yards wide and 1,000 feet high cascading over Echo Summit. Echo Lake's low-walled dam, built of loosely placed granite at its natural outlet, had succumbed to water pressure from melting snow. Breakwater logs protecting wave action were washed away. After the dam was replaced, it was rebuilt in 1928 and again in 1992. (Courtesy of Dorothy De Mare.)

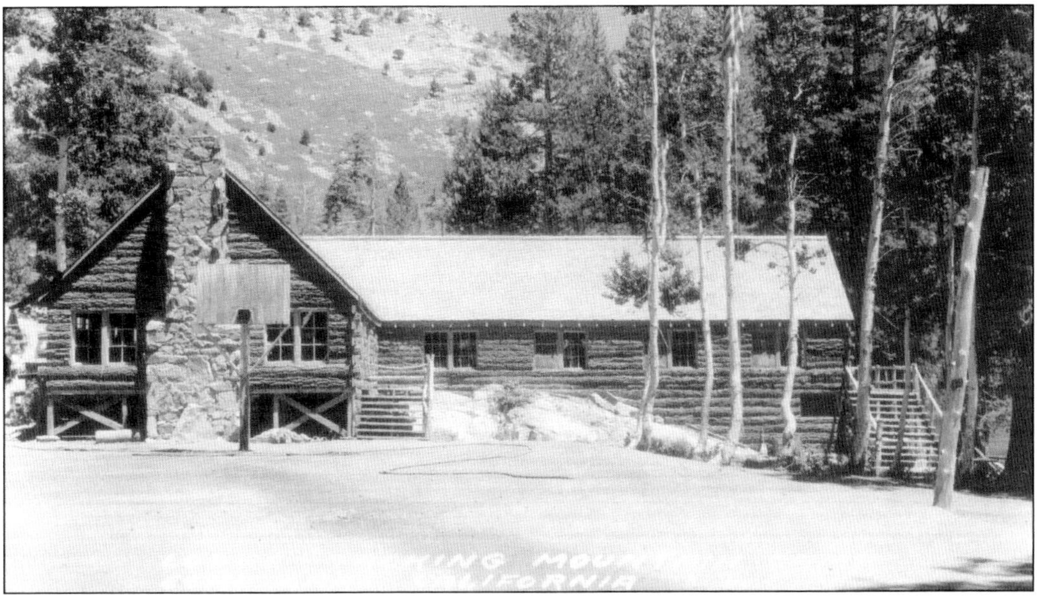

UC Berkeley professor Frank Kleeberger and his wife, Helen, founded Sierra Camps in 1923. Privileged boys attended Frank's Talking Mountain Camp (shown here); girls attended Helen's Laughing Waters Camp adjacent to Talking Mountain Camp on the other side of Tamarack Creek. Attending each six-week session throughout summer, at a cost of $350, were 150 children. Ralph Proctor and Ralph King helped build this lodge. Former attendee Wally Haas Sr. occasionally stopped to visit King at Echo Portals when in the area. (Courtesy of Dorothy De Mare.)

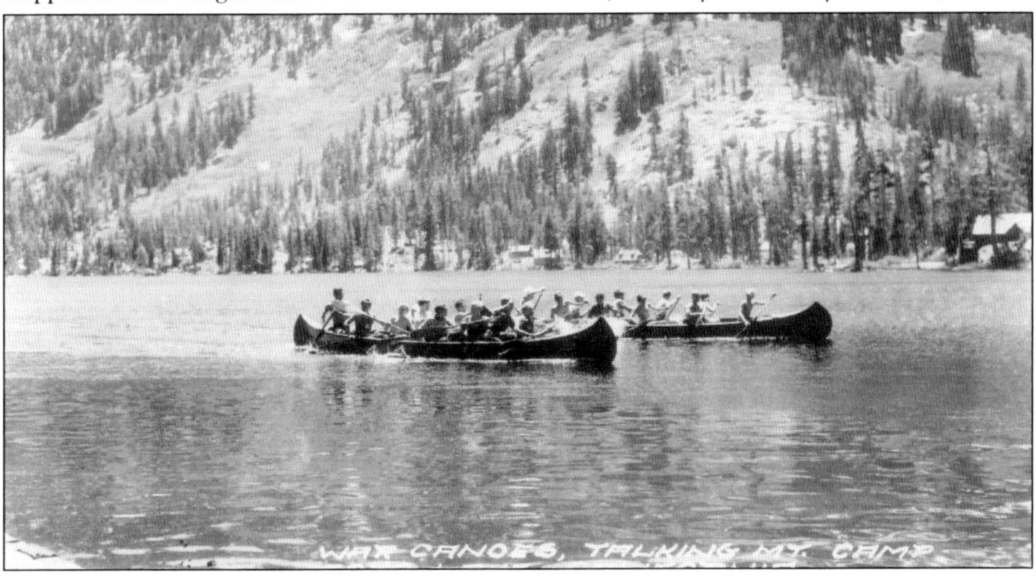

Attendees paddle war canoes at Camp Talking Mountain. The camp was sold in 1941 to Mount Diablo Boy Scouts Silverado Council. With World War II and membership struggles, it operated from 1946 through 1947. Golden Empire Council asked philanthropist Harvey West in 1948 to purchase Camp Talking Mountain for them, due to a polio outbreak and low water at Camp Audrain. Now called Camp Harvey West, a lakefront building, cigar store Indian, and totem pole were added. By 1970, environmental concerns reduced attendance, building dismantling began, and operations were phased out. (Courtesy of Dorothy De Mare.)

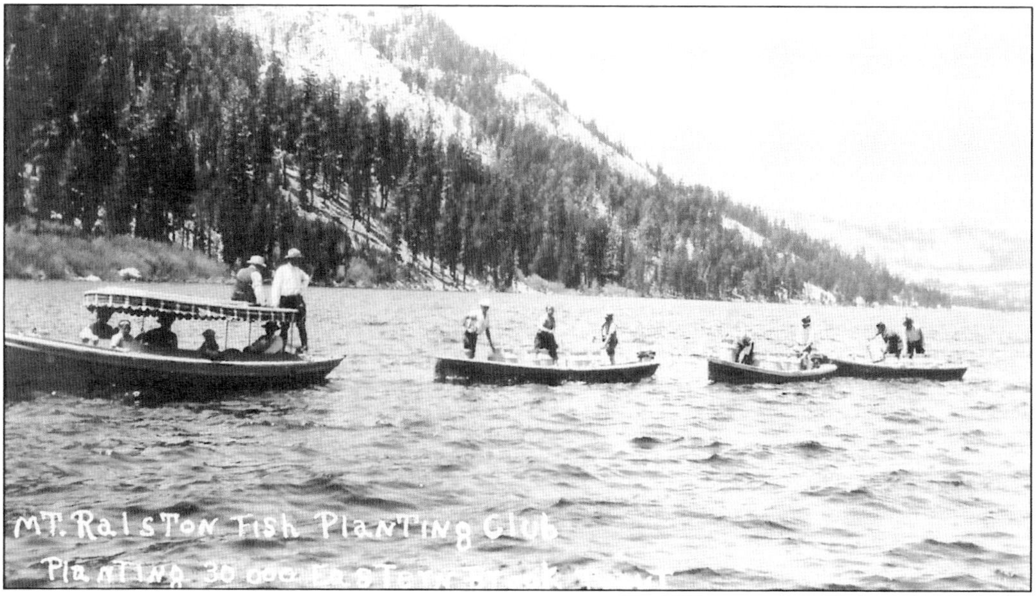

Mount Ralston Fish Planting Club was formed in 1925 by Walter Campbell and Ross Pierce to stock lakes in Desolation Valley. Unnamed lakes were given Indian-sounding names for club officers: Waca (Walter Campbell), Ropi (Ross Pierce), Jabu (Jack Butler), Gefo (George Foss), Frata (Frank Talbot), Toem (Tom Emeral), and Osma (Os Mackey). A plaque at Ralston Lake honors Ross Pierce's fish-planting dedication. Restocking by air began around 1951. In 1960, Echo Lake's trash fish were poisoned. (Courtesy of Dorothy De Mare.)

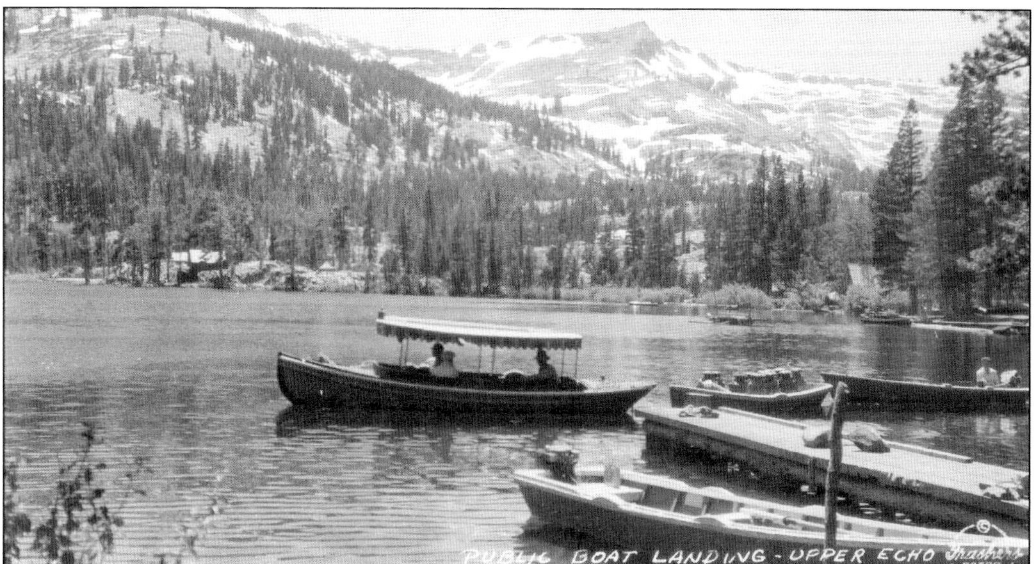

Walter Campbell's canopied boat tows Mount Ralston Fish Planting Club's boats containing milk cans filled with fingerlings that Ralph King picked up from Taylor Creek and Markleeville hatcheries. From Upper Echo's public boat landing, the fish were transported by Euell Gray's horses to Desolation Valley lakes and released. To ensure survival, check dams were built on the lakes, controlling water levels and thus protecting fish from predators. In addition, aquatic plants were introduced as food to sustain them. (Courtesy of Paul DeWitt.)

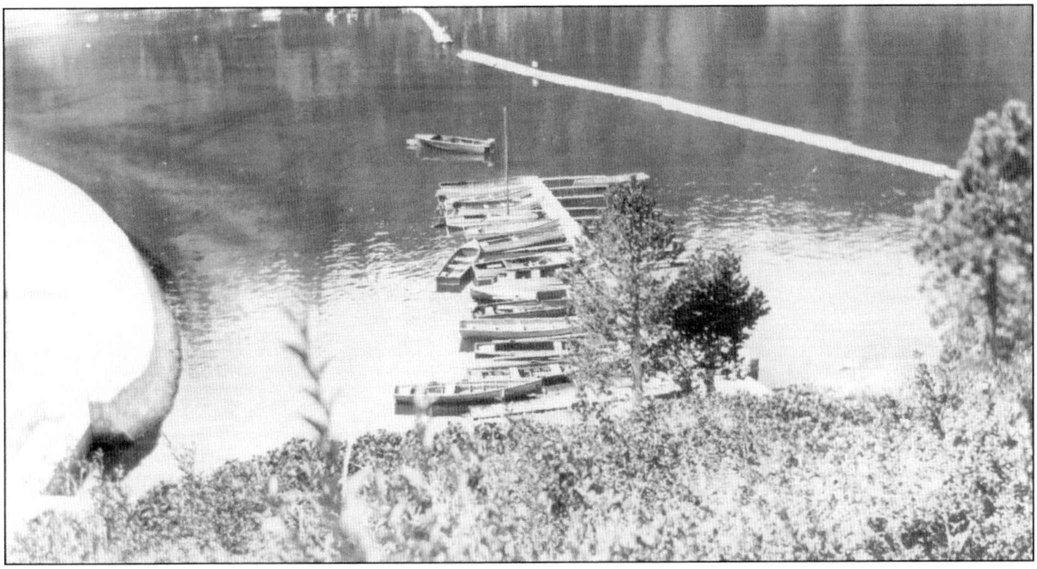

Finger piers and logs function as a dam breakwater adjacent to the north shore of Lower Echo Lake. Dam caretaker Tom Swansborough tended Echo's dam and spillway, removing debris from in front of the outlet to prevent wave action from battering the dam. Swansborough, in his mid-70s and with a wooden leg, and accompanied by his wife, Mary, walked weekly to another dam in Desolation Valley to read its meter and report evaporation. (Courtesy of Dorothy De Mare.)

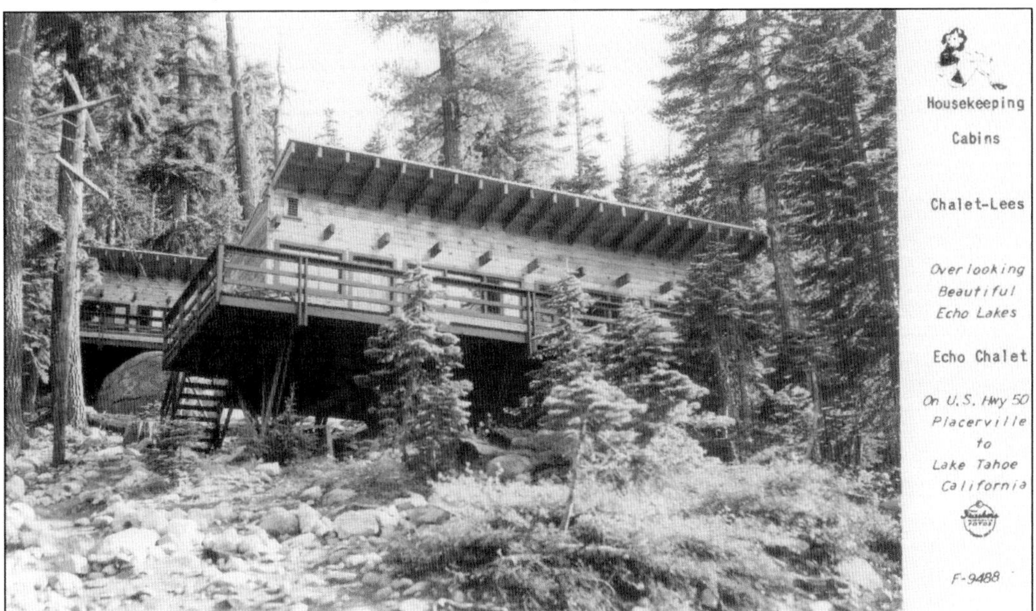

Under Haven "Jorgy" Jorgensen's ownership, Echo Chalet Resort opened its newly developed winter sports area, including three ski tows, in winter 1947 to enhance the Sierra experience for year-round vacationers. Their advertising brochure described newly constructed Chalet-Lees, pictured on this postcard with spacious duplex cabins matching Echo Chalet's original Swiss-style architecture, overlooking Lower Echo Lake. Offering beginning to advanced skiing with a fully equipped ski shop, the resort also conducted ski touring on slopes in the Crystal Range Mountains. (Courtesy of Paul DeWitt.)

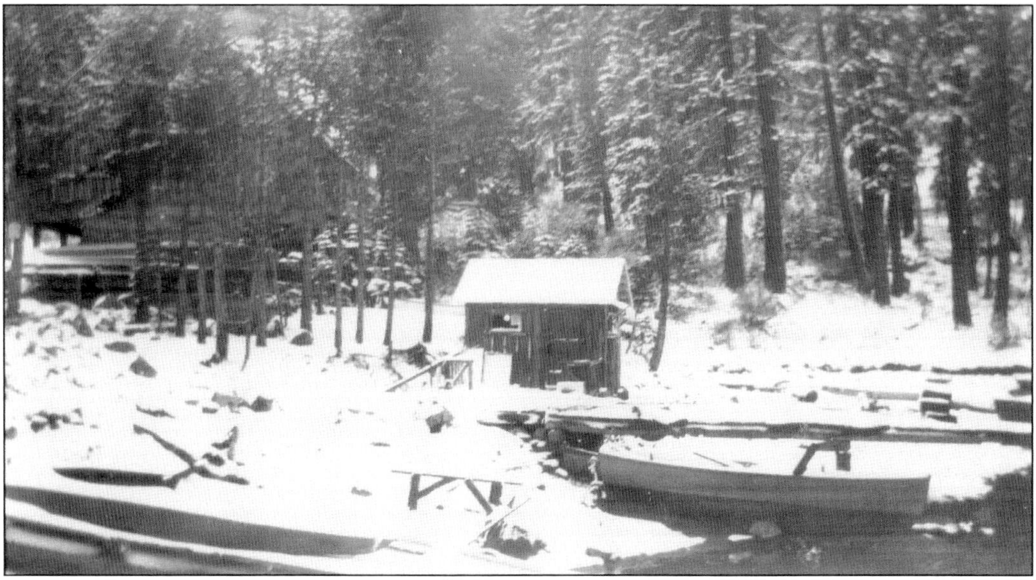

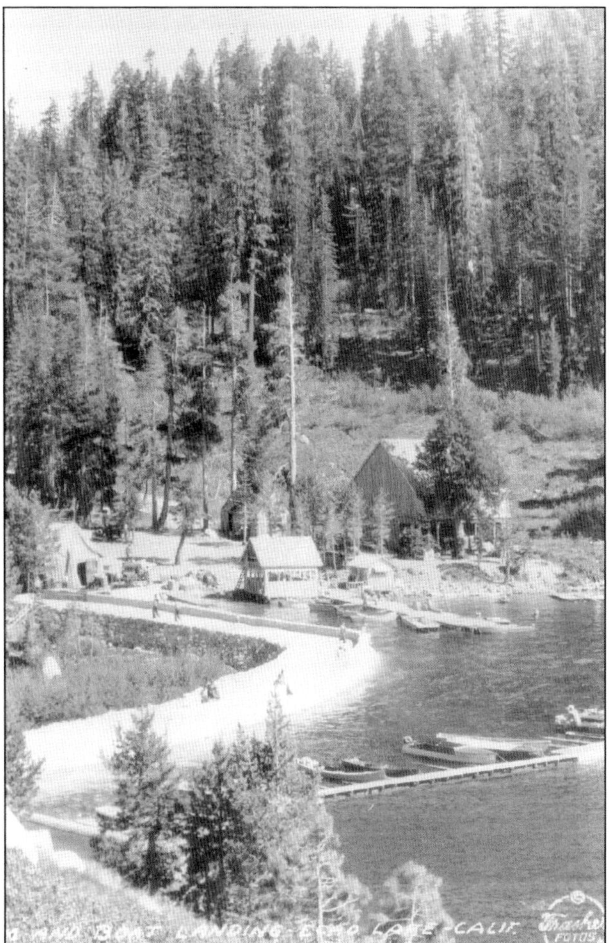

Early snow covers Ralph King's Echo Lake office in September 1930. On June 19, 1926, dam caretaker and boat taxi owner Tom Swansborough rescued King from drowning, deepening their friendship. Called Aunt Mary and Uncle Tom, the Swansboroughs were loved by all. In 1927, they retired to Placerville, giving King their boat operations. Evelyn and John Smith, who opened Echo Portals Store a mile away in 1927, briefly operated competing boat services in 1928. (Courtesy of Dorothy De Mare.)

The two-story lodge, stable, store, and post office at Echo Lake was owned by Euell Gray. In 1928, Ralph King took over Swansborough's boat services. In this 1932 photograph, King's existing boathouse is dwarfed between Gray's lodge, store, and new boathouse, under construction to the left of the commercial freight pier. A tent is nearby to assist with construction activities. By 1938, a homeowner's pier, finger piers, and more breakwater piers had been constructed. (Courtesy of Paul DeWitt.)

Ralph King, pictured here in 1930, lived year-round at Echo Lake, overseeing boat operations at the commercial pier, installing water systems, and constructing many cabins for leaseholders. Lumber was supplied by Celio & Son's mill near Meyers. At one time, 29 employees comprised King's summer crew, including boat boys, stonemasons, cook Edith Young, and secretary Ada Ackler. During winter, King provided general maintenance, cabin patrols, and snow removal. Ralph King and many other Echo Lakers were UC Berkeley graduates and associates. Ralph and others skied out to attend Cal football games. Many at nearby Fallen Leaf Lake were with Stanford University enabling a local rivalry. (Courtesy of Dorothy De Mare.)

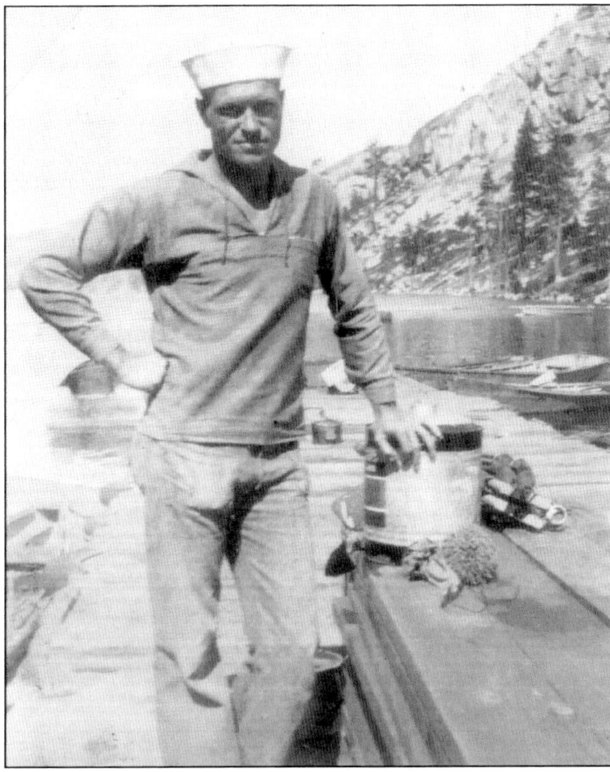

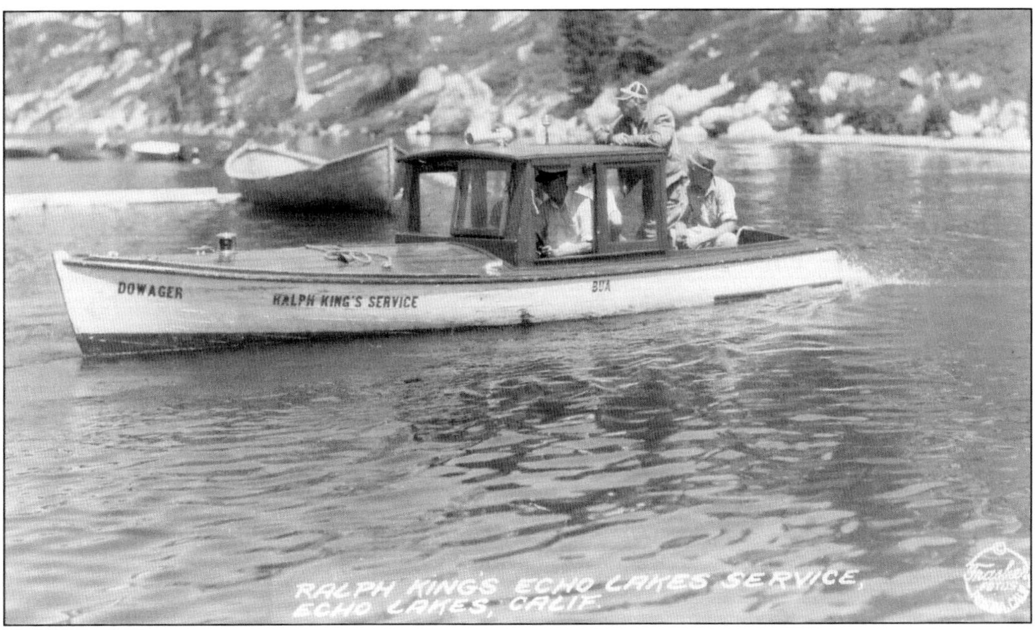

John Wiley pilots the *Dowager* on Lower Echo Lake in 1936. Ralph King's boats were named *Nellie*, *Dowager*, *Duchess*, *Prince Robert*, and *Princess*. With the exception of *Nellie*, the boats were built in a Berkeley garage during the winter of 1927–1928 by Ralph King and his fellow UC Berkeley Kleeberger Camp staff associates, colleagues, and friends. Cabin owners enjoyed all the great service they received from competing boat concessions. (Courtesy of Beverly King.)

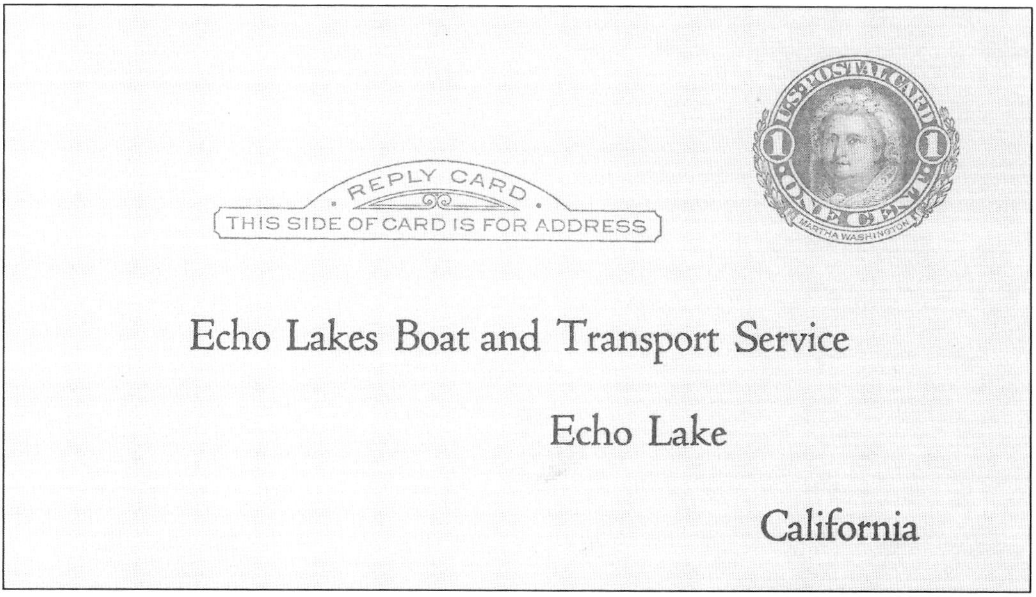

REPLY CARD

THIS SIDE OF CARD IS FOR ADDRESS

U.S. POSTAL CARD 1 ONE CENT 1

MARTHA WASHINGTON

Echo Lakes Boat and Transport Service

Echo Lake

California

An advocate of providing the best customer service for his patrons, Ralph King sent out a variety of preprinted, perforated reply postal cards to the Echo Lake and Echo Summit communities. These Echo Lake Boat and Transport Service mailings requested cabin owners to fill in their individual needs and mail the postal card back to King, who would then arrange better organization of the services he offered them. (Courtesy of Dorothy De Mare.)

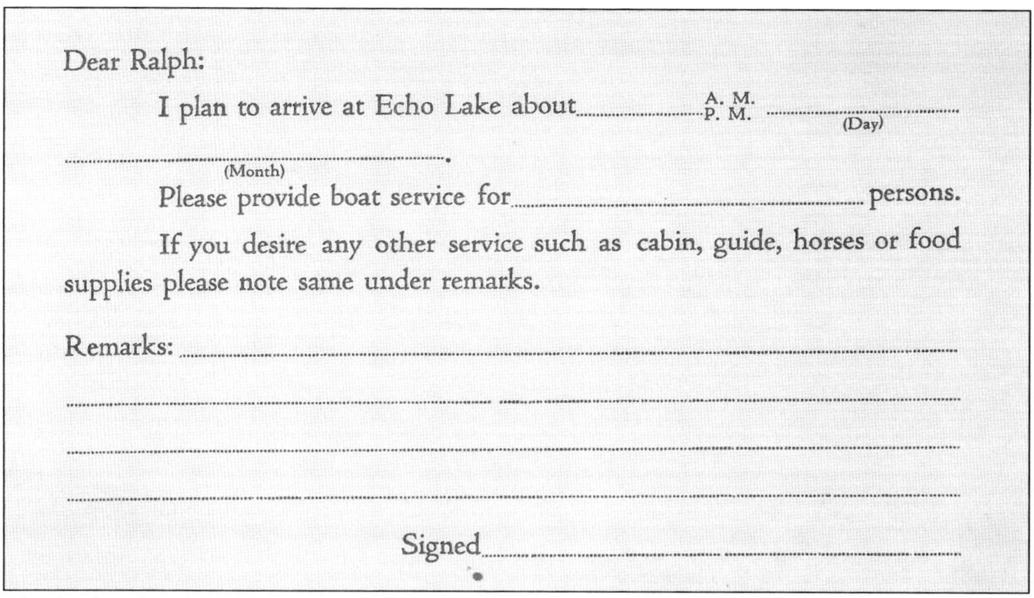

Dear Ralph:

I plan to arrive at Echo Lake about............A. M. P. M. .... (Day)

.... (Month).

Please provide boat service for............persons.

If you desire any other service such as cabin, guide, horses or food supplies please note same under remarks.

Remarks: ....

....

....

....

Signed............

The backs of Ralph King's preprinted postal cards varied, being tailored for customers' needs. Each had room for individual requests and their date of arrival. Boxes could also be checked for "Boat, Motor or Canoe," "Cabin Construction," Cabin Alteration/Repair," "Painting," "Refill Natural Gas Tank," and "Water System." Other customized cards not listing boating needs were sent to customers along the road or on the summit if they wouldn't be needing boating service. (Courtesy of Dorothy De Mare.)

Shirley King's husband, Ralph, and his crews teased her and cook Edith Young, known as "the Duchess" for using crude fishing gear. Shirley was given a 15-pound striped bass in 1935. She could not resist saying she caught it in Echo Lake, and she was horrified when Ranger Raleigh Bryan reported it. Maury McLaughlin said that, around 1900, Ham Cagwin transplanted netted shrimps and stripers from Antioch's delta as food to allow Echo's trout to grow bigger. Maury's grandmother Harriet caught one of the stripers in 1908, so Shirley's story seemed plausible. Articles about Shirley's catch appeared in newspapers from San Francisco to Reno. She was inundated with requests and information about what style of lure she used. Years later, Shirley shared the real story with Ralph. (Courtesy of Dorothy De Mare.)

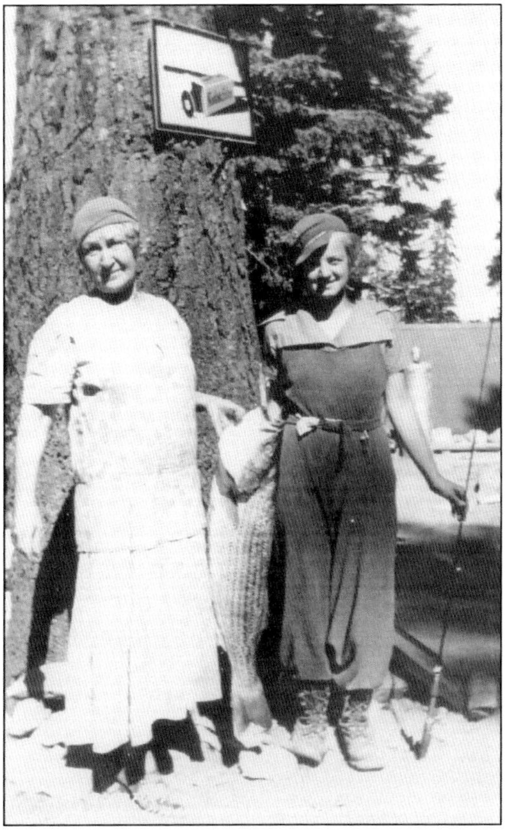

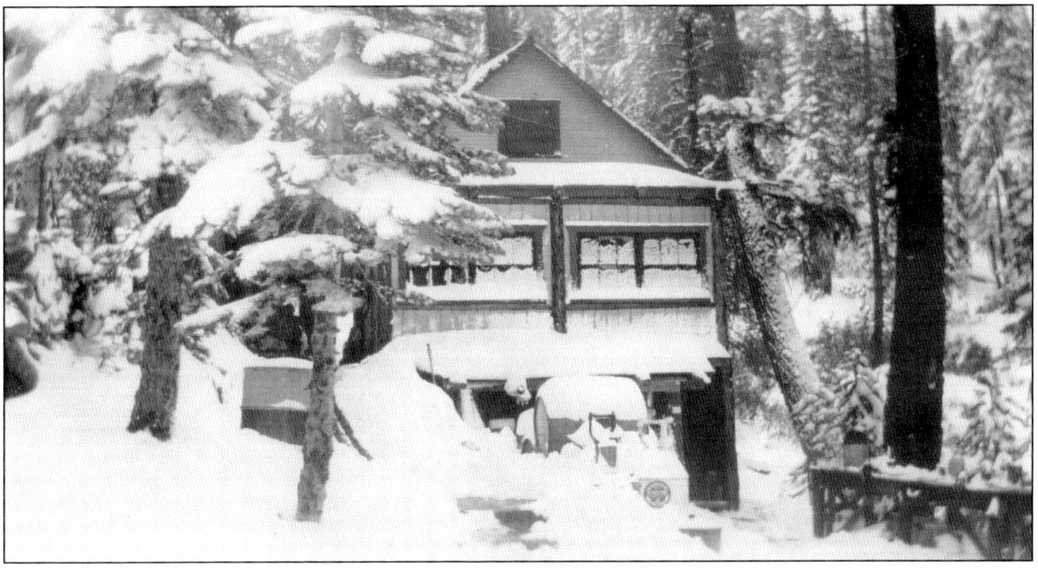

Ralph King's cabin overlooking Lower Echo Lake was built in 1930 by Ralph and his father, Clyde King. Next to the cabin on the hillside were four tent platforms with canvas tops available for guests. The cabin was located on the old road across from the PG&E cabin occupied by Tom and Mary Swansborough, near the stairs leading down to Echo Chalet and just below Kathleen and Tom Fashinell's present residence. (Courtesy of Dorothy De Mare.)

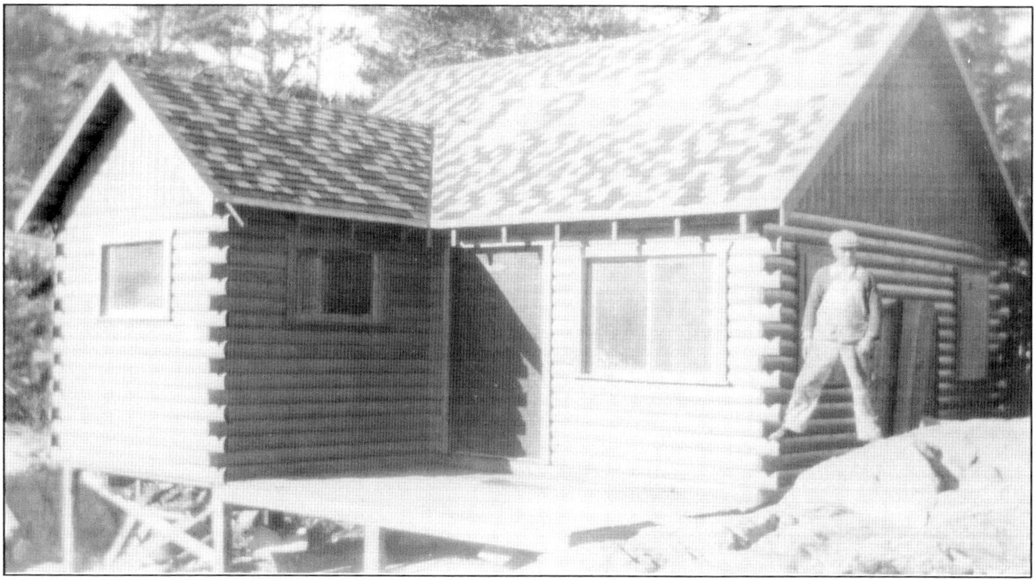

Ralph King's father, Clyde, stands by the cabin they built at the upper end of Lower Echo Lake. The year 1930 is creatively displayed by the arrangement of oil-dipped roof shingles. Clyde, Ralph, and their crews built many of the cabins at Echo Lake. Clyde worked other jobs, and he built the wooden access stairs from the parking lot to the beach at Bijou, South Lake Tahoe. (Courtesy of Dorothy De Mare.)

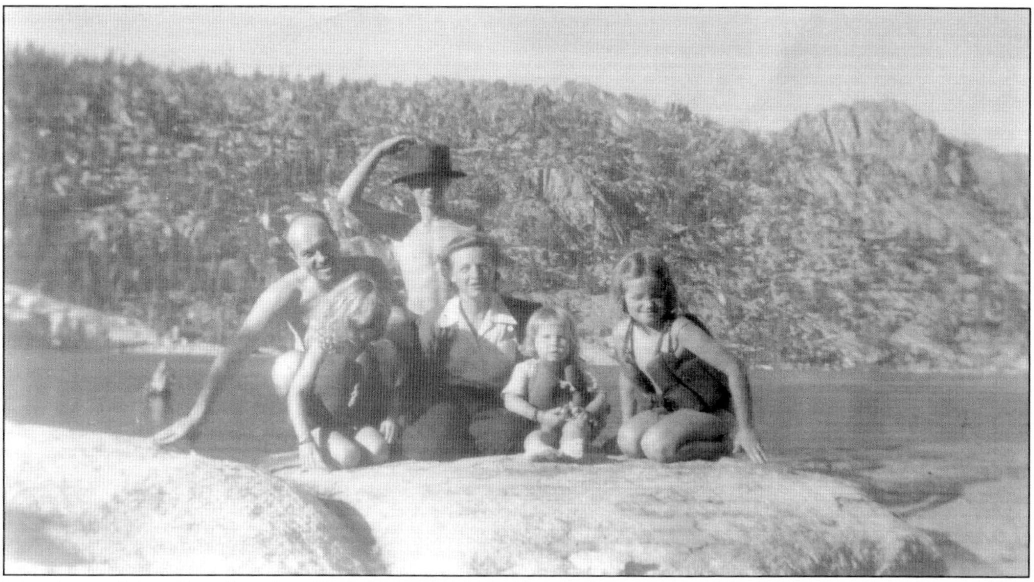

Members of the King family—Ralph, Marylee, Robert, Shirley, Dorothy and Beverly—are pictured in July 1949 at lifetime friends Ethel (Booch) and Relzy Aikin's South Shore Tract cabin on Lower Echo Lake. Roommates at UC Berkeley decades earlier, Relzy suggested Ralph visit Professor Kleeberger's camp, which Ralph did, arriving there on June 25, 1925. Ralph became general superintendent of grounds and buildings and remained there until acquiring Swansborough's Echo Lake Boat Service. Ralph later described the Echo area as a "Silent Symphony" and his association there lasted his lifetime. (Courtesy of Marylee King Larson.)

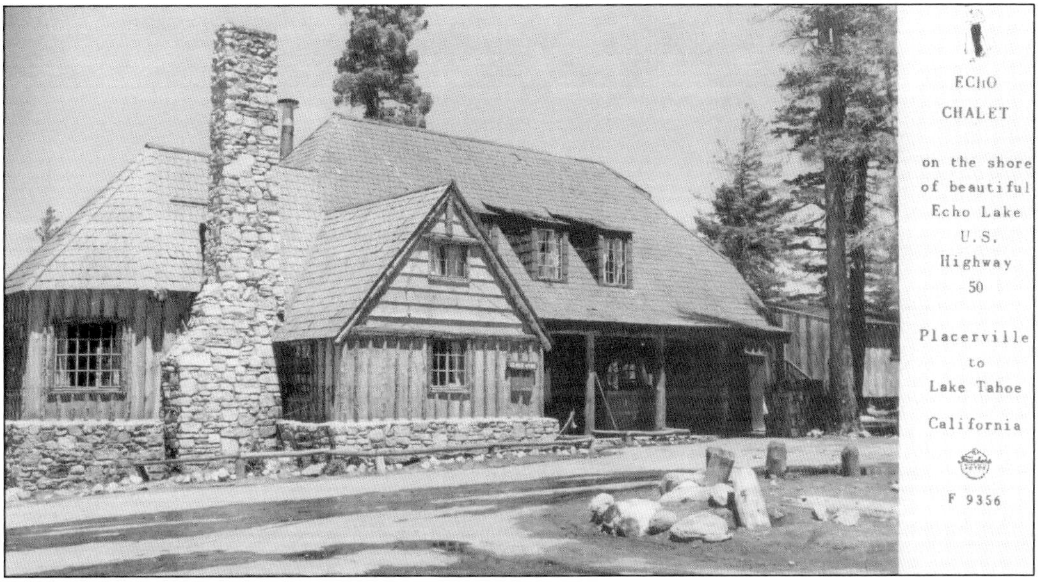

Blanche and Curt Rocca opened Echo Chalet in February 1939, offering expanded boat services. In 1946, after World War II, Haven "Jorgy" Jorgensen bought Echo Chalet and, by winter 1947, converted it into a year-round resort. He reintroduced recreational skiing, which the Roccas had introduced in 1939. A colorful brochure with a map of Echo Lake and Desolation Valley advertised Echo Chalet's indoor resort amenities, outdoor adventures, and convenient Greyhound bus services. Jorgensen stopped operating year-round in 1955. (Courtesy of Paul DeWitt.)

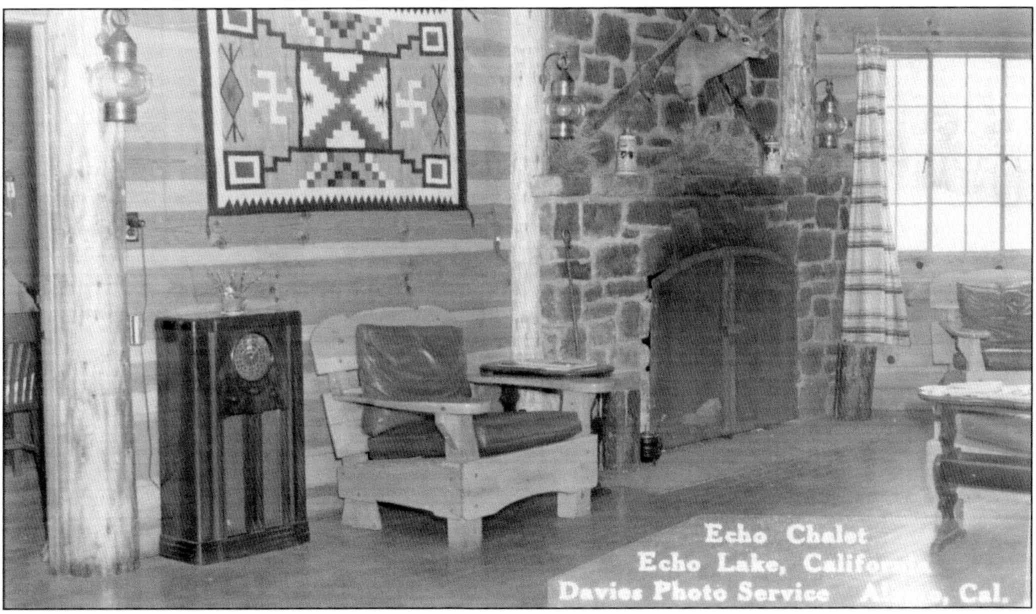

With World War II looming, Curt Rocca enlisted in the Navy. Motor parts and supplies were unavailable. Blanche's efforts and adaptability allowed her to continue operations for those who could find gas rations to travel to Echo. Commercial power services were not available on the lake. Cabin owners enjoyed comfortable lobby accommodations. And, while picking up mail from inside the Echo Lake Post Office, they could catch up on war news and other programs from an old console radio. (Courtesy of Paul DeWitt.)

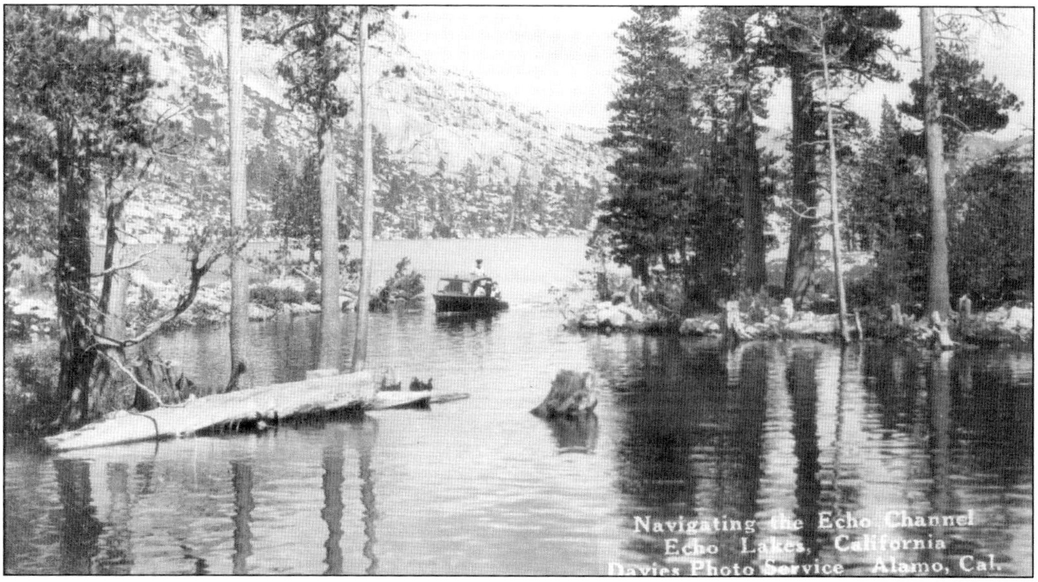

Echo Lakes were two lakes with a land bridge until 1876, when a dam was operational at Lower Echo's natural outlet. A shallow channel was created, and the lakes were renamed Upper and Lower Echo Lake. Granite rocks were dynamited and first removed from the channel by the US Forest Service in 1924, and later by Ralph King's Service and the Boy Scouts, allowing for easier boat passage. In the 1930s, a public camp was located on the right of this photograph. (Courtesy of Paul DeWitt.)

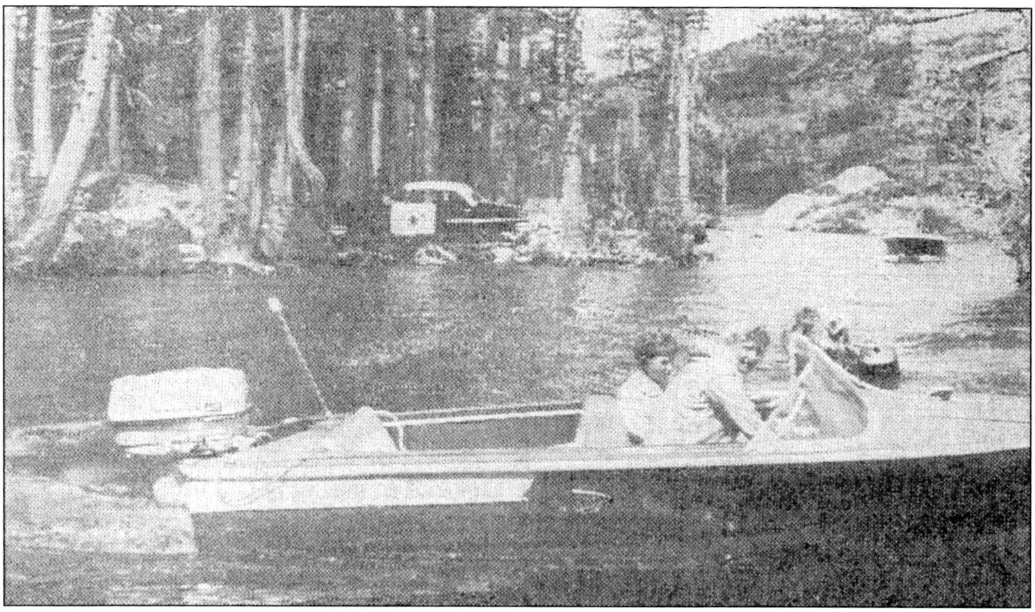

The *Tahoe Daily Tribune* of August 13, 1962, showed a painted California Highway Patrol cruiser, placed as a prank, at the Echo Lake Channel, over a mile from the nearest road. Concerned about speed, Harvey West commissioned billboards along Highway 50 from Placerville to Lake Tahoe. The channel cruiser, borrowed from Little Norway by Echo Chalet boat boys Rich Best, Bruce Brown, John Durein, Jeff Nunn, and Tom Phair, slowed the boaters. Hearing of its effectiveness, West dispatched a news photographer, then asked that the billboard be returned. He later received Pres. Lyndon Johnson's commendation. (Courtesy of *Tahoe Daily Tribune*.)

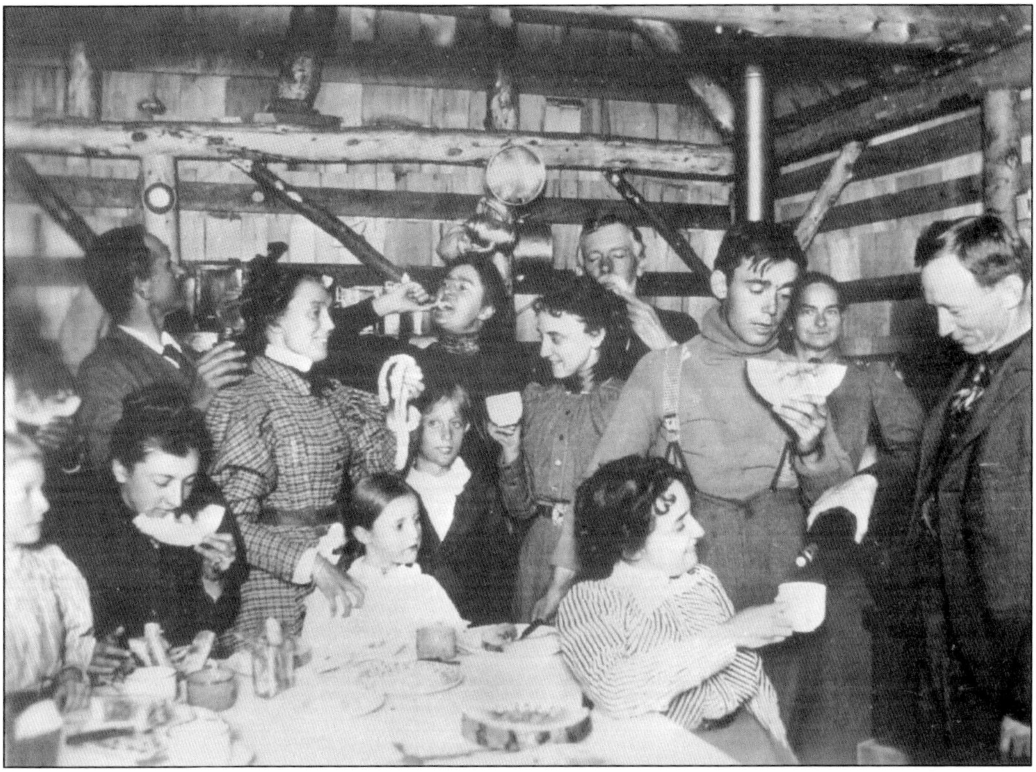

A candy pull takes place in August 1898 inside John Becker's two-room homestead cabin, which once stood where Echo Chalet was later built. It was a speakeasy during Prohibition. Shown here are, from left to right, (seated) Sylvia Swissler, Mabel Swissler, Bernice Cagwin, and possibly Mrs. Lamphere; (standing) George Cagwin, Fannie Cagwin, Master Aubrey Cagwin, Miss Grant, Mrs. John (Grace Huntley) Becker, James H. Burnham, E.R. Lamphere, and Mabel Huntley. John Becker pours drinks for his guests. (Courtesy of Dorothy De Mare.)

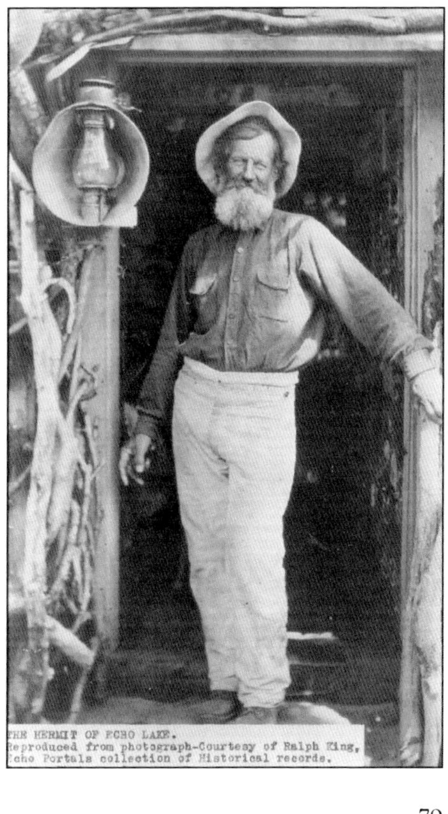

Hamden Eldorado Cagwin is photographed around 1908 by Mabel Swissler. His cabin doorway is adorned with a lantern, horseshoe, driftwood, moss-covered limbs, and a weathered sign that reads "Heather Bell." In 1900, Charles and Mabel Swissler acquired the island in Upper Echo Lake where the Lowery boys' cabin stood, naming it Heather Bell Island. By 1906, Ham Cagwin finished helping build their cabin. Their friendship is evidenced by Ham's naming his cabin Heather Bell. (Courtesy of Dorothy De Mare.)

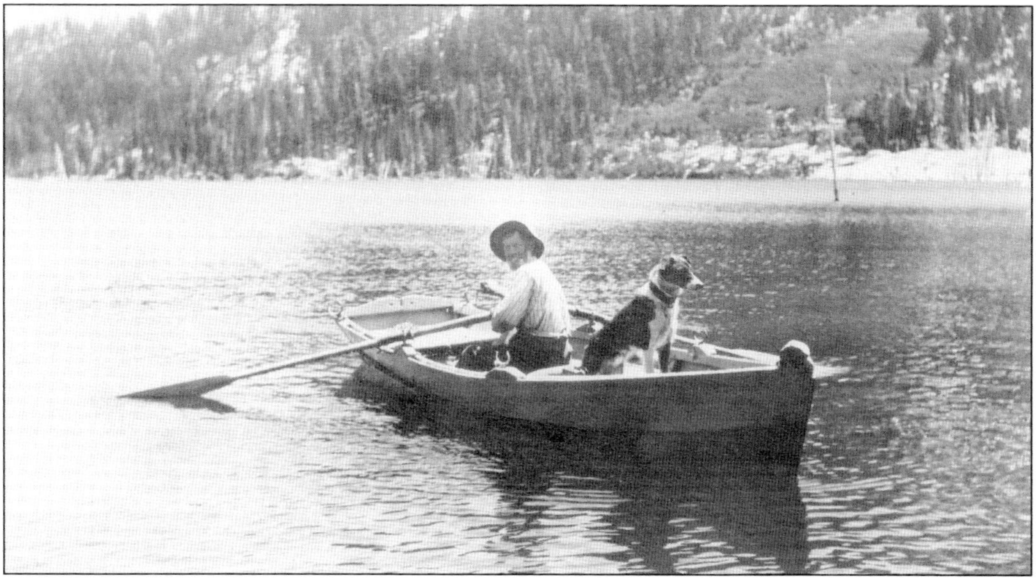

Ham Cagwin and his dog Saint were photographed in 1904 on Lower Echo as he prepared to beach his boat, *Ferry*, at a site he named Rocky Roost. It was Cagwin's favorite place, discovered years earlier when family and friends camped there. He suggested that friend Dr. George McLaughlin choose this lease site in 1907. McLaughlin's grandson Maury said that their guest cottage was built on the Rocky Roost site, 200 yards below the McLaughlin cabin. (Courtesy of Dorothy De Mare.)

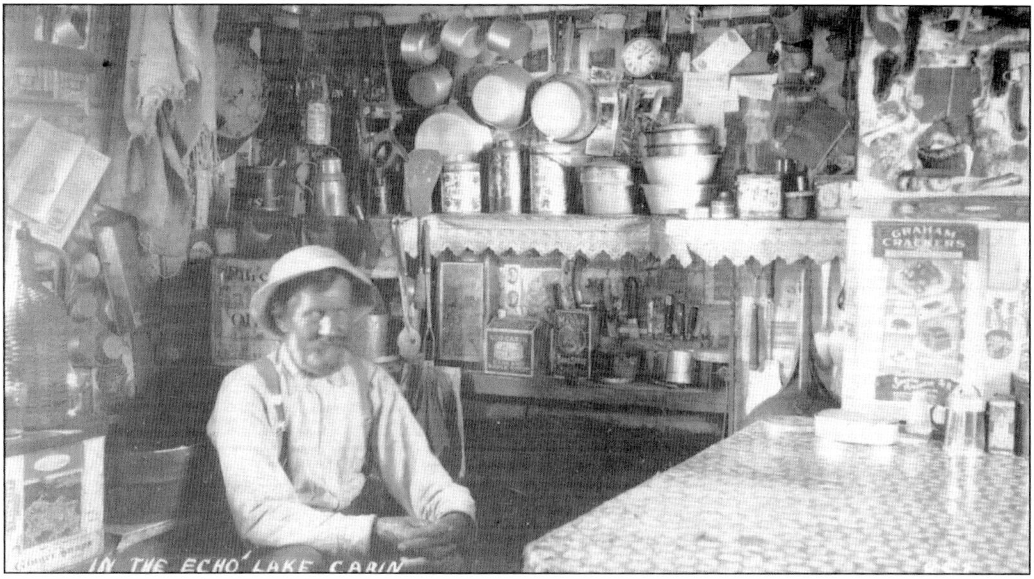

Photographer William Pillsbury visited Ham Cagwin in 1909. Cagwin's beard and hair were neatly trimmed for Pillsbury's camera. This is the only known interior image of Cagwin's cabin. Cagwin mastered merchandising while at Cagwin & Noteware's Carson City store, owned by his brother George and Dorsey Noteware. Labels, pictures, postcards, and newspapers became wallpaper insulating interior walls. A clock, almanac, Triscuit Ginger Snaps tin, knives, pots, tools, Graham Cracker and Van Camp's Macaroni charts all hang for storage, functionality, and decoration. (Courtesy of Ed Herny.)

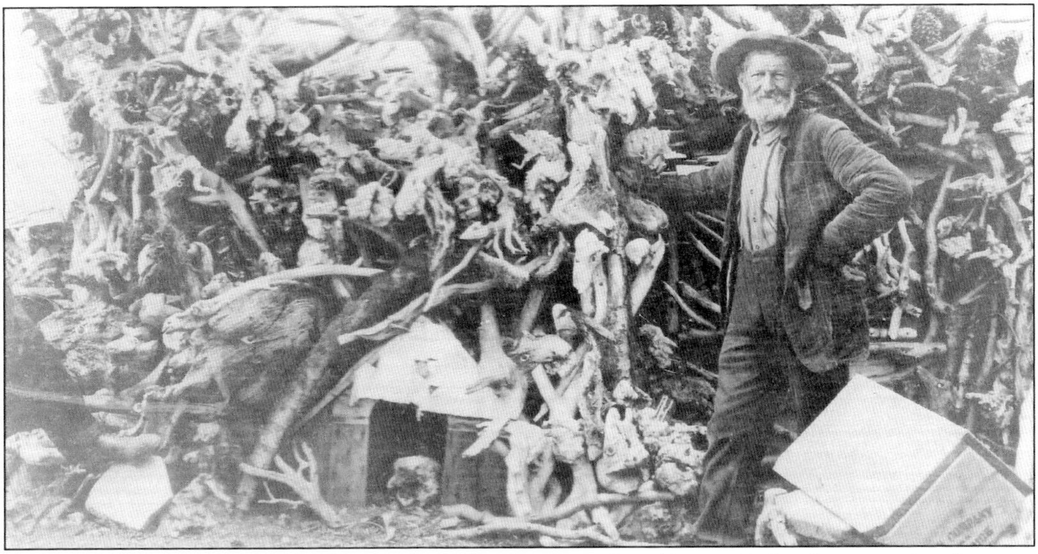

Cagwin's harmless driftwood fence of wooden beasts infests Rustic Dale, the name he chose to describe his compound. Everywhere are the eyes of critters, including a camel, dog, anteaters, hippos, birds, and dinosaurs. According to the *Stockton Daily Evening Record* of July 21, 1913: "By placing buttons or tacks indicating eyes, Cagwin makes you see laughing foxes, kingly lions, graceful deer, growling bruins, ugly rhinos, grinning crocodiles, and venomous reptiles. You immediately see the resemblance. Cagwin has been invited to duplicate *Rustic Dale* at the 1915 exposition." Cagwin died on October 6, 1914, before the San Francisco Panama Pacific International Exposition opened. (Courtesy of Dorothy De Mare.)

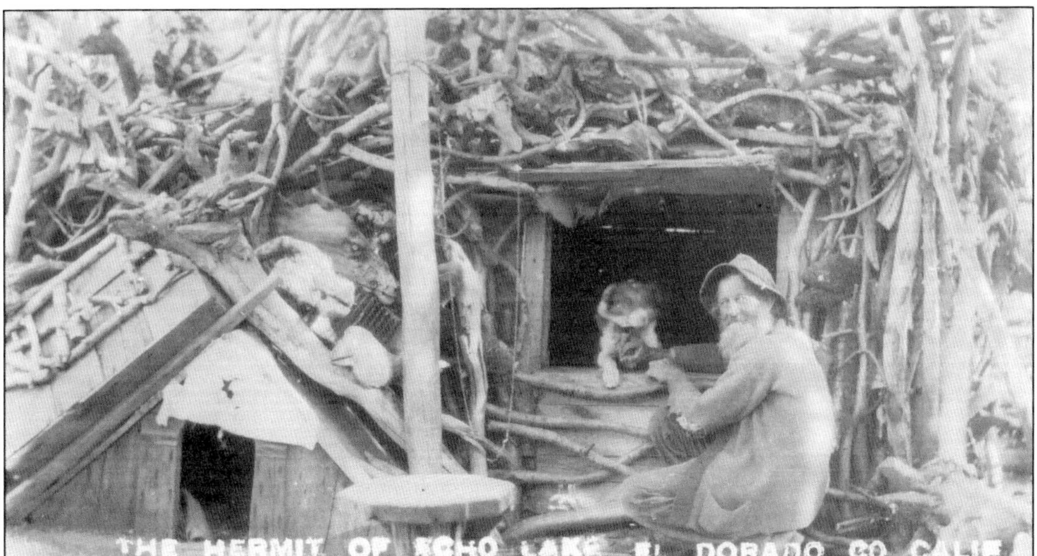

Cagwin is pictured petting his dog, Saint. During idle time, Cagwin, Robert Shorrock Sr., and others created artistic animals from abundant driftwood, with buttons and tacks used to create realistic eyes. In the 1930s, when Shirley and Ralph King lived in their cabin overlooking Echo Lake, Shirley and cook Edith Young visited Cagwin's compound annually, reattaching eyes that fell off during harsh winters. (Courtesy of Paul DeWitt.)

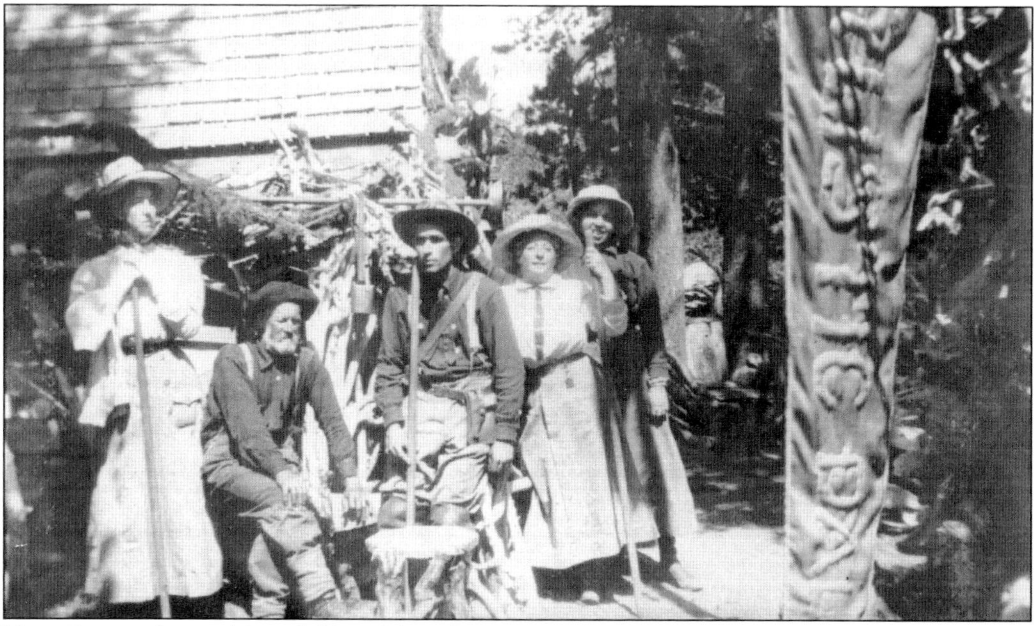

Ham Cagwin (second from left) and friends pose near his handcrafted "Rustic Dale" canvas sign around 1914. Jim Darrington's and Ralph King's Echo Lake neighbor Ralph Cross Sr., researching *The Early Inns of California,* interviewed them around 1940. Darrington revealed then "on October 6, 1914, I helped pack Cagwin's body out." In 1927, Cagwin's nephew Fred Phelps erroneously revealed to King that "Indians found Cagwin's body in 1916," details King published on a 1936 postcard. Thanks to Darrington, history is corrected. (Courtesy of Dorothy De Mare.)

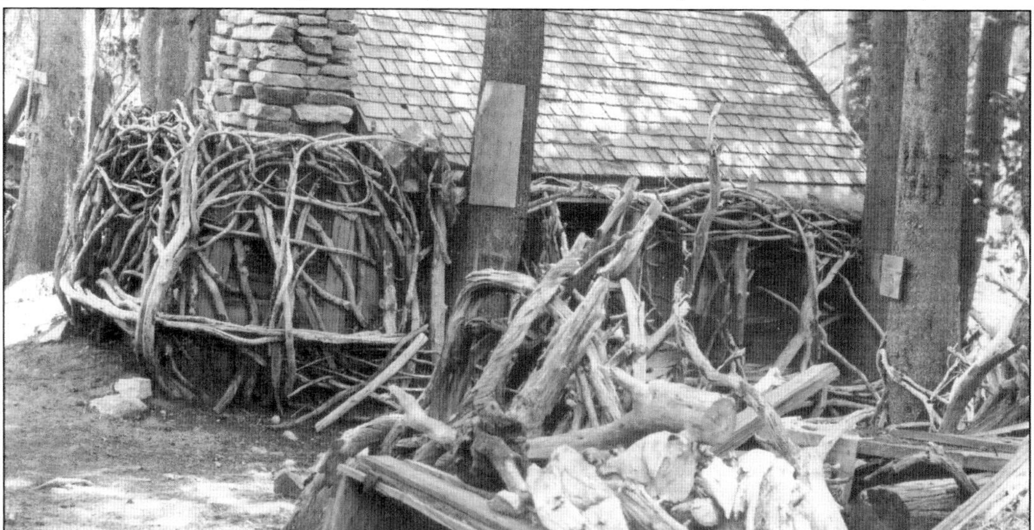

Cagwin's driftwood is still abundant in this 1947 image taken about a year before the cabin was lost in a fire. Haven "Jorgy" Jorgensen recollected the cabin looked like this before the US Forest Service arrived, he believed, in the fall of 1948 and burned it down thinking it was a detriment. Jorgy recalled hearing, at 5:00 a.m., a tall fellow who had already set it on fire holler, "'Fire!' His pump had quit. By the time we got the Chalet crew up and set up a bucket brigade, the fire took out four structures plus trees and bushes." (Courtesy of Louisa Cagwin.)

Five

Berkeley Echo Lake Camp

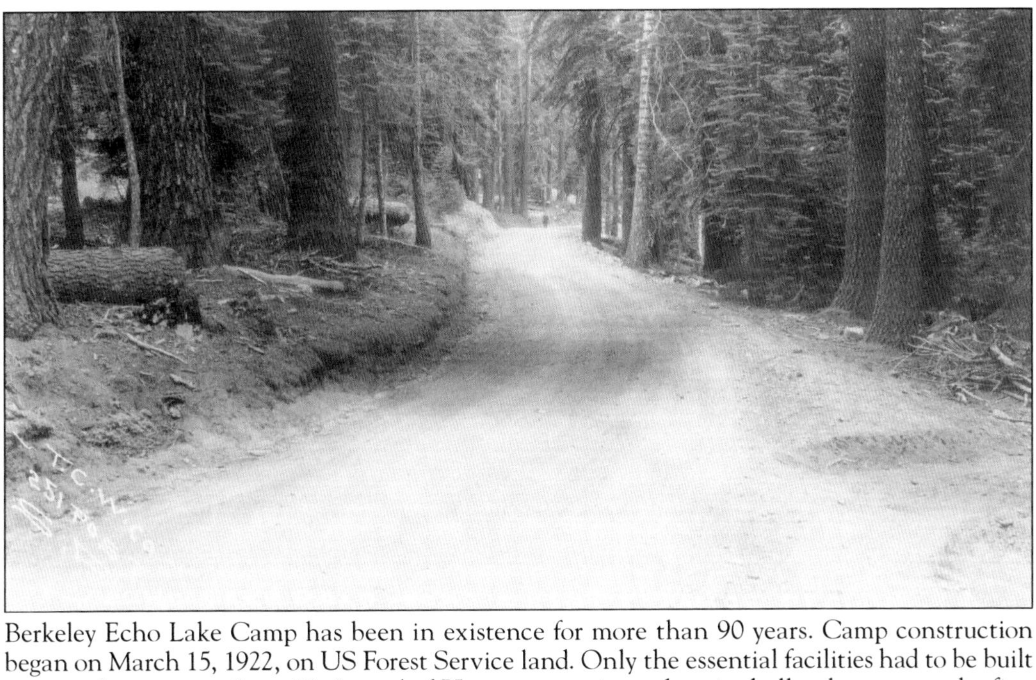

Berkeley Echo Lake Camp has been in existence for more than 90 years. Camp construction began on March 15, 1922, on US Forest Service land. Only the essential facilities had to be built to open the camp on June 15. A total of 75 campers registered at city hall to be at camp the first day. They wanted to experience living in the wilderness. The first manager was William Morrison, a student in forestry and agriculture at UC Berkeley. As visitors drove toward Echo Lake, they would see, just around the bend shown in the distance, the entrance to the camp on the right. Over the years, there have been many changes to the camp, but it is still owned and operated by the City of Berkeley. (Courtesy of Dorothy De Mare.)

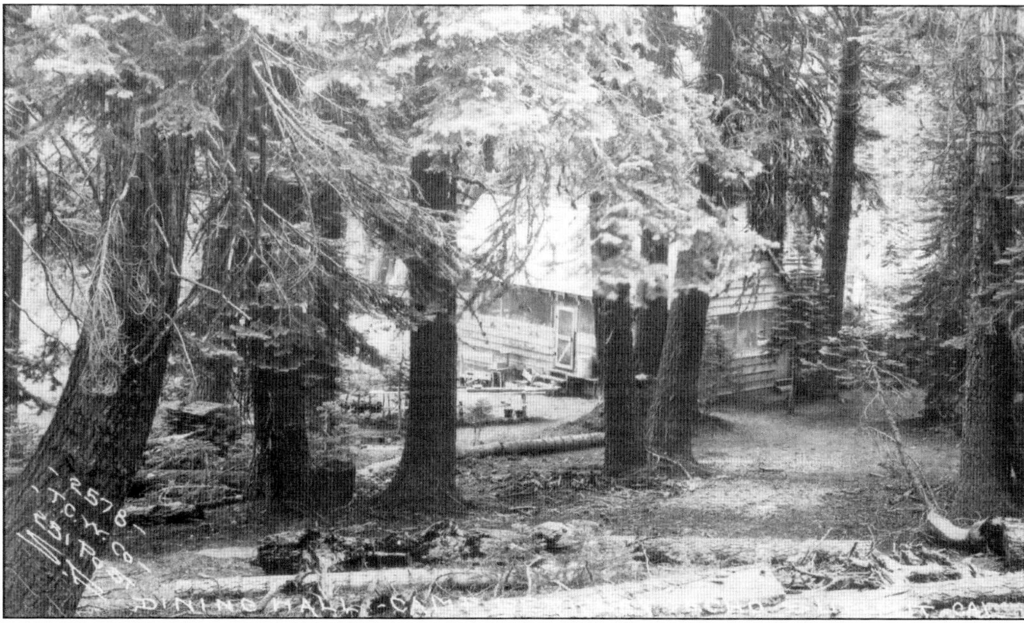

The first entrance to Berkeley Camp was down this dirt road that led to the small dining hall. Over the years, there have been four different entrances to the camp. This entrance is about 100 feet toward Echo Lake from the current entrance. Studying the area now, one can still just make out this old entrance from Echo Lake Road and from the parking lot by the dining hall. (Courtesy of Paul DeWitt.)

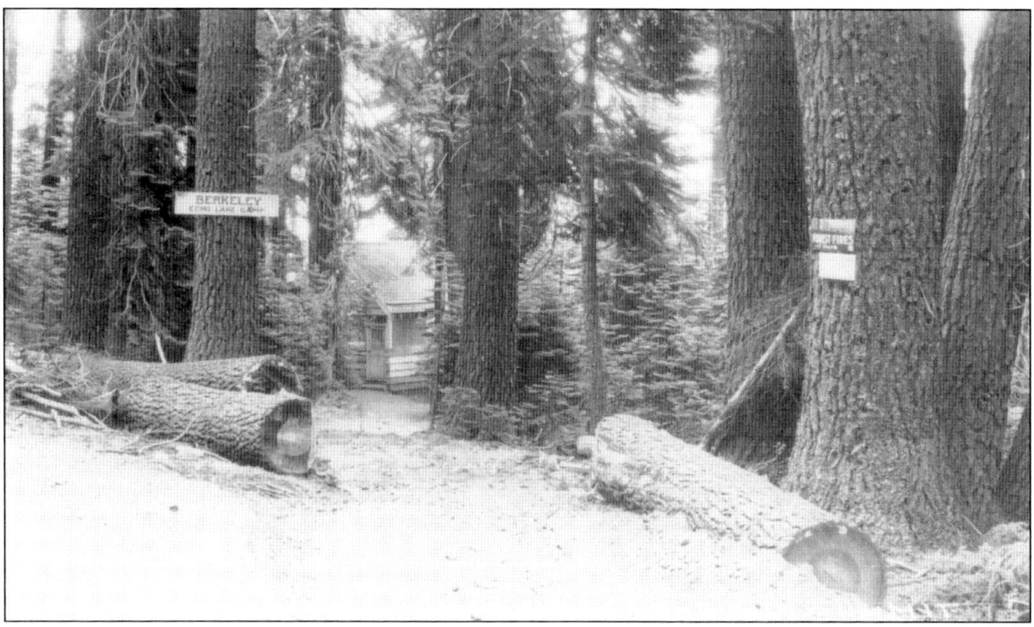

The first dining hall was small. The cook, Frank Greenwood, often complained and would be on the verge of leaving, but he was a master chef who served three delicious meals a day. The meat, butter, and milk came from the Celio ranch in the Upper Lake Valley of the Lake Tahoe Basin. It was difficult getting good fruit and vegetables, which had to come from Sacramento, often spoiling because of packaging and transportation. (Courtesy of Paul DeWitt.)

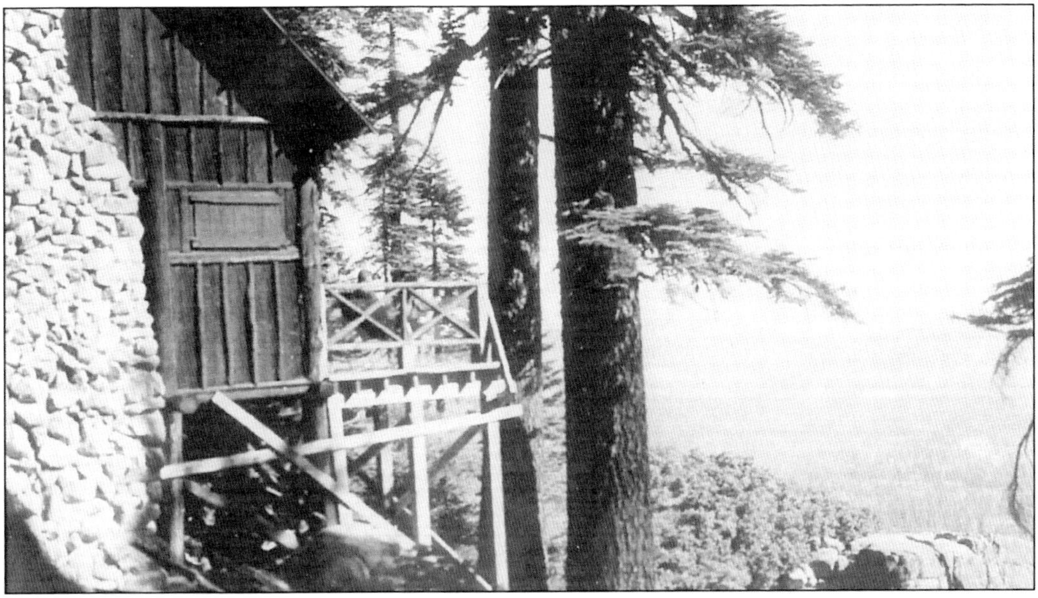

Besides the dining hall, other structures to be built were the lodge and tent platforms along the ridge. Afterward, more tent platforms were built away from the ridge. The ridge tents were the more desirable, because they provided spectacular views of the Lake Tahoe Basin. The lodge had a deck from which campers had a panoramic view of Tahoe as well. Inside, there was a library, and tables on which campers could play board games and cards. (Courtesy of Berkeley Echo Lake Camp.)

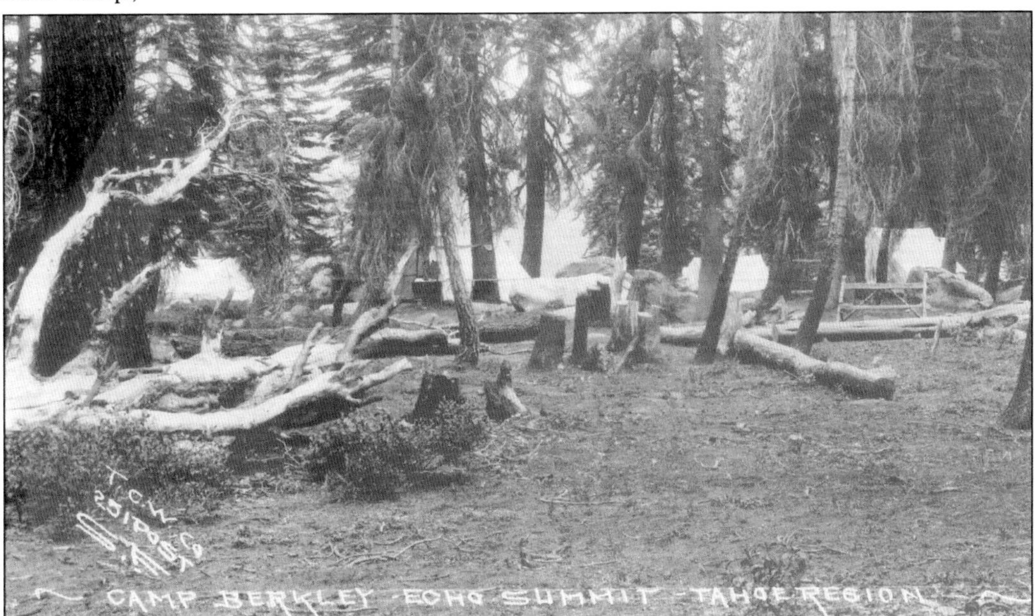

The concept of Berkeley Camp was to preserve the quality of camping in the wilderness instead of creating an urban environment. Guests at camp spent their vacations living a life of forest luxury. They could go anywhere or just sit around camp. "EKR" wrote to a friend, "We like it here and are glad we came. Hazel is off to Desolation Valley today. Gaye has gone swimming with the camp crowd. I am enjoying a real loafing time." (Courtesy of Paul DeWitt.)

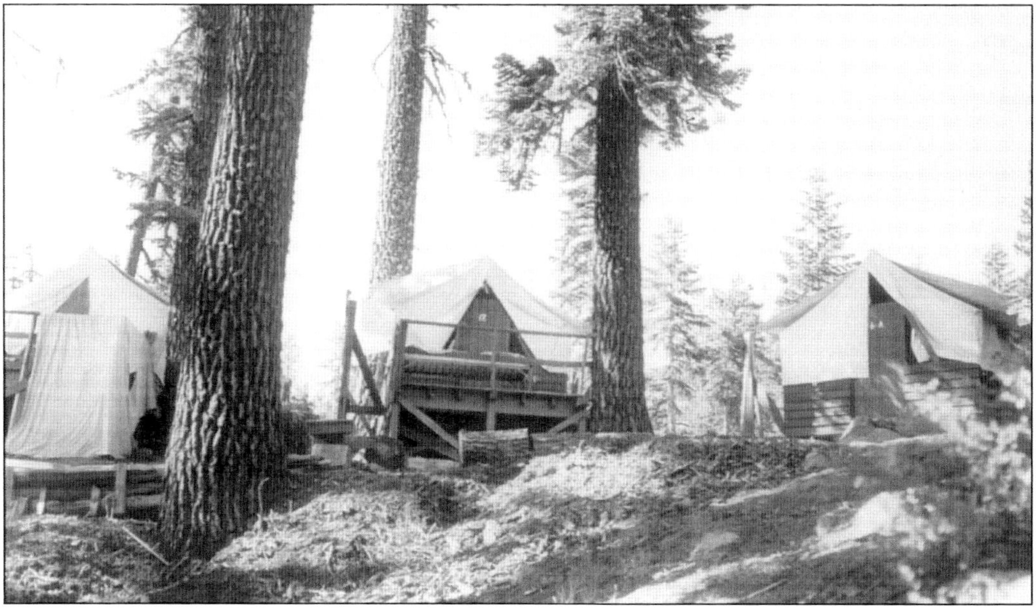

At first, campers had individual evening campfires near their tents to heat water for drinks and to warm their feet. Soon, there were two or three main fires in the camp around which everyone joined, to be entertained by staff and fellow campers. Campfires became a prominent form of socialization, as campers talked about their interests and where they might go for day hikes, swimming, fishing, bird-watching, or any other activities. (Courtesy of Berkeley Echo Lake Camp.)

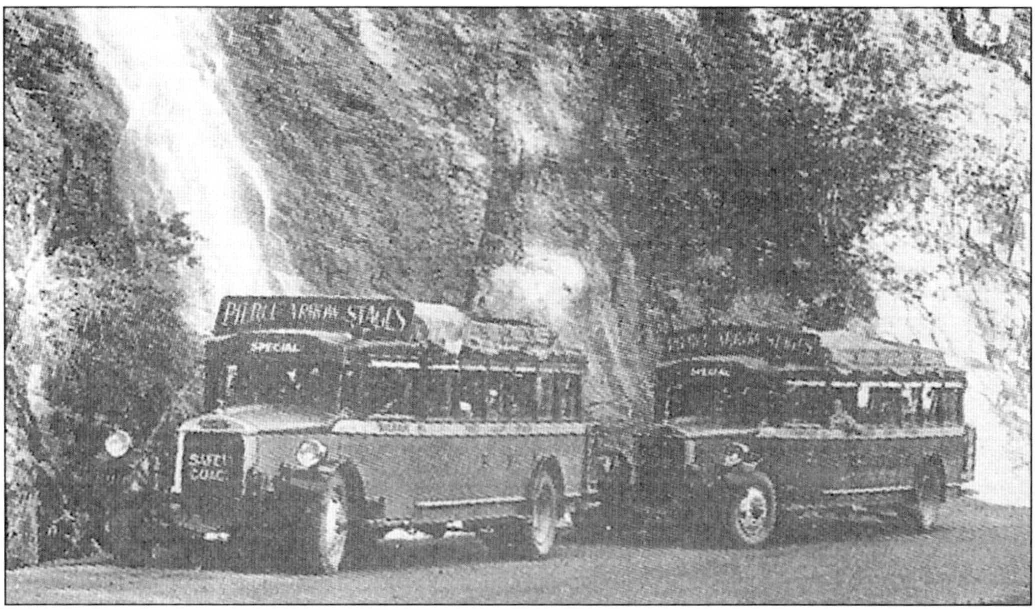

In the 1920s, it was an all-day trip to get to Berkeley Camp. Campers would board the Sacramento Northern Railroad early in the morning for the trip from the Bay Area to Sacramento. In Sacramento, they would catch the Pierce Arrow Stage at 10:45 a.m., leaving for Tahoe. In Placerville, campers would eat lunch and continue their journey over a bumpy sand, dirt, and gravel road until arriving at the Berkeley Camp Junction at 5:30 p.m. Pierce Arrow Stages are seen here passing Bridal Veil Falls en route to Tahoe. (Courtesy of Paul DeWitt.)

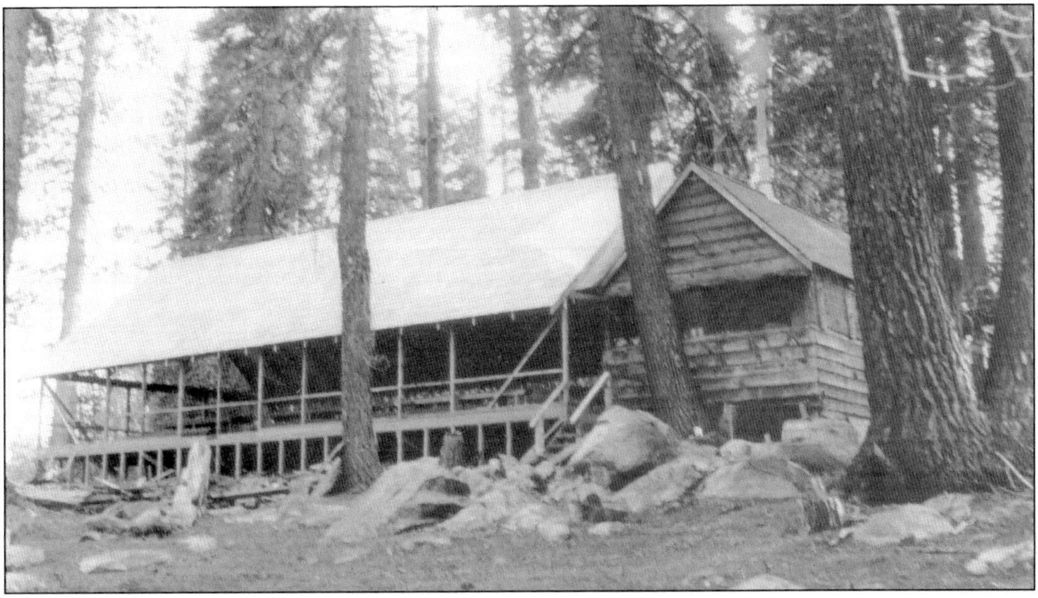

The number of campers had increased so much during the first eight years that Berkeley decided to build a larger dining hall, extending from the side of the original dining hall. Construction began in 1931 and was completed during the fall, before the first winter snows. (Courtesy of Berkeley Echo Lake Camp.)

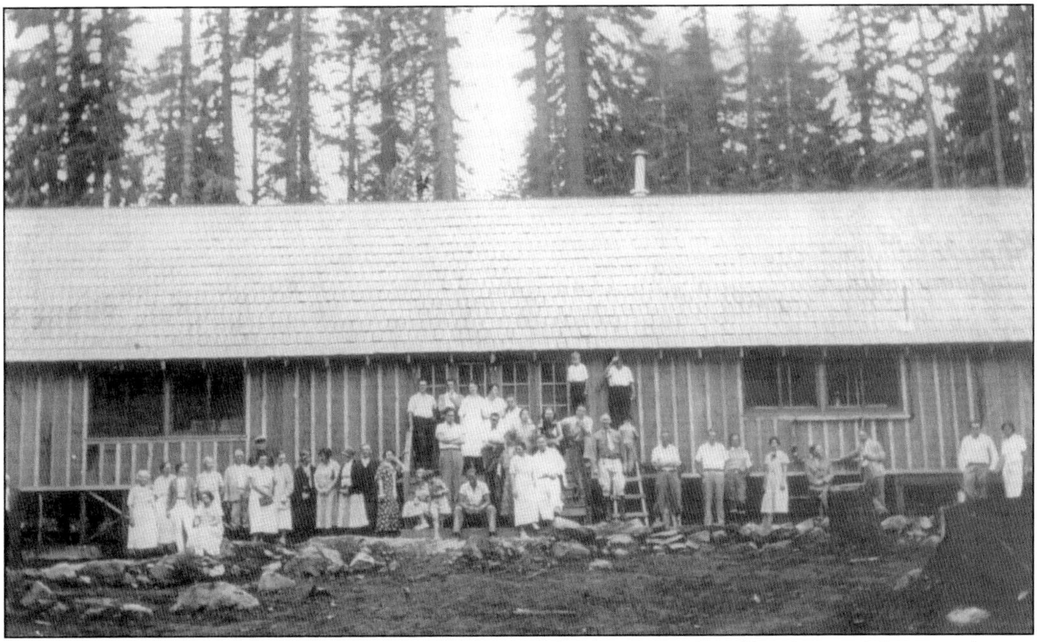

This is probably the first group photograph taken of campers and staff in front of the new dining hall in 1932. The building had vertical board and batten siding. Visible are two large windows and two double doors that led into the dining hall. The roof was shingled. Everyone probably felt they had a new dining hall that was beautiful and would last forever. (Courtesy of Berkeley Echo Lake Camp.)

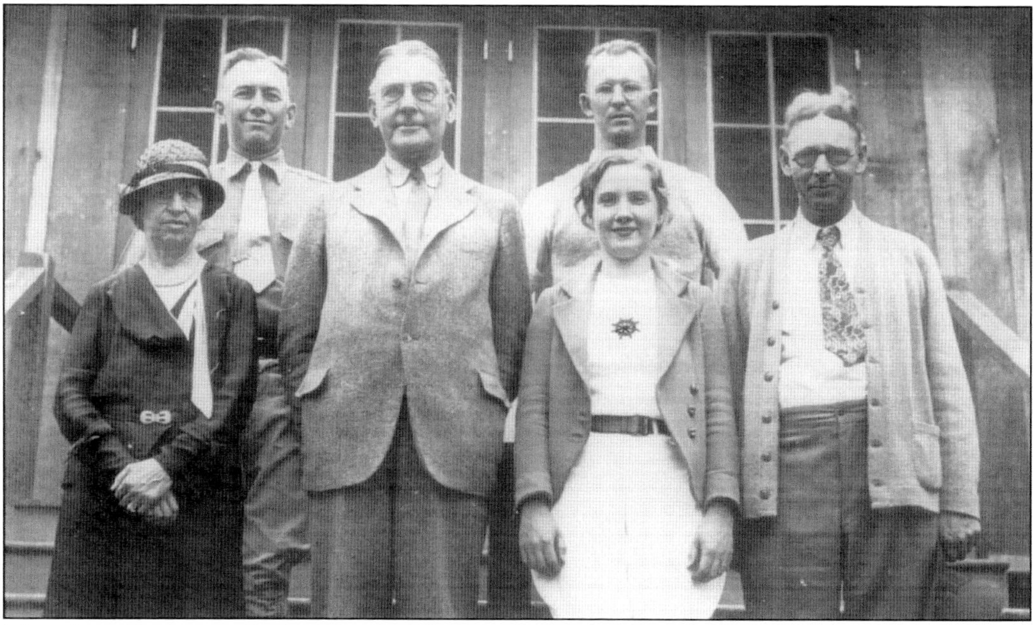

This photograph was taken in front of the new dining hall in 1932. In the second row at right is camp manager Harry Stoops. Harry's wife and camp nurse, Eileen Stoops, is second from right in the first row. Also in the first row are Judge Curtis Wilbur (second from left) and his wife, Olive. Judge Wilbur served as chief justice of the California State Supreme Court and was secretary of the Navy. He was nominated to the Federal Ninth Circuit Court of Appeals in 1929. The other individuals are unidentified. (Courtesy of Berkeley Echo Lake Camp.)

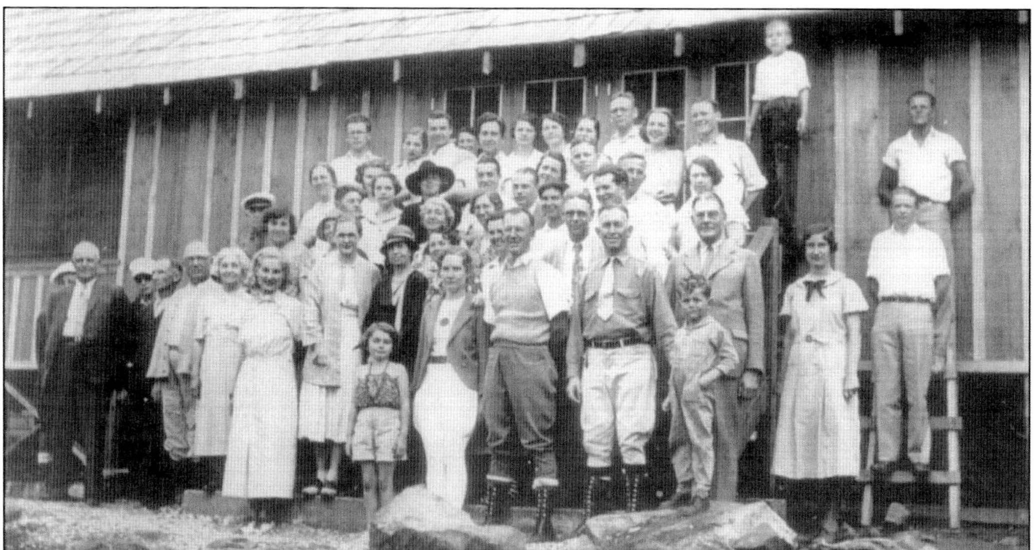

This is a group photograph of the campers at Berkeley Camp. Judge Wilbur stands behind the young boy on the right. The Wilburs stayed at Berkeley Camp for the summer of 1932 while their cabin and Curtis's law library were being built on US Forest Service land. During the summer months, Judge Wilbur would stay at his cabin and drive to Carson City to serve on the Nevada Federal District Court until he retired in 1945. The man standing on the bottom ladder rung at right is David Brower (see next page). (Courtesy of Berkeley Echo Lake Camp.)

David Brower became a nationally and internationally renowned environmentalist and conservationist. As a camp staff member from 1930 to 1932, he loved the wilderness. Campers told him about the Sierra Club, which he joined in 1933. In his lifetime, he held leadership positions in the Sierra Club, Friends of the Earth, and the Earth First Institute. (Courtesy of Berkeley Echo Lake Camp.)

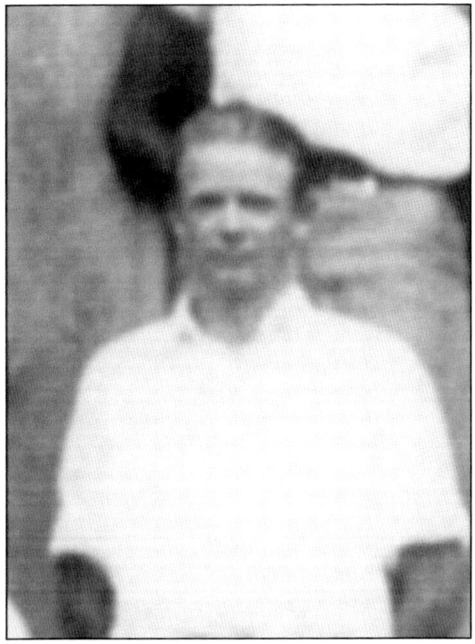

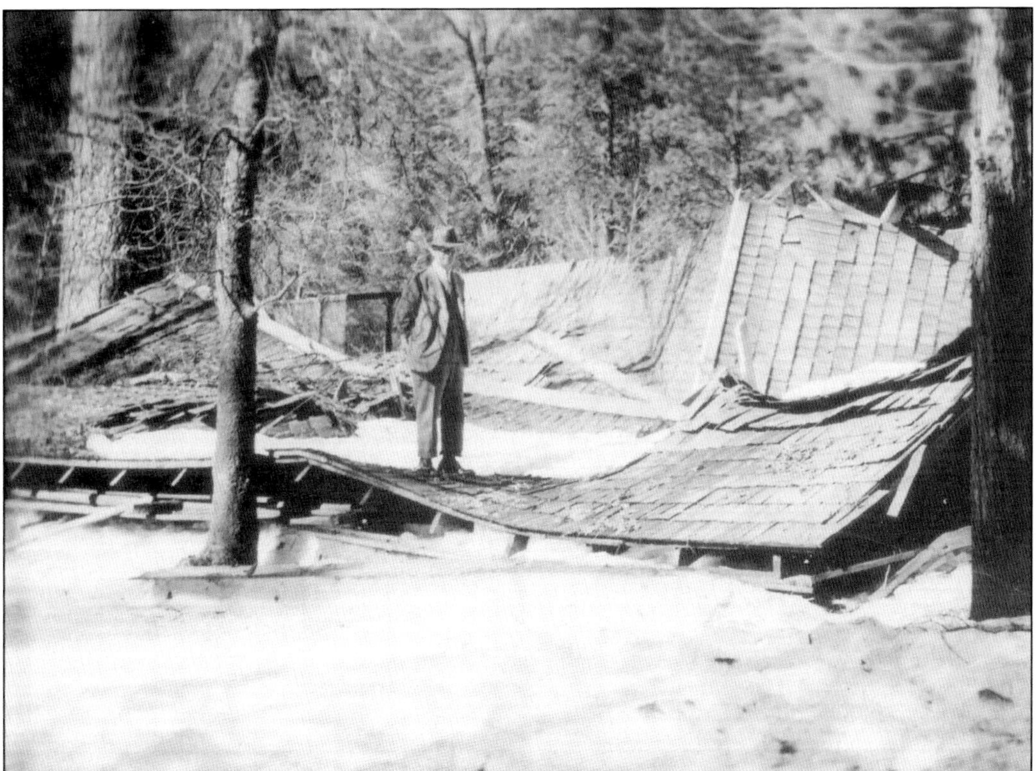

Heavy snowfall in the winter of 1932–1933 completely collapsed the new and old dining halls. A city official stands on the flattened roof of the original dining hall. Behind him, the new dining hall roof is tilted upward. (Courtesy of Berkeley Echo Lake Camp.)

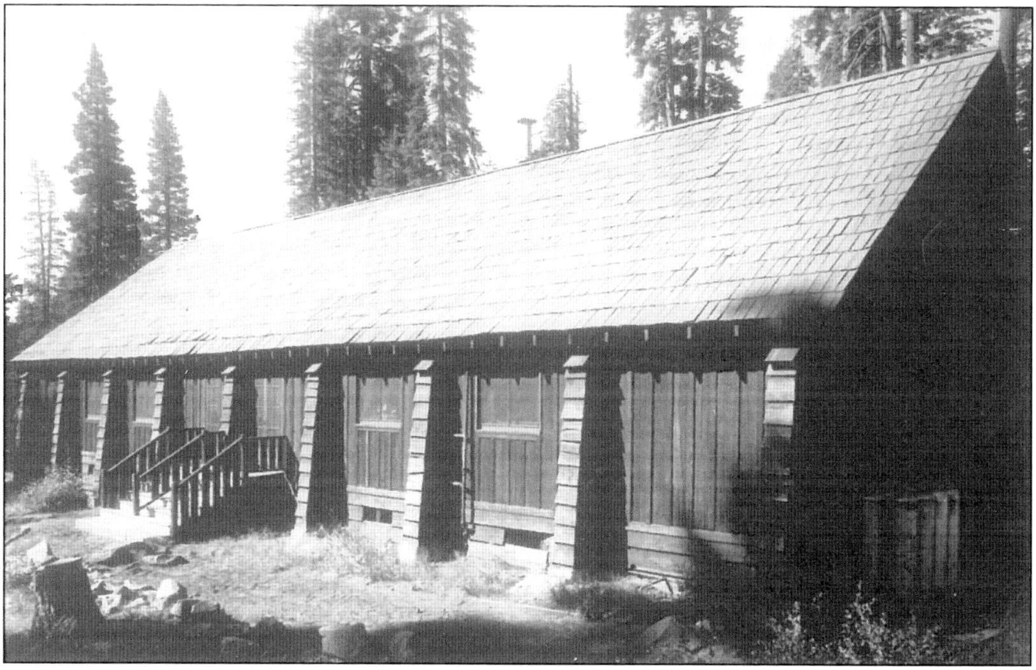

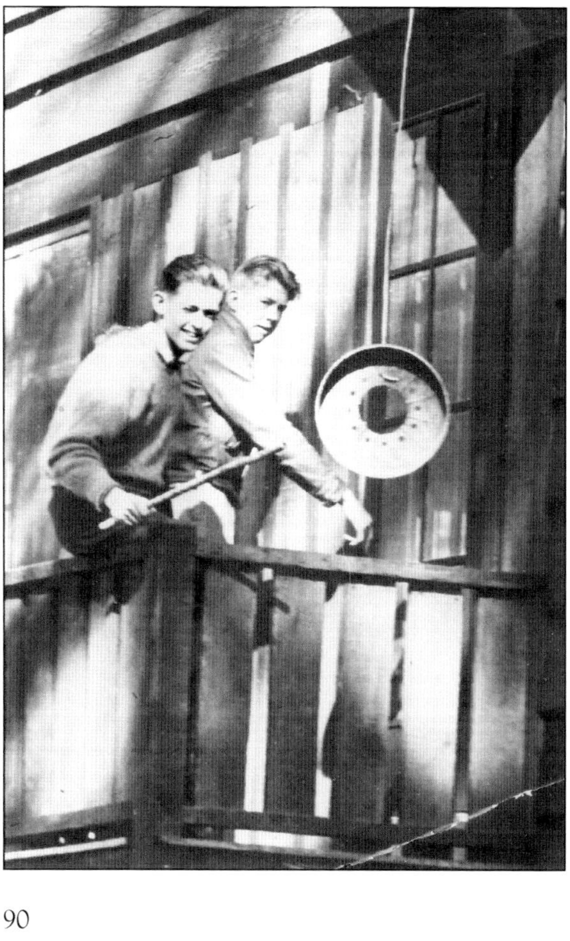

With the dining hall destroyed by snow, Berkeley Camp was closed for the 1933 season. Another dining hall was being built that could withstand the conditions of a severe winter. The new dining hall included buttresses to support the walls and roof. Harry Stoops returned as the camp manager in 1934 to serve his last summer. Beginning in the 1940s, he returned with his family as campers until the 1960s. (Courtesy of Berkeley Echo Lake Camp.)

The new dining hall had an unusual dinner gong for the 1934 season. These two boys are playing with the gong and a half-inch pipe to make it ring. The gong itself looks like an old brake drum from a large truck. This gong did not last long, replaced by a completely different-looking gong. (Courtesy of Berkeley Echo Lake Camp.)

153

July 18, 1935

Athletics Hold Interest at Camp

ECHO LAKE CAMP, July 15 (By Mail)—Berkeley Echo Lake Camp's interest in athletics is steadily increasing as the Garfield Playground boys, under the direction of Dave Luce, widen their camp program to include inter-camp baseball, volleyball and tennis. The Garfield boys played the Sacramento Y. M. C. A. Camp in a game of baseball and were nosed out in the ninth inning by a score of 10-9.

New guests arriving in camp today include Clifford H. Bissell, Mrs. A. H. Kroeber, Mrs. C. H. Brown, Clifton Kroeber, Teddy Kroeber and Mr. M. B. Rosekrans and family, Ruth Popper, Mr. and Mrs. Michael Arnando and Miss E. Constance Douglas, all of Berkeley.

Mr and Mrs B. J. Bennett, Oakland
Andrew Clough Palo Alto

July 19, 1935

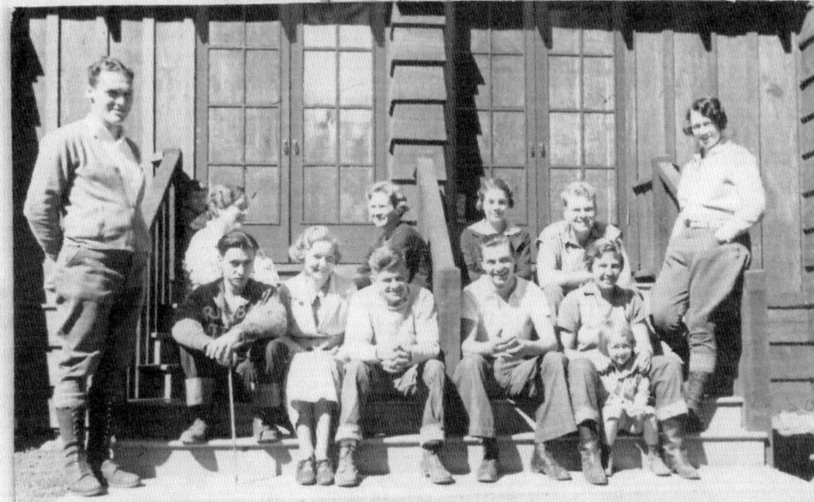

1935 Season - Camp Staff
(Taken by Dr. N. S. Marshall)

Carlton "Duke" DeWitt and his wife, Harriett, managed Berkeley Camp beginning in 1935. In this photograph, Duke is standing on the far left, and Harriett is leaning on the stair railing at right. The camp staff members are seated on the steps between them. At the top of this page is an article about sporting events at the camp. Athletics and other physical activities have always played a major role in the life of Berkeley Camp. (Courtesy of Paul DeWitt.)

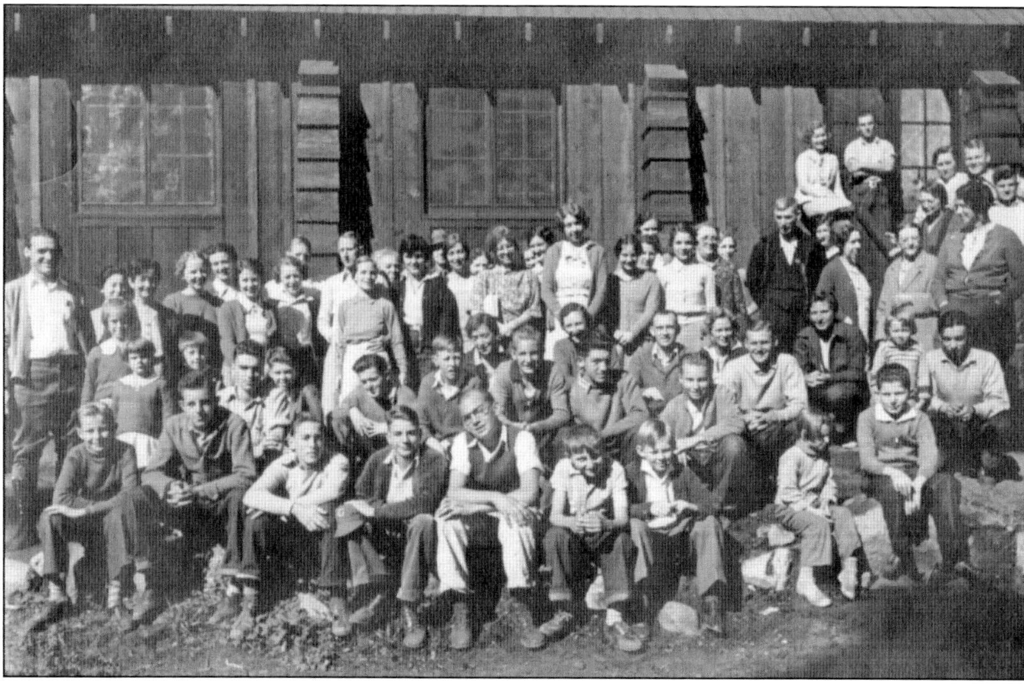

Campers pose in front of the new dining hall on July 9, 1935. This was a special year for Duke and Harriett, as his parents drove out from Iowa to be with them for the opening of camp. Duke is standing on the far left. Harriett is standing on the far right at the end of the fourth row wearing a white blouse and dark sweater. Carl DeWitt, Duke's father, is the third person standing from Harriett, wearing a white shirt with a dark sweater and jacket. Mable DeWitt, Duke's mother, standing next to Carl, is wearing glasses and a patterned jacket. (Courtesy of Paul DeWitt.)

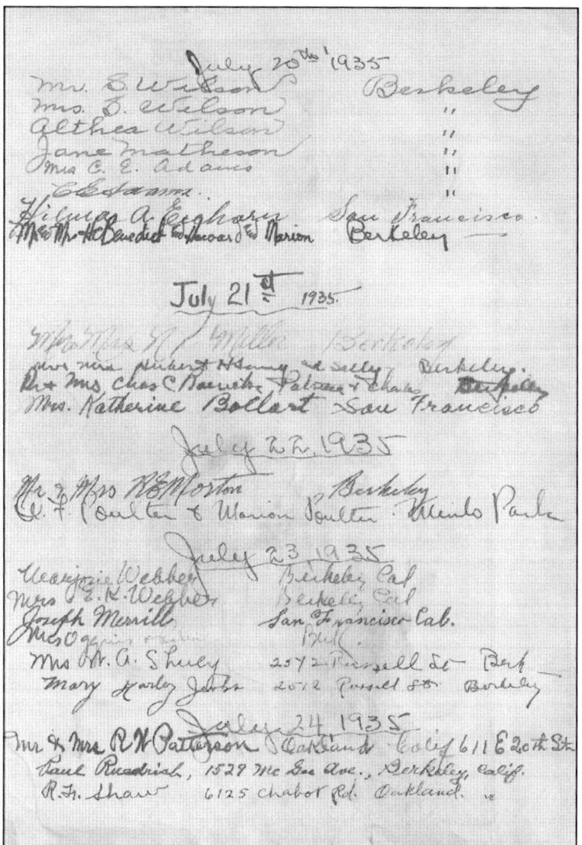

July 20th 1935
Mr. [illegible] Wilson Berkeley
Mrs. [illegible] Wilson "
Althea Wilson "
Jane Matheson "
Mrs C. E. Adams "
C E Adams "
Wilma A. Eighorn San Francisco
Mr & Mrs H C Benedict [illegible] & Marion Berkeley

July 21st 1935.
[illegible] Berkeley
[illegible] Berkeley.
Dr & Mrs Chas C [illegible], Patricia & Charles [illegible]
Mrs. Katherine Bollart San Francisco

July 22. 1935
Mr & Mrs [illegible] Morton Berkeley
[illegible] Coulter & Marion Coulter Menlo Park

July 23 1935
Marjorie Webber Berkeley Cal
Mrs [illegible] Webber Berkeley Cal
Joseph Merrill San Francisco Cal.
Mrs [illegible] Berk.
Mrs [illegible] 2572 Russell St Berk
Mary [illegible] 2572 Russell St Berkeley

July 24 1935
Mr & Mrs R W Patterson Oakland Calif 611 E 20th St
Paul [illegible], 1529 Mc Gee Ave., Berkeley, calif.
R. F. Shaw 6125 Chabot Rd. Oakland.

This is a typical page from the roster on which guests signed their names when arriving at Berkeley Camp. The use of a typewriter for registration and running the office was unheard of until the 1960s. From the names and addresses, one can tell that campers did not come just from Berkeley but from other cities in the San Francisco Bay Area: San Francisco, Palo Alto, Menlo Park, Oakland, and other cities. (Courtesy of Paul DeWitt.)

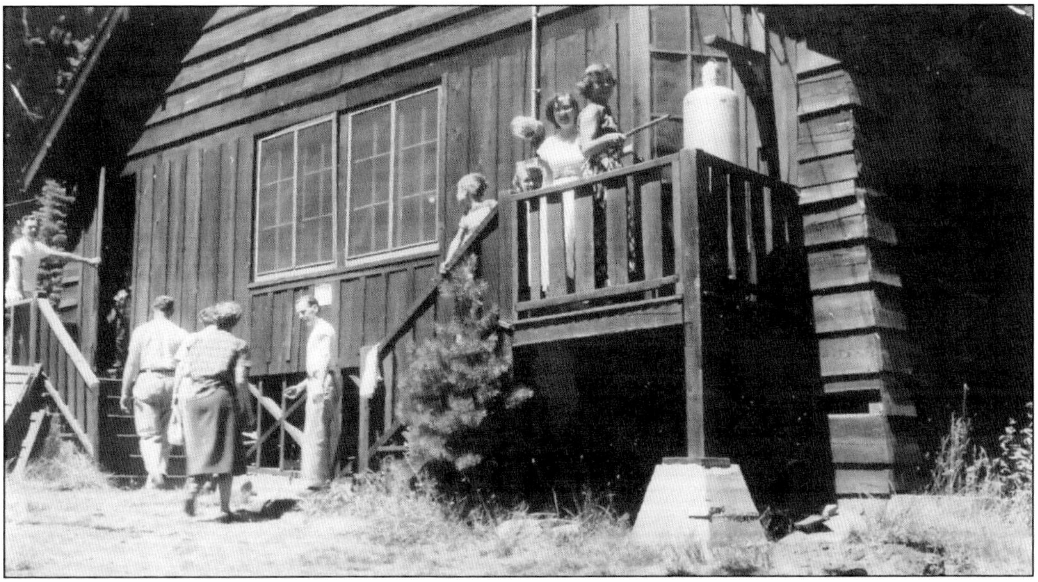

A dining hall girl uses a half-inch pipe to strike the side of a large, empty propane tank hanging from a wooden support. Announcing mealtimes at Berkeley Camp, the sound of the gong could be heard throughout the whole camp. In the morning, the gong was rung an hour and a half-hour before breakfast, and then again at mealtime. For lunch and dinner, the gong was rung a half-hour before and at mealtimes. (Courtesy of Berkeley Echo Lake Camp.)

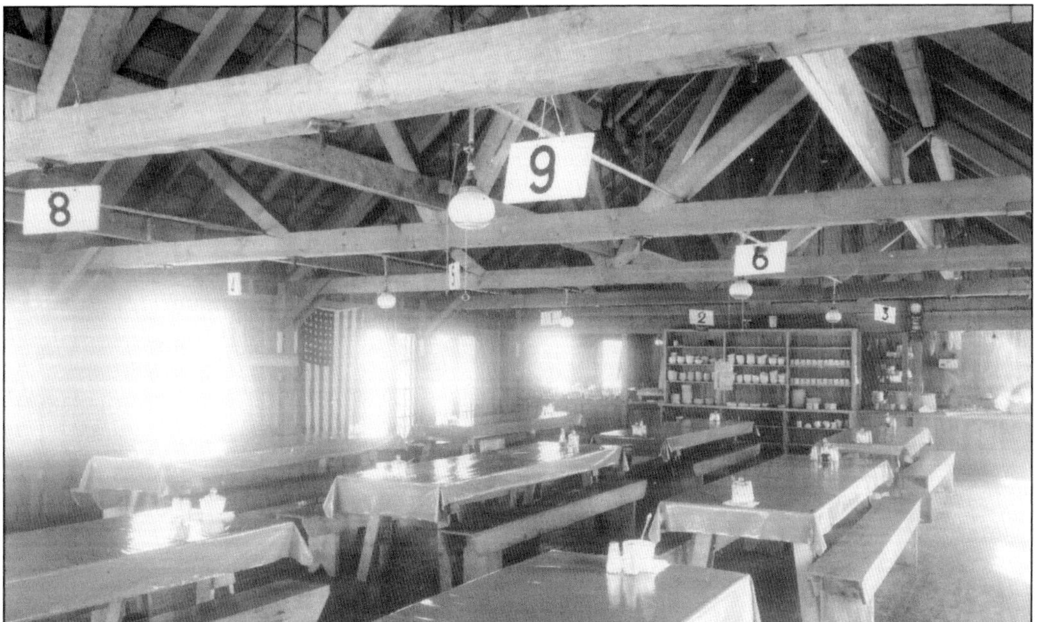

This is the dining hall as it appeared in the 1940s. In the 1950s and 1960s, more tables were added, expanding the seating from three rows to four to accommodate more campers. The camp staff always sat at table No. 2. Families and individuals were assigned specific tables. Dining-hall girls set the tables and served platters of food. A raised empty platter meant more food was desired by the campers at the table. Campers carried their dishes to the counter (right), where kitchen boys rinsed them and loaded the dishwasher. (Courtesy of Berkeley Echo Lake Camp.)

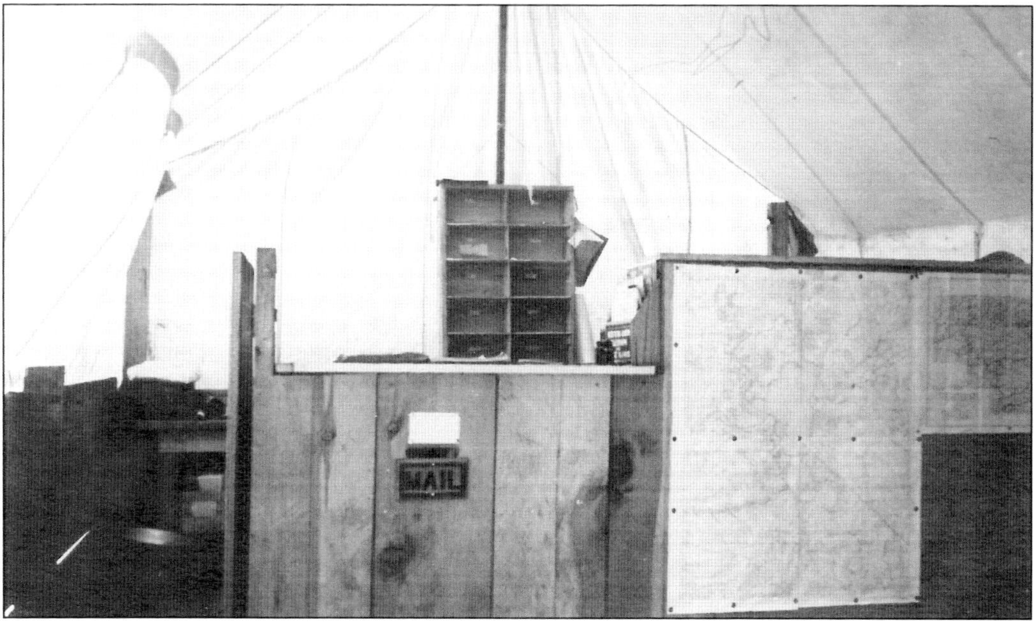

The camp office was just like any other tent on the grounds. It was located between the lodge and the volleyball court. Arriving campers would check in to get the number and location of their tents. They would learn their assigned tables in the dining hall. Campers could send out and receive mail at the office, and they could purchase stationary, toiletries, batteries, film, and other items to make their stay comfortable. Children could buy candy. (Courtesy of Berkeley Echo Lake Camp.)

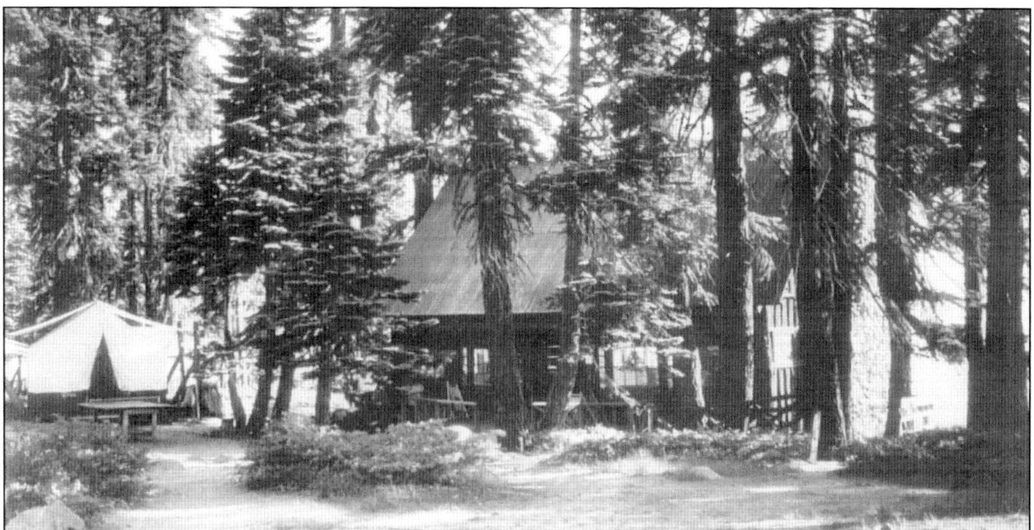

The lodge has always played a major role in Berkeley Camp life. Besides the library and tables for board games and card games in the 1920s, a ping-pong table and conversation circles were added. There were deck chairs on the porch for campers to view the Lake Tahoe Basin or to talk with each other. On cold evenings, recreation leaders would lead campers in folk, square, and social dancing in the lodge. On warm evenings, the dancing would be held outdoors on the volleyball court. (Courtesy of Berkeley Echo Lake Camp.)

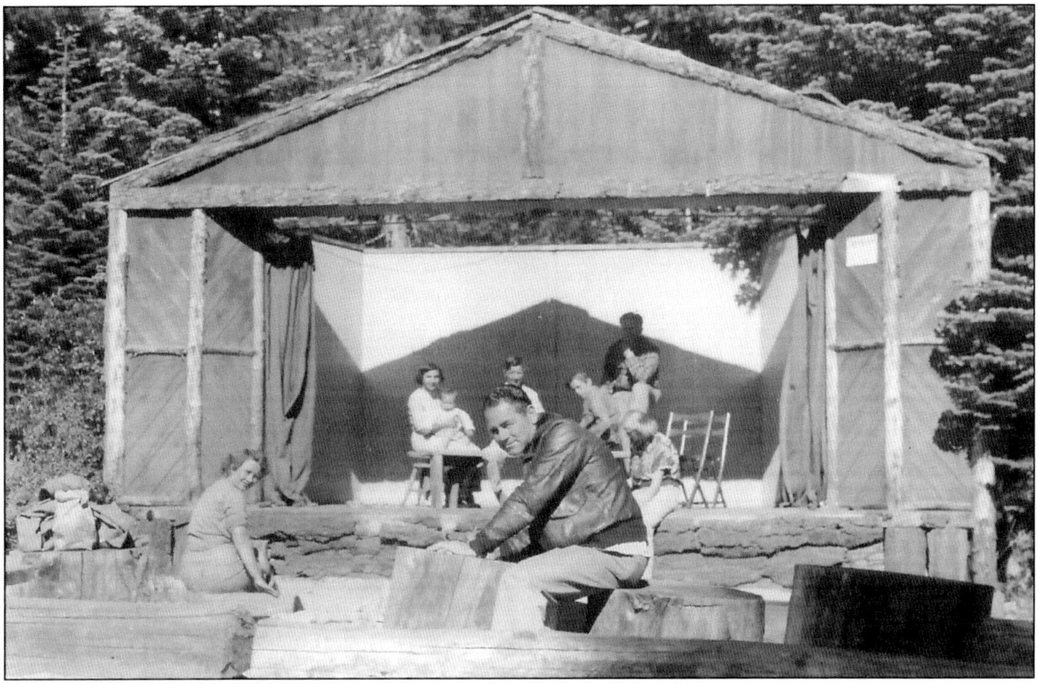

This stage survived for more than 40 years at Berkeley Camp. It stood in front of a campfire, with benches and logs providing seating for the audiences. Saturday night was staff night, with the camp staff performing skits and leading campers in songs. Wednesday night was table night, with each dining table performing skits. During the day, children would create their own skits to entertain themselves and anyone who might be watching. (Courtesy of Berkeley Echo Lake Camp.)

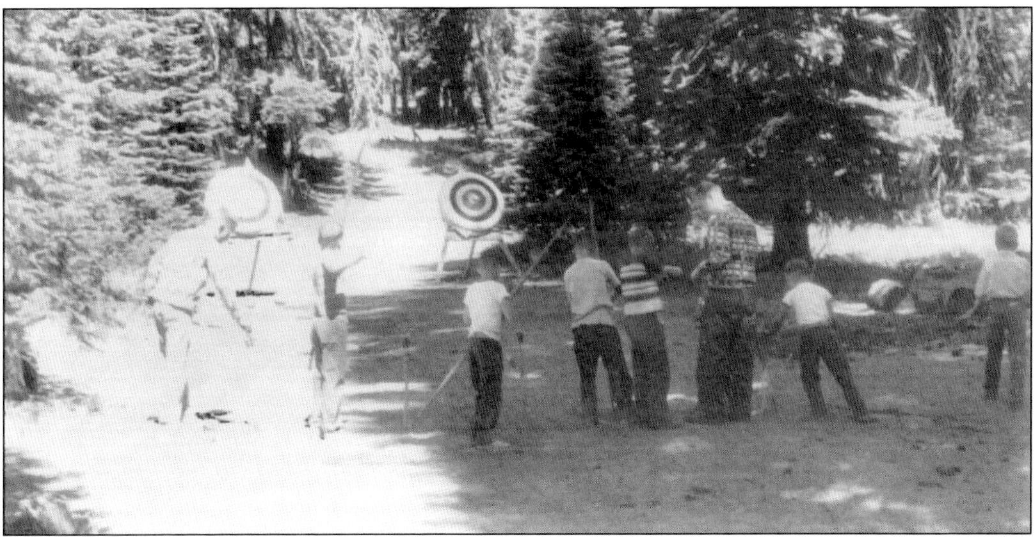

Many recreational activities were offered within the camp setting. There was an archery range just across Echo Lake Road. There were badminton, volleyball, and basketball courts, a croquet field, and a mountain golf course played with croquet balls, mallets, and—for holes—buried number-10-size cans. The arts and crafts building had all kinds of projects for young children to make, using watercolors, crayons, paper, glue, pinecones, pine needles, and different sizes and shapes of small branches. (Courtesy of Berkeley Echo Lake Camp.)

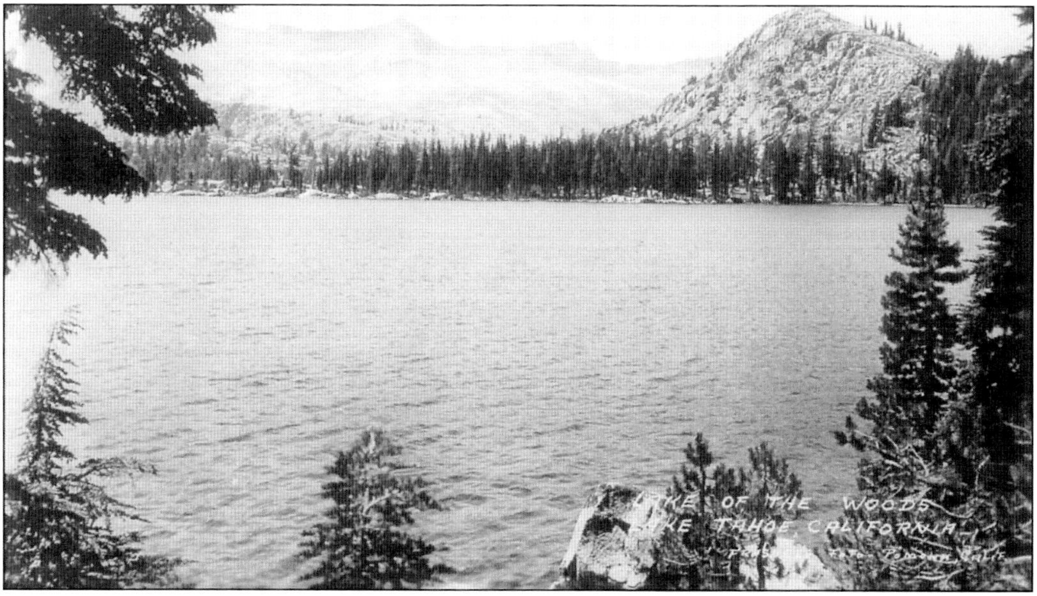

Numerous recreational activities were offered outside of Berkeley Camp. Recreation leaders would take campers on all-day hikes to places like Lake Audrain, the old Hawley Grade, and the Desolation Wilderness Area. Destinations in Desolation included Tamarack Lake for a short, easy hike, and Lake of the Woods and Aloha Lake for longer trips. Hour and two-hour horseback rides were scheduled once a week at Chet Mitchell's Echo Summit Stables, across the road from Berkeley Camp. (Courtesy of Paul DeWitt.)

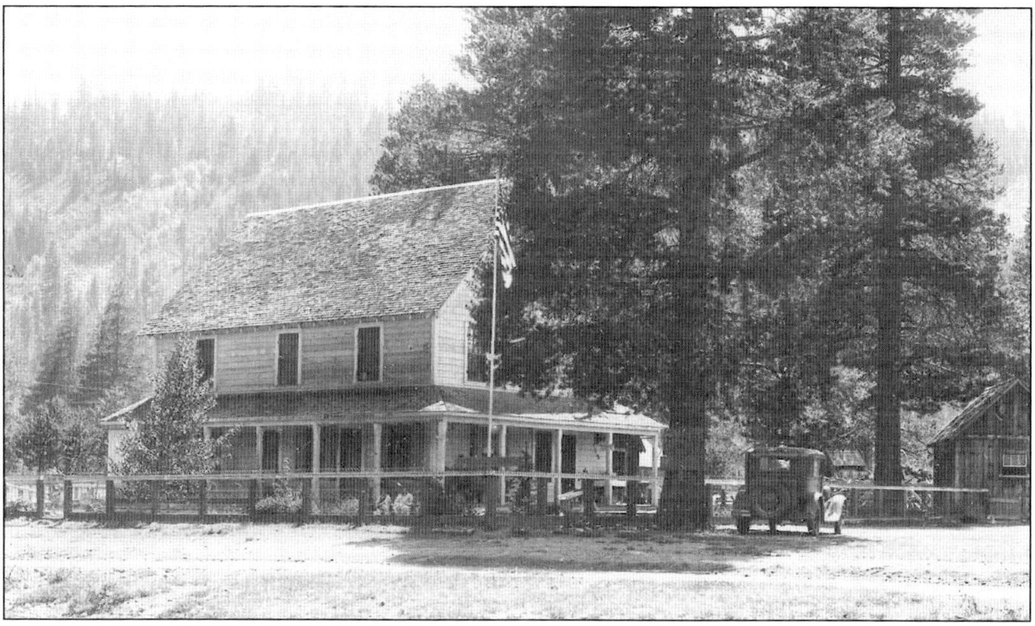

Before the 1950s, much of the food and supplies for operating Berkeley Camp came from the Celio Ranch (seen here), the Smith Dairy Ranch, and other businesses in the South Lake Tahoe Basin. When food rationing began in World War II, it was hard to buy food and supplies without ration stamps. During the summer of 1943, many campers gave their stamps to Berkeley Camp, to help purchase food for camp guests eating in the dining hall. (Courtesy of Shirley Taylor.)

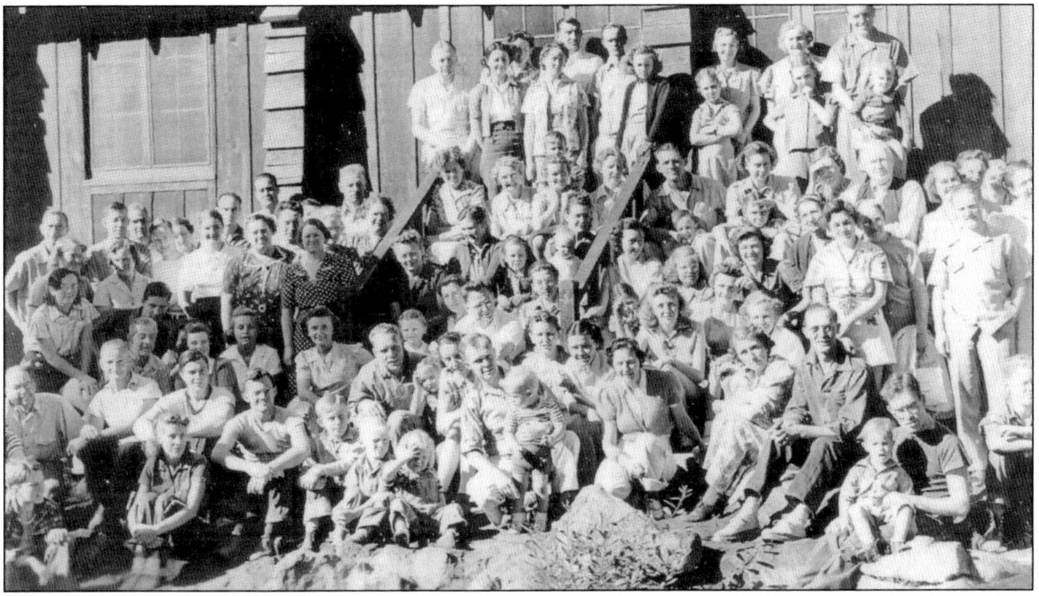

Because of the shortage of food and fuel in the summer of 1944, Berkeley Echo Lake Camp was closed for the season. Duke and Harriett DeWitt managed Berkeley Tuolumne Camp that summer. They returned to Berkeley Echo Lake Camp in 1945 as managers for their last season. As usual, group photographs of campers were taken in front of the dining hall. This one was taken the last week of camp in 1945. (Courtesy of Paul DeWitt.)

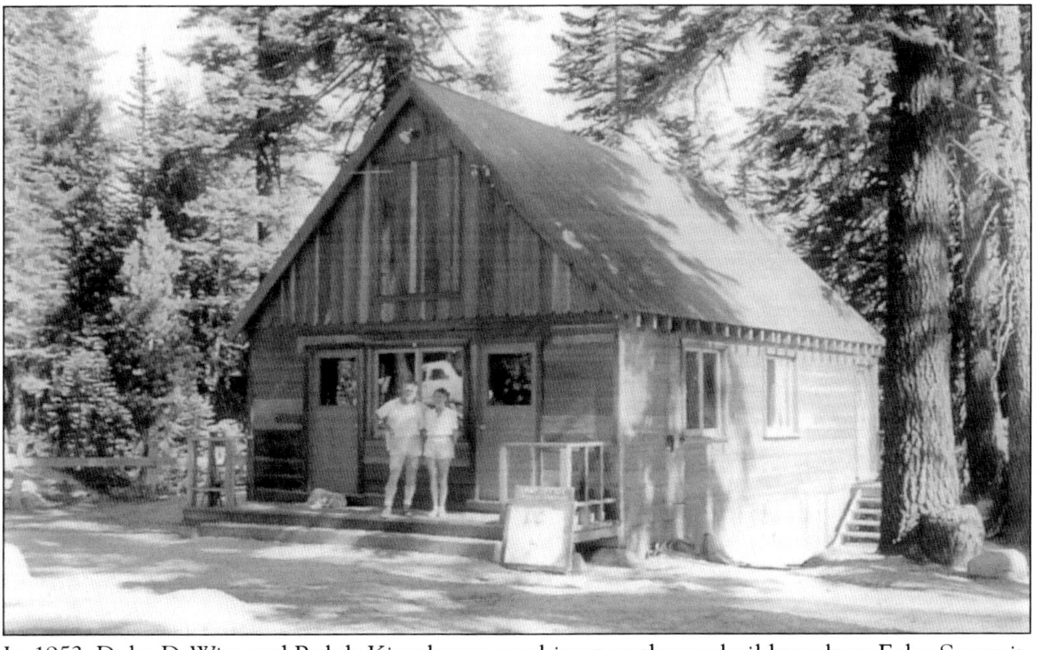

In 1953, Duke DeWitt and Ralph King began working together as builders along Echo Summit. Their first job was the construction of the new Berkeley Camp office, seen here with Emery Curtice, camp manager from 1946 to 1957, and his wife, Minerva. The old office tent became the new recreation office. (Courtesy of Berkeley Echo Lake Camp.)

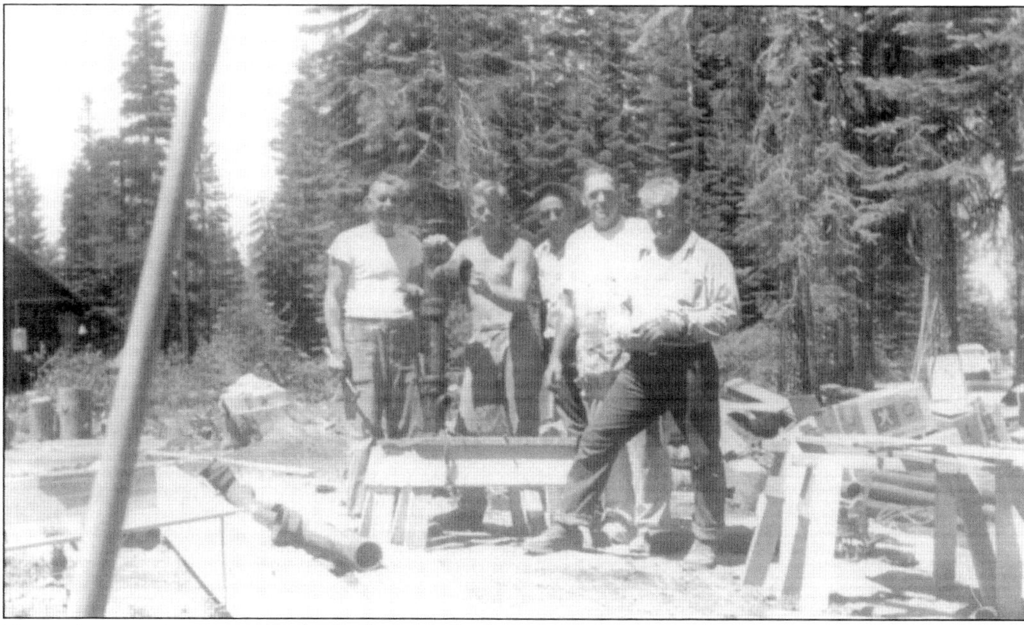

Over the next few years, Duke built tent platforms, a building with showers and a laundry room, a building with bathrooms and two showers, a cook's cabin, and the bathrooms and changing rooms for the new swimming pool. Here, Emery Curtis, on the far right, and Duke DeWitt, second from the right, are working on a plumbing project. The other men are unidentified. The dining hall is in the background. (Courtesy of Berkeley Echo Lake Camp.)

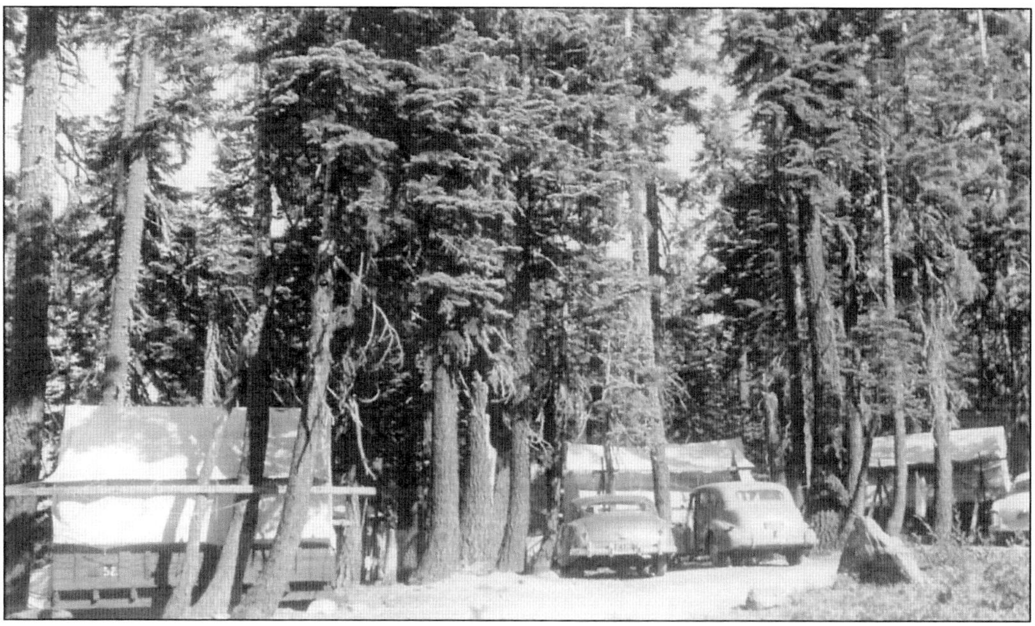

Until the late 1970s, campers arriving at Berkeley Camp would drive down the entrance road that had a sign in bold, carved, and painted letters—"BERKELEY CAMP"—on a 30-inch-diameter log. They would proceed to the office to register and get their tent and table numbers. From there, they could drive to their tent and park their cars, as seen in this 1950s photograph. This entrance was where the bocce ball court is today. (Courtesy of Berkeley Echo Lake Camp.)

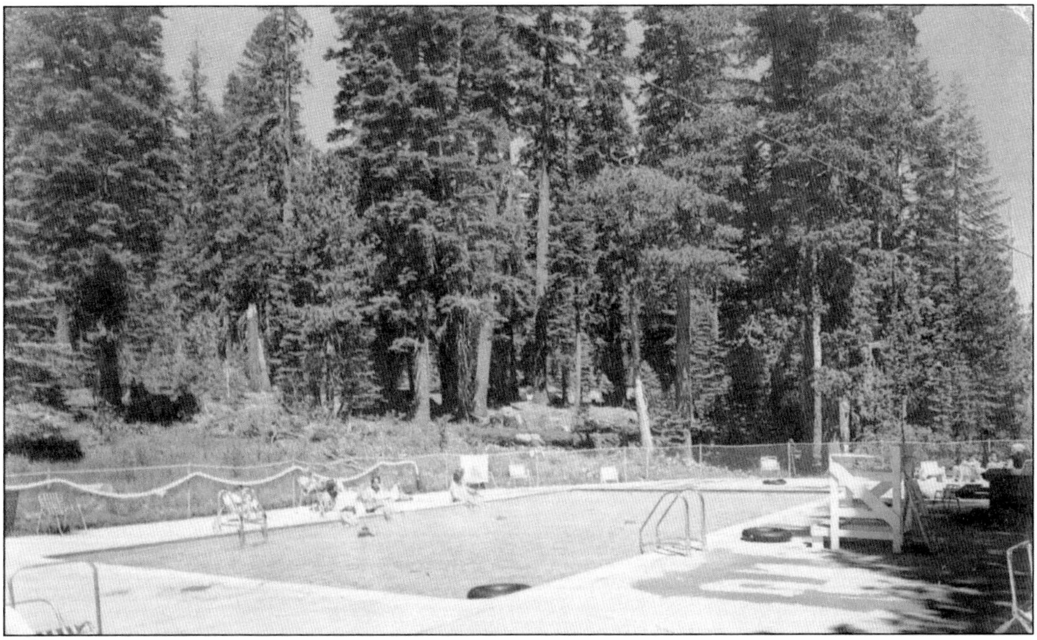

In 1958, swimming and children's wading pools were constructed at Berkeley Camp. Over the years, things have changed. The wading pool was covered in the 1990s, with a spa installed on top of it. The filtering system was changed. Although the swimming pool does not look different today than when it was built, in the fall of 2013, it received a major face-lift to modernize it. (Courtesy of the El Dorado County Historical Museum.)

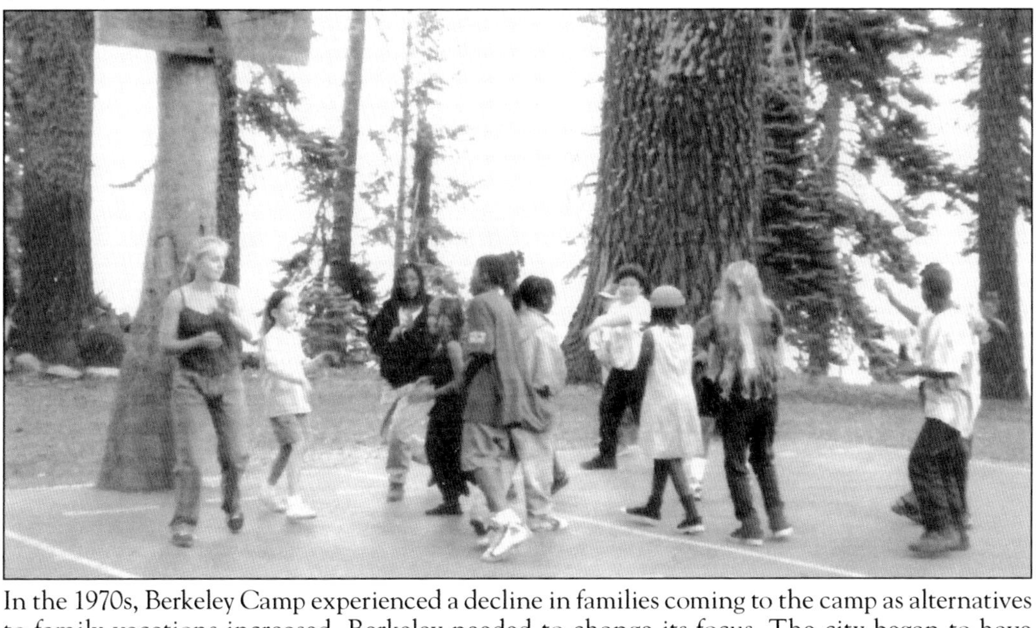

In the 1970s, Berkeley Camp experienced a decline in families coming to the camp as alternatives to family vacations increased. Berkeley needed to change its focus. The city began to have specialized sessions for young teenagers, senior citizens, and different organizations. Today, there are at least four weekly sessions of teens, and a session for older adults. Several cross-country and running organizations have weekly sessions at the camp. One has been using the camp for 25 years. (Courtesy of Berkeley Echo Lake Camp.)

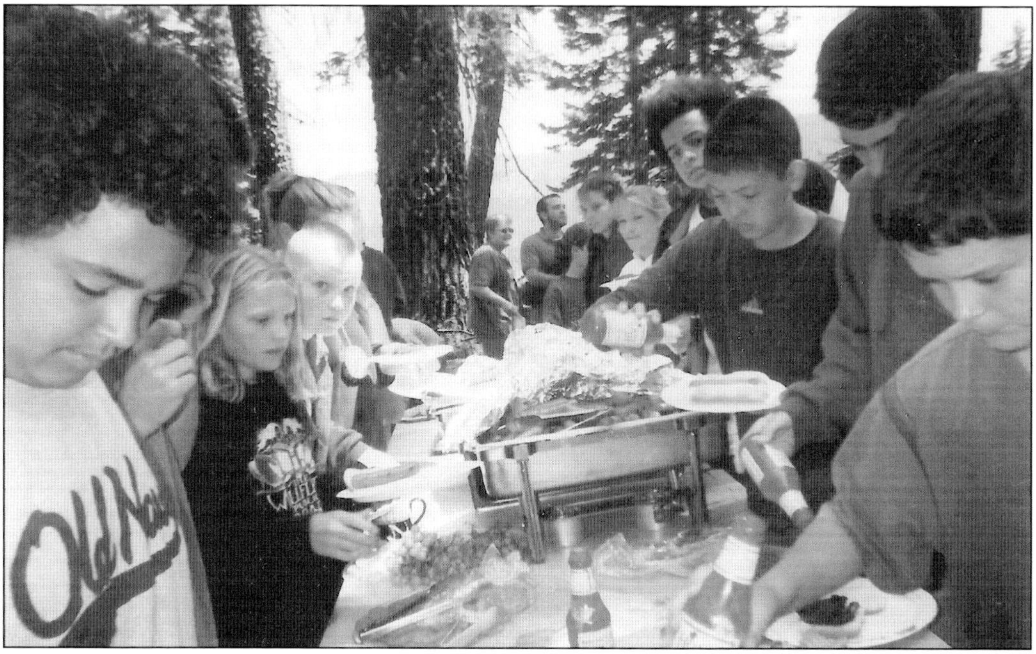

Teenage camping sessions begin when they arrive by bus on Mondays. There is a young adult counselor for about every 16 youths. Daytime activities include walks to Echo Lake, swimming, basketball, volleyball, and a three-hour hike. In the evenings, teens participate in a night hike, a campfire, a dance, and a pajama party. On Friday, they help clean up the camp, have a hot dog and hamburger barbecue-style lunch, and board the bus for home. (Courtesy of Berkeley Echo Lake Camp.)

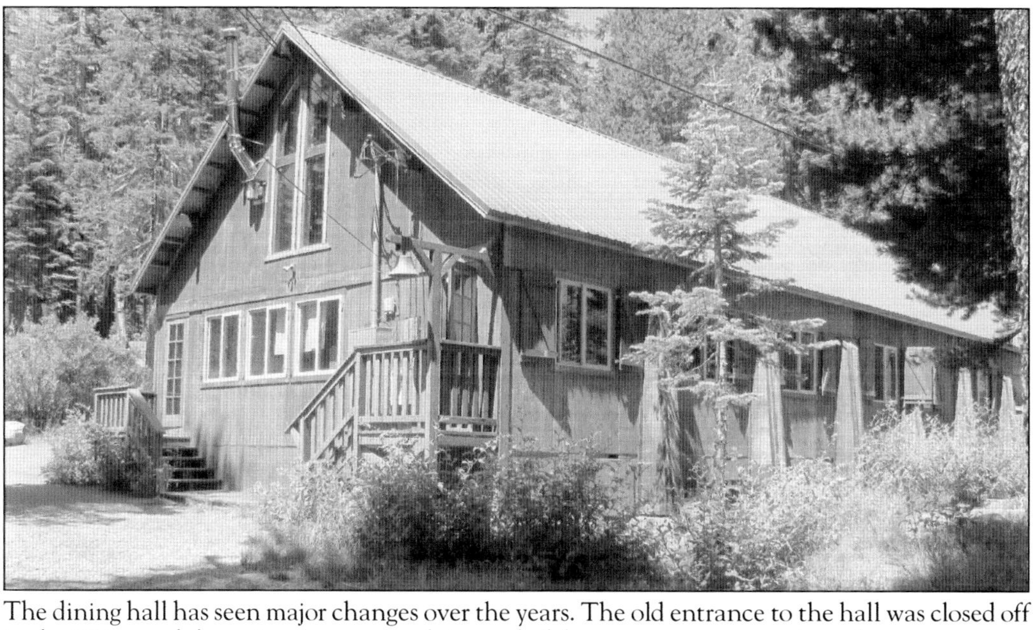

The dining hall has seen major changes over the years. The old entrance to the hall was closed off in the 1980s, and the stairs were removed. Instead of the empty propane tank used as a gong, there is now a brass bell. To get more natural light into the dining hall, large windows were built into the gable end. A wood-burning stove now heats up the interior. (Courtesy of Paul DeWitt.)

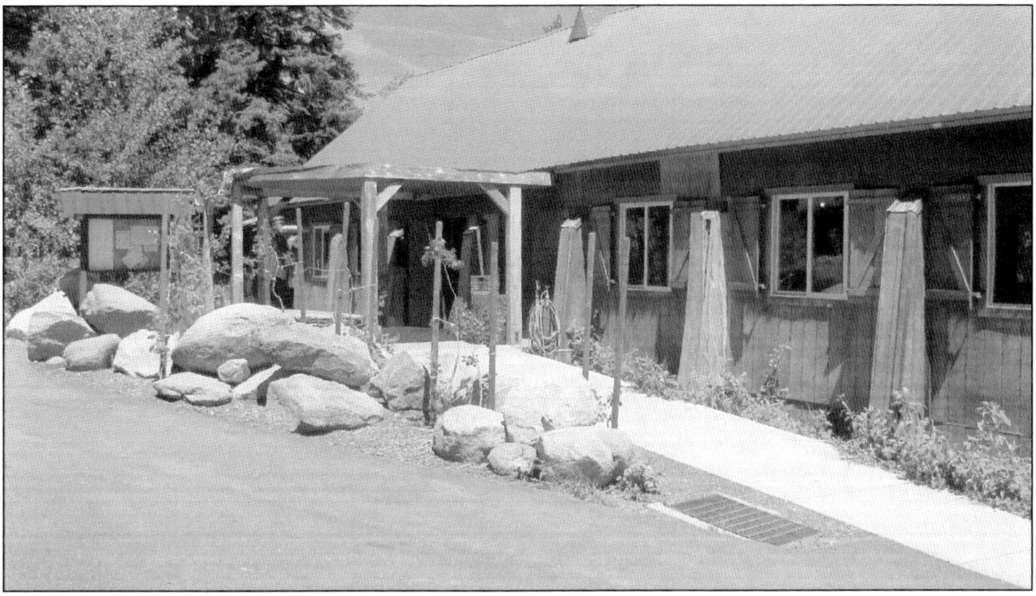

The entrance to the dining hall is now on the east side of the building. There is a ramp for disabled persons to access the entrance. Unlike the old days, when food was purchased from local ranches and stores, food is carefully planned and ordered from one concessionaire, who delivers twice a week. The cost of food per person has declined, from $16 a day five years ago to $9 a day. (Courtesy of Paul DeWitt.)

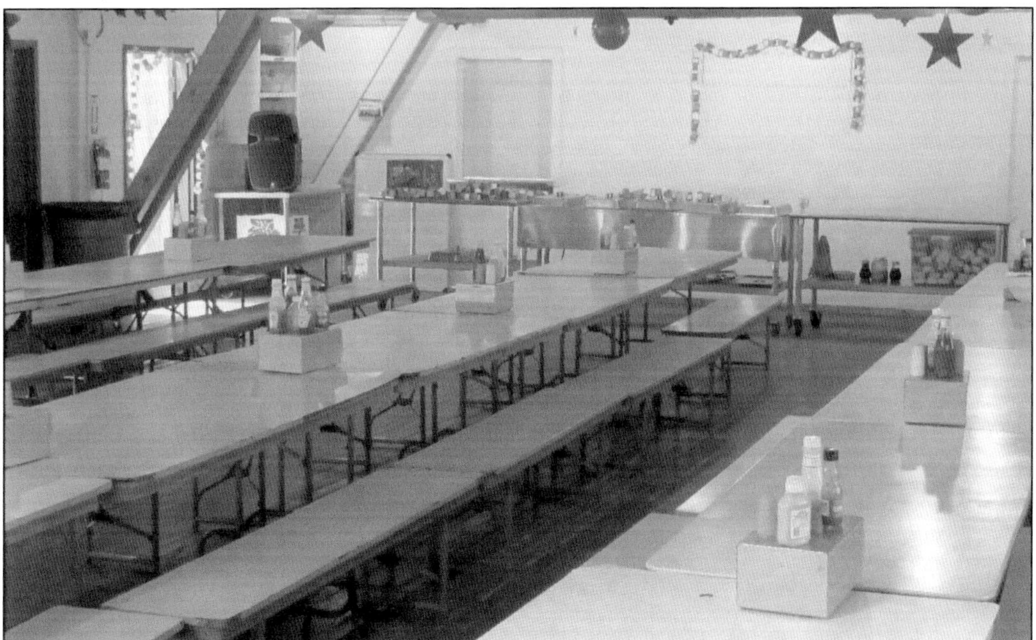

The interior of the dining hall has changed. Food is now served cafeteria-style. No longer do dining-hall girls serve food to individual tables, nor do kitchen boys collect dishes to be washed. Today, four or five cooks prepare the food in the new kitchen, serve the food to the campers, and clean and wash the dishes. The new kitchen replaced one that had been used for 60 years. (Courtesy of Paul DeWitt.)

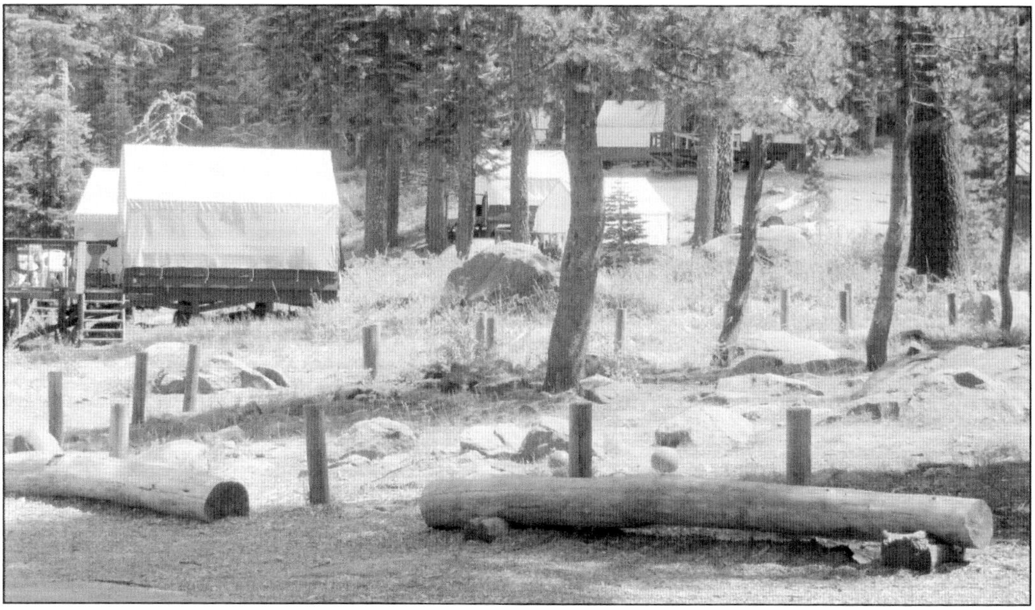

This is today's layout of tents and walkways. The tents no longer have flies, as they did in the old days, because the canvas roofs are now waterproof. The smaller tents can sleep eight people in bunk-style beds. The sides of the tents can be rolled up to allow more light and greater circulation of air. Some walkways are lined with vertical posts so that campers will stay out of natural areas. (Courtesy of Paul DeWitt.)

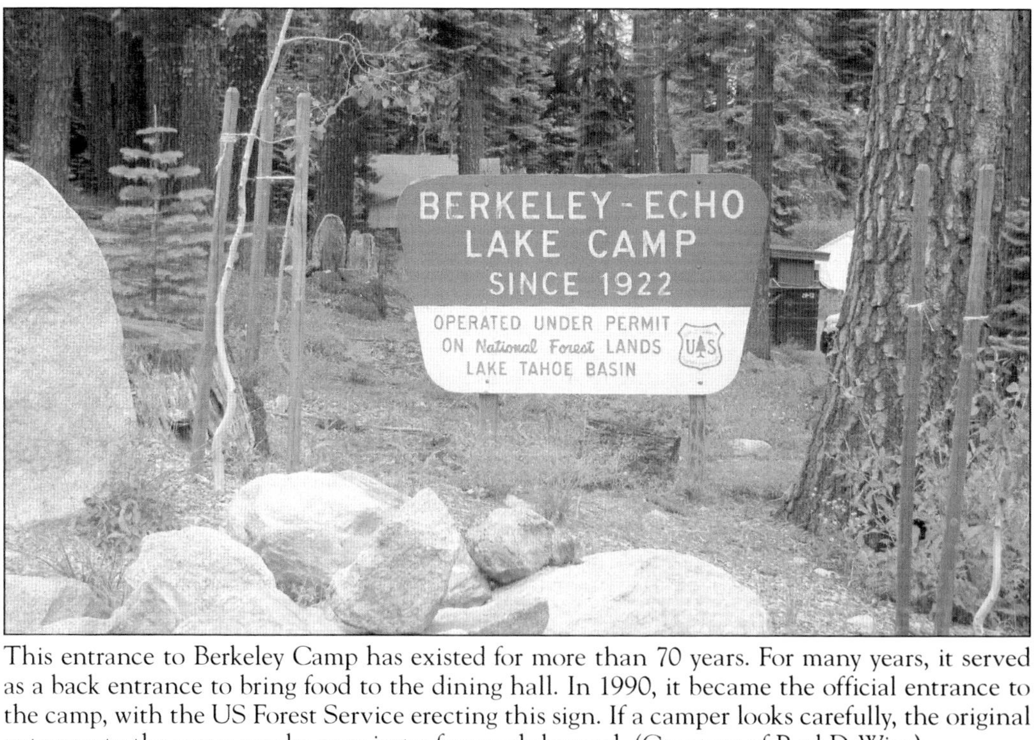

This entrance to Berkeley Camp has existed for more than 70 years. For many years, it served as a back entrance to bring food to the dining hall. In 1990, it became the official entrance to the camp, with the US Forest Service erecting this sign. If a camper looks carefully, the original entrance to the camp can be seen just a few yards beyond. (Courtesy of Paul DeWitt.)

Six

ECHO PORTALS

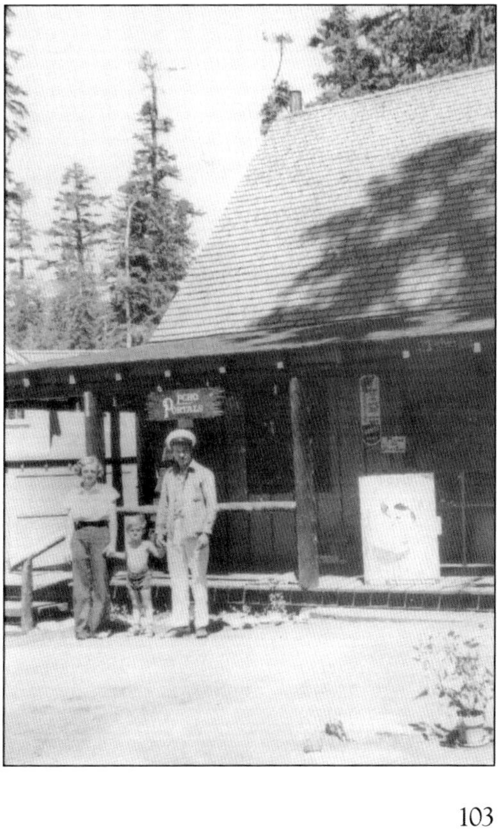

Prior to Echo Portals being built in 1926, North America House was built there in 1859. Little is known about the early roadhouse, which existed for about eight years. Shirley and Ralph King acquired Echo Portals Store in 1936. They offered a restaurant, dormitory, rooms, and platform tents for campers. Ranger Ed Smith approved Echo Summit's first rope-tow ski operations at Echo Portals in the winter of 1936–1937. Here, Shirley, Robert (center), and Ralph stand by Shirley's newly planted hop vines in 1940. During World War II, they moved to San Francisco, returning in 1945. Greyhound began regular stops there, and plans were approved for a three-story lodge addition. After the new highway bypassed Echo Portals and business declined, Ralph King provided real-estate services, offering cabin rentals and sales. His sign read, "If you're looking for land that's for more than mere mortals, talk to the mayor of Echo Portals." In disrepair, Echo Portals was dismantled in the late 1990s. (Courtesy of Dorothy De Mare.)

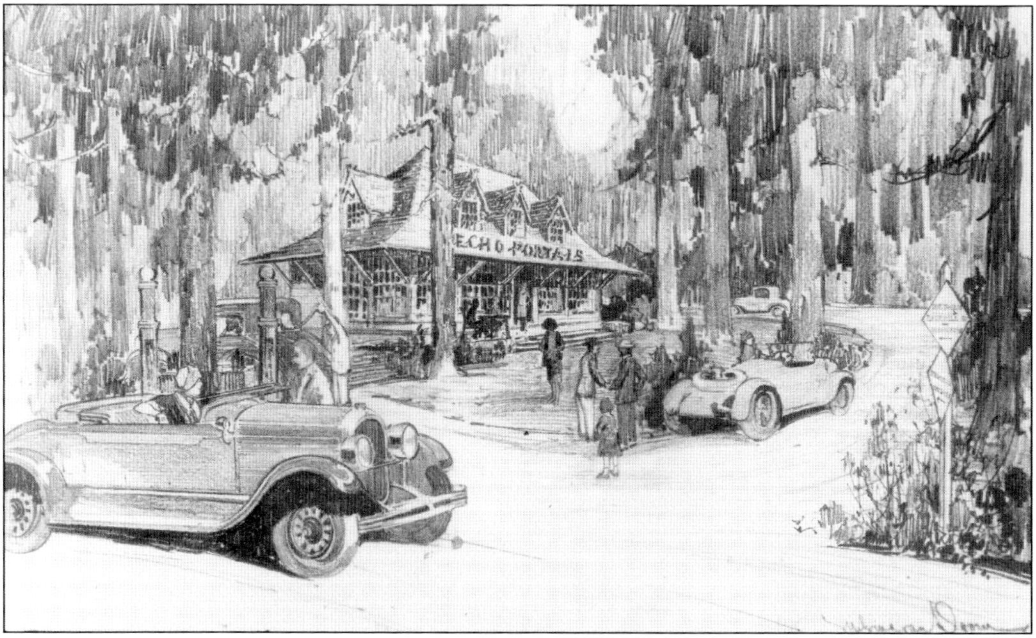

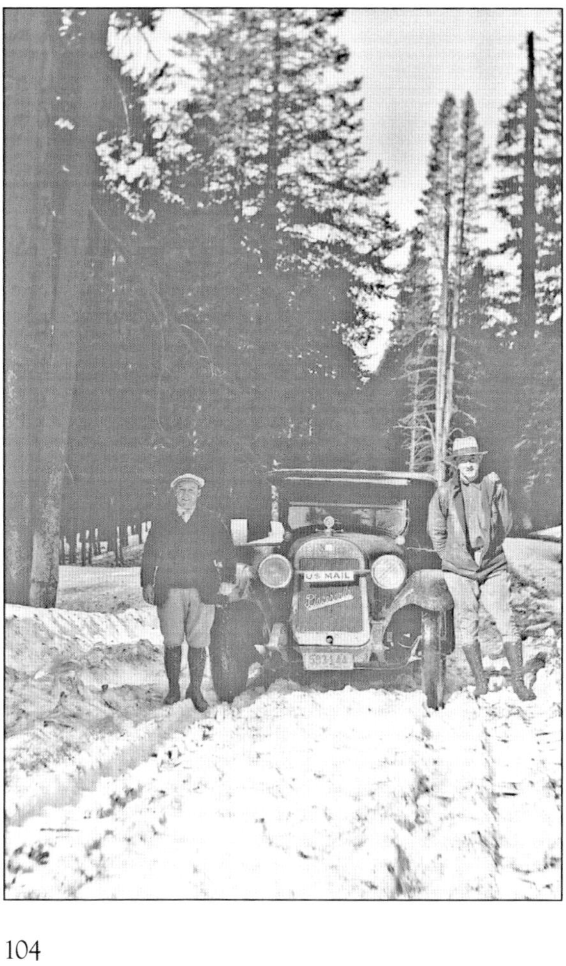

Dr. John Jacob Smith intended to build a resort named Echo Portals, commissioning artist Melvina Van Doorn to create this rendition. The fancy cars and stylish guests fit more with the old-style elegance and architecture of Lake Tahoe than the modest and rustic style of Echo Summit. A diamond-shaped sign advises travel distances. By 1930, the Depression and financial hardships caused Smith to abandon Echo Portals and other Echo Summit investments. (Courtesy of Dorothy De Mare.)

Echo Post Office was established on August 16, 1886, and was transferred to Meyers on December 15, 1910. Echo Lake reestablished postal deliveries on December 11, 1926, via Echo Portals, one mile away, due to poor road conditions. The mail car, opposite Echo Portals, may commemorate this event. Euell Gray continued daily mail trips to the mailbox at the Portals "triangle," carrying mail back to Echo Lake. This lasted until 1936, when the Civilian Conservation Corps's new road allowed access into Echo Lake. (Courtesy of El Dorado County Museum.)

Hamden Cagwin, a Celio family friend and expert skier, is pictured in Lake Valley in 1911, near the Celio homestead. Like John "Snowshoe" Thompson, Cagwin sometimes carried mail in emergencies, if in the area, between Strawberry and Carson City and Echo Lake, Meyers and Tallac. It is likely Cagwin carries mail in his backpack from the new Meyers post office that opened in December 1910. He also carried mail to and from the original Echo Lake mailbox at the junction of Echo Lake and Johnson Pass Road. Note the Echo Portals mailbox (seen below) at the same site. Over the 17 years Cagwin was at Echo Lake, he preferred vacating his cabin in winter, choosing to spend time with family in Larkspur and friends in Sacramento and Carson City. (Courtesy of Miles Celio.)

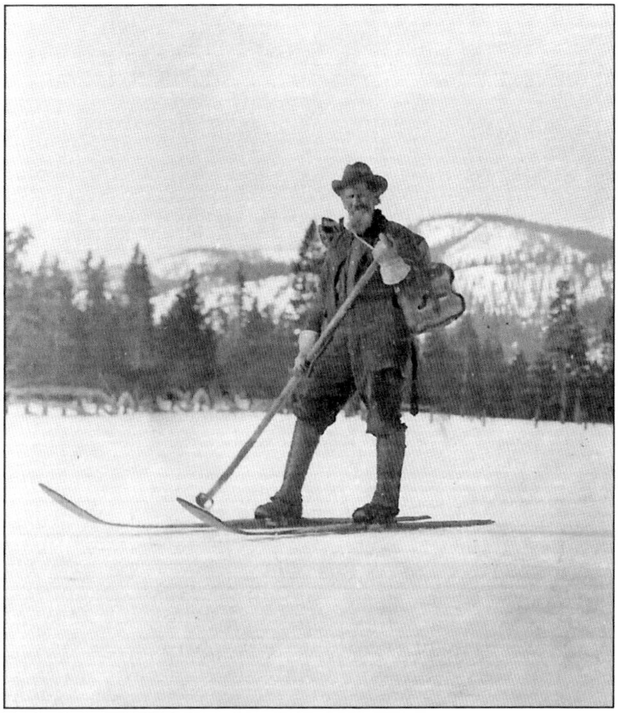

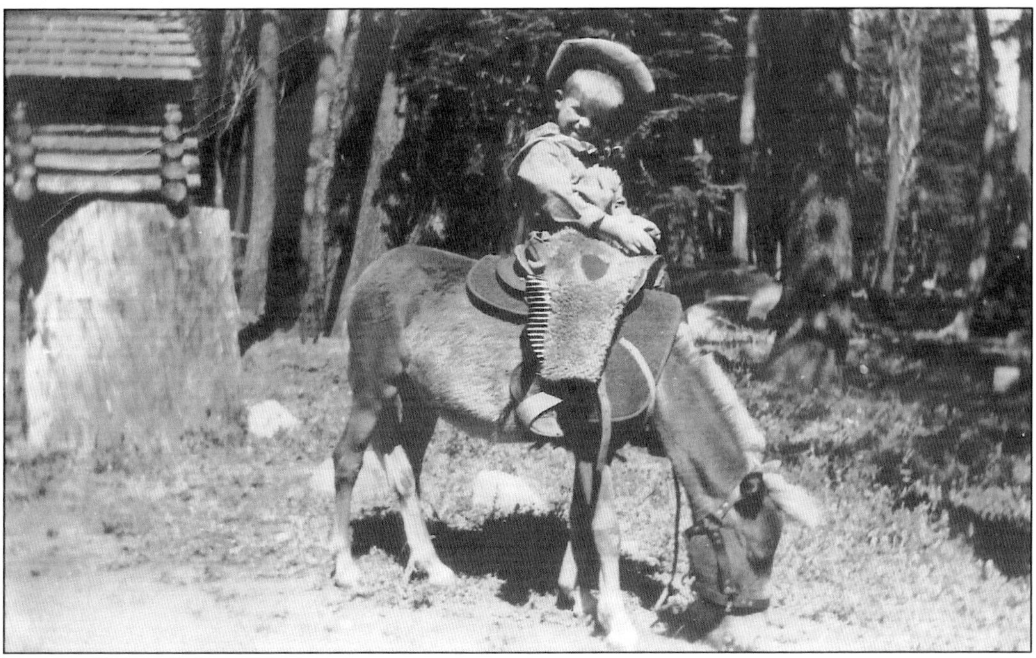

Pictured in August 1940, Robert King sits atop Petite near the Echo Portals mailbox, which was built by Harold Trunk in 1936. This triangle junction at Echo Lake and Johnson Pass Roads was where mail destined for Echo Lake was originally delivered until road conditions could be improved. Ham Cagwin mentioned this site on a 1906 postcard he sent Dr. George McLaughlin in San Francisco stating, "Best wishes to Hattie. Snow one to four feet still on road to mailbox. HE Cagwin." (Courtesy of Dorothy De Mare.)

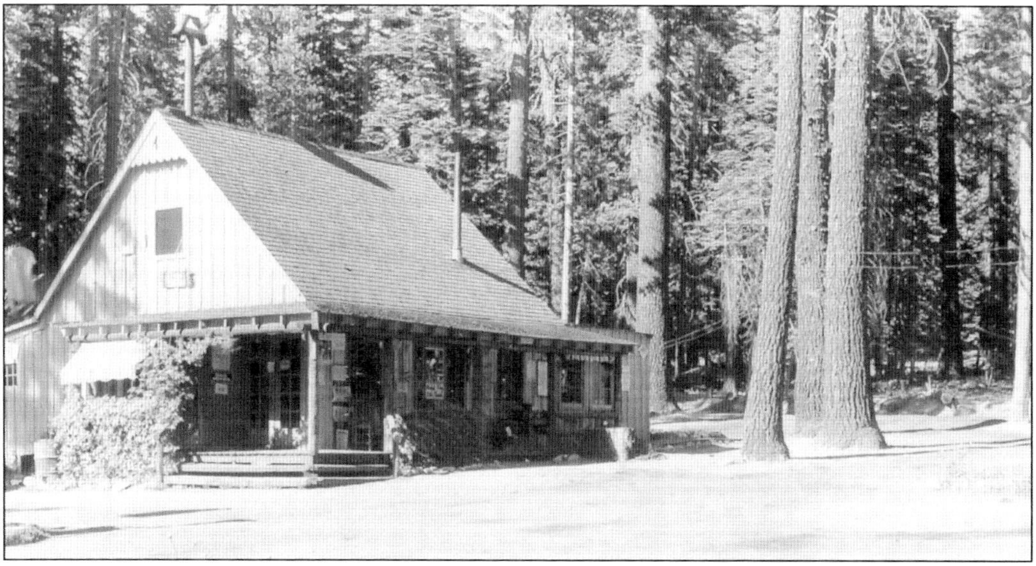

Shirley and Ralph King acquired Echo Portals Store in 1936. Newspapers are displayed on the porch in this 1948 photograph. Hop vines planted by Shirley in 1940 now trellis both porches. A mystery hop vine growing one-fourth of a mile away at Echo Summit Lodge is pictured in *The Wasmann Journal of Biology*, reprinted by California Alpine Club member Gladys L. Smith. Speculation was that the hop vine was a volunteer or was carried by birds. Actually, Shirley took a cutting from Echo Portals and transplanted it at the Echo Summit Lodge around 1953. (Courtesy of Dorothy De Mare.)

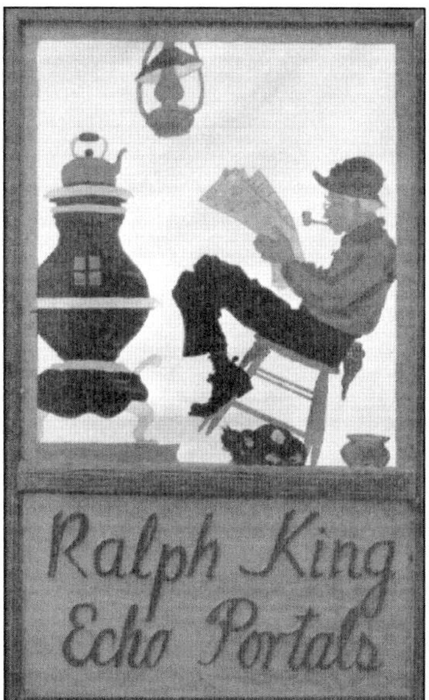

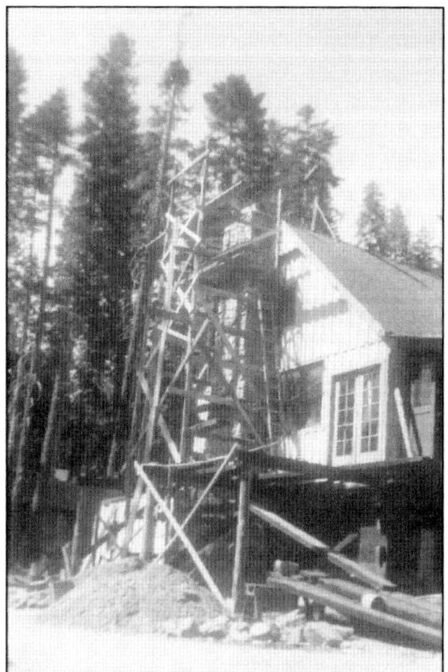

Harold Trunk's hand-carved sign (left) shows Ralph King reading a newspaper, something few ever witnessed in King's early days. Later, King broadcast stories from newspapers and road conditions on KTRB Modesto, KNBR San Francisco, and for Tom DuHain at KCRA-TV in Sacramento. Author Earl Stanley Gardner enjoyed listening to King's radio broadcasts on KTRB and mentioned King in *Gypsy Days on the Delta*. Robert King built a fireplace (right) in 1956 during the Echo Portals expansion. (Courtesy of Dorothy De Mare.)

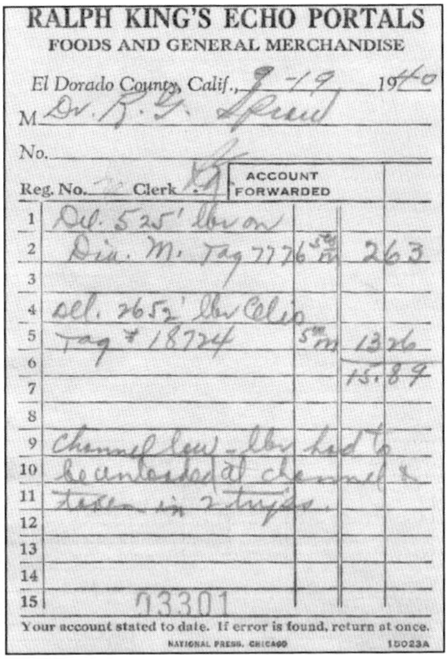
RALPH KING'S ECHO PORTALS
FOODS AND GENERAL MERCHANDISE
El Dorado County, Calif., 9-19 1940
M. Dr. R. G. Sproul
Reg. No. — Clerk — ACCOUNT FORWARDED
1 Del. 525' lbr on
2 Div. M. Tag 7776 5m 263
4 Del. 265½' lbr Celio
5 Tag # 18724 5m 1326
6 15.89
9 Channel low – lbr had to
10 be unloaded at channel &
11 taken in 2 trips.
15 13301
Your account stated to date. If error is found, return at once.
NATIONAL PRESS, CHICAGO 15023A

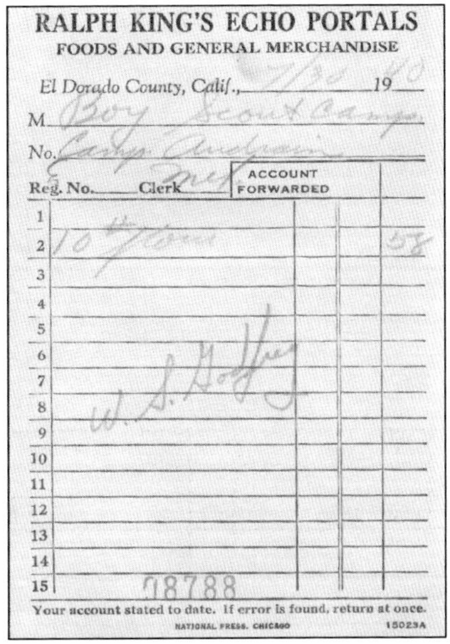
RALPH KING'S ECHO PORTALS
FOODS AND GENERAL MERCHANDISE
El Dorado County, Calif., 7/30 1940
M. Boy Scout Camp
No. Camp Audrain
Reg. No. Clerk — ACCOUNT FORWARDED
2 10 # flour 58
W. S. [illegible]
15 18788
Your account stated to date. If error is found, return at once.
NATIONAL PRESS, CHICAGO 15023A

Ralph King's receipts show difficulties delivering lumber to Robert Sproul, UC Berkeley's chancellor, and Camp Audrain's flour on its account. Echo Portals employee Roderic McCuish worked for Celio & Son's and Young's at Elk Point and was South Lake Tahoe's justice of the peace. Employees Pat Collins and Betty and Rosemary Dick were Shirley and Ralph's neighbors. Ralph worked many years building and maintaining cabins with lifelong friend and summit resident Carlton "Duke" DeWitt. (Courtesy of Dorothy De Mare.)

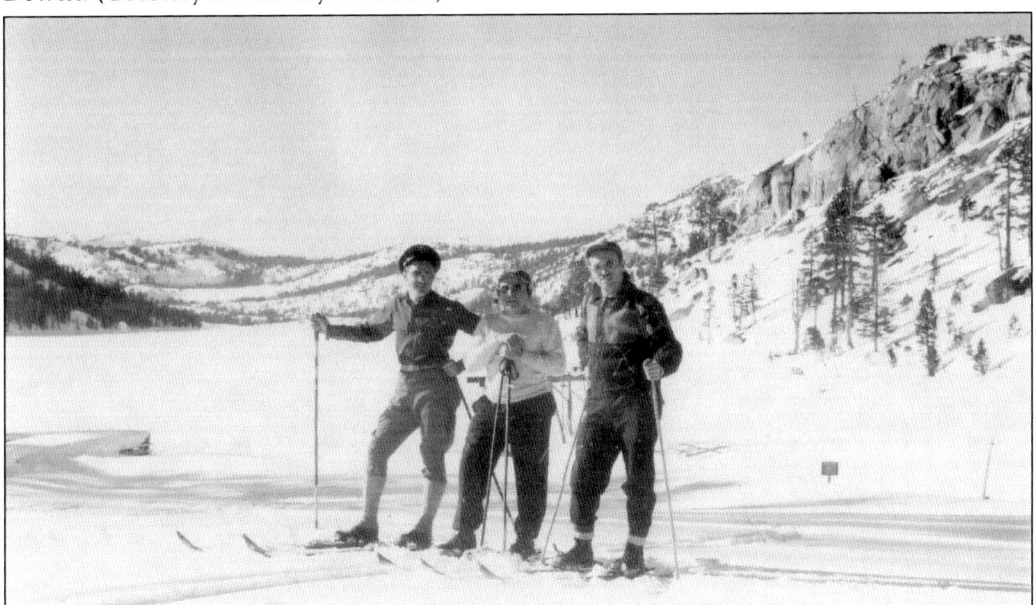

Ralph King (right), wearing a Norwegian sweater that Shirley King knit for him, poses with Lower Echo Lake visitors. The Kings, year-round Echo Lake and Echo Portals residents, skied to Meyers or Fred's Place to get mail and provisions. During winter, the first three feet of lake surface freezes, facilitating cross-country skiing. In the late 1970s, Robert King rescued five cross-country skiers who fell into melting ice covering Echo Lake. (Courtesy of Dorothy De Mare.)

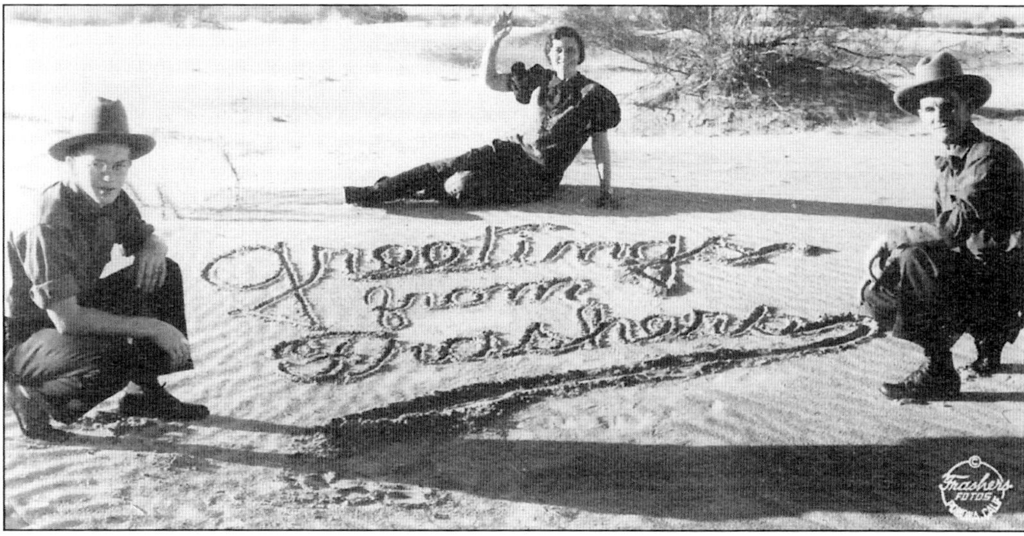

This New Year's message—"Greetings From Frashers"—was written in desert sand by Burton Frasher Jr. (left), Josephine, and Burton Frasher Sr. (right) This greeting, along with additional correspondence sent to Ralph and Shirley King over five years, discussed planned area visits, family projects, and business inquiries. The Frashers stayed at Echo Portals when photographing nearby areas. Sample postcard views for sale were sent to resort owners to purchase and display in their postcard racks. (Courtesy Dorothy De Mare)

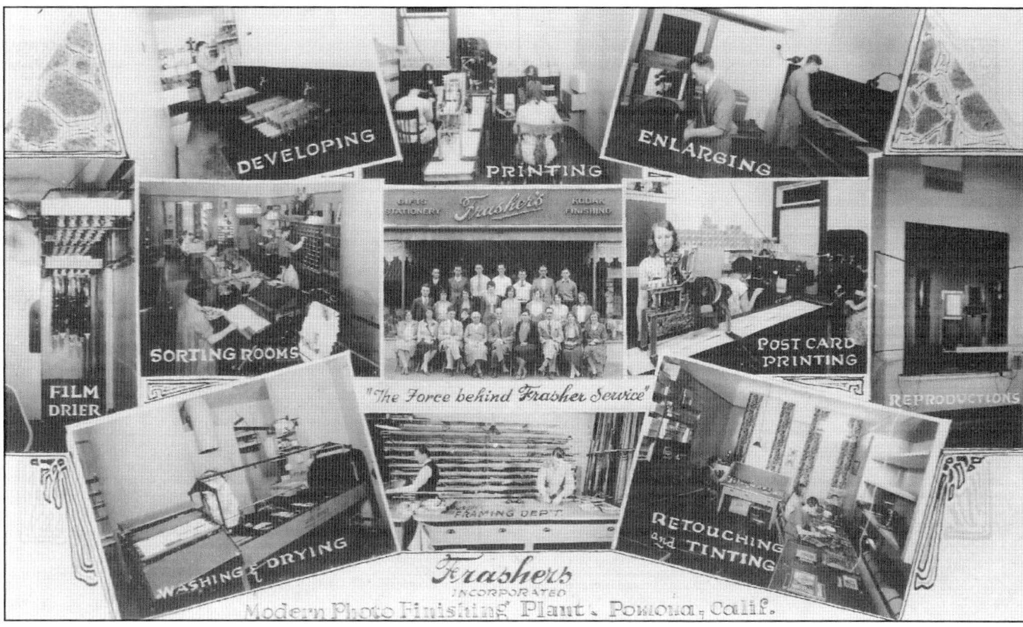

This is a vignette postcard of the Frashers' "Modern photo finishing plant, Pomona, Calif." Josephine and Burton Frasher Sr. were some of the Southwest's most prolific photographers. The postcard shows washing and drying, film drying, developing, sorting, printing, enlarging, reproductions, retouching, tinting, and an employee group photograph. Contacted by chamber secretary Ralph King regarding business support for the new chamber of commerce, Josephine sent a donation and, in a letter to Norman Celio, discussed ups and downs in their business. (Courtesy of Dorothy De Mare.)

Ranger Ed Smith approved Echo Summit's first ski area opening in 1936 at Echo Portals. Shirley and Ralph King's patrons parked at Highway 50 and were transported to Echo Portals Resort. Ski lessons were taught by Roderic McCuish. The cost of $5 included accommodations with two meals; one being all-you-can-eat fillet mignon provided by meat wholesaler Harvey Gross. (Courtesy of Dorothy De Mare.)

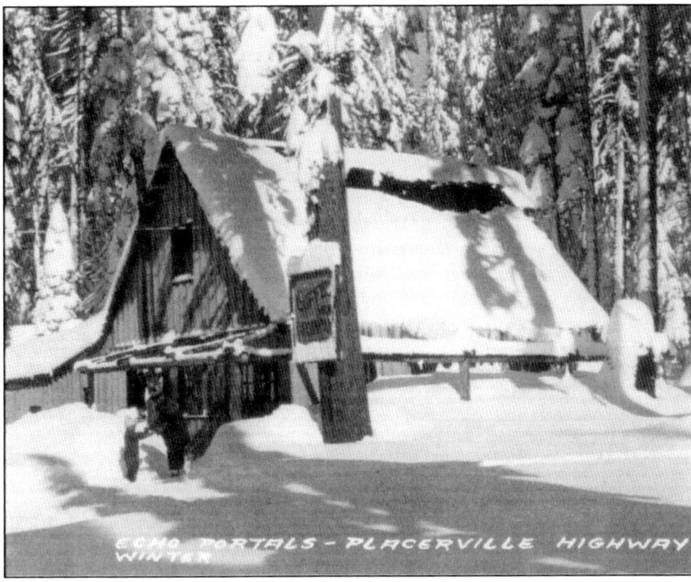

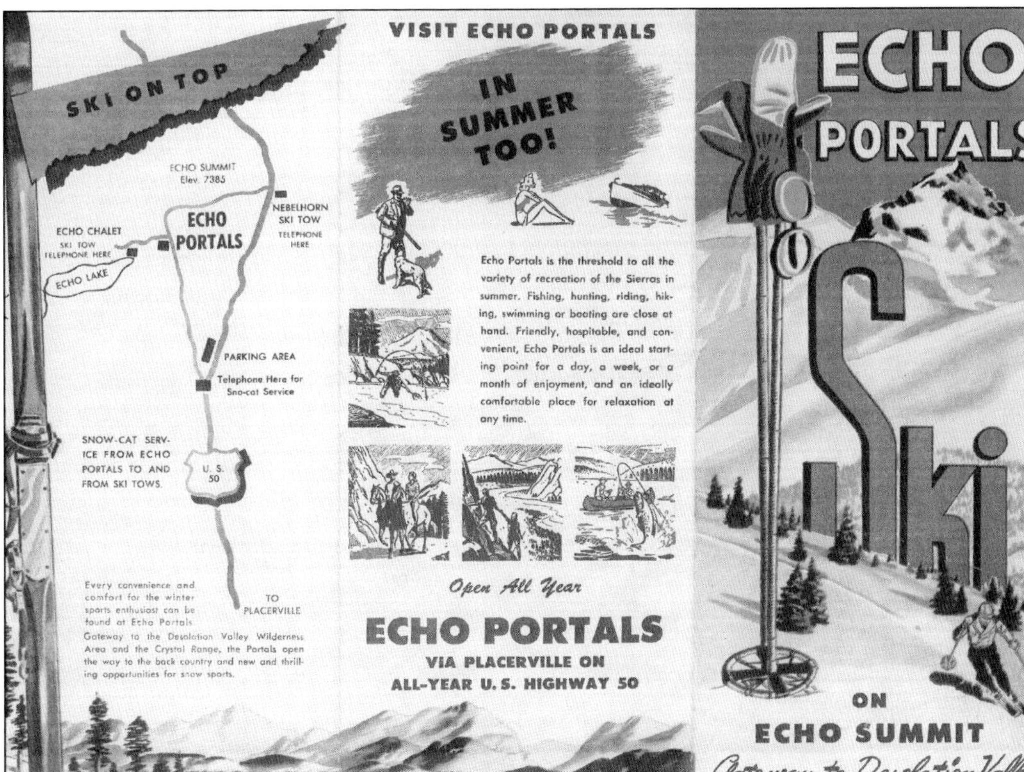

The Echo Portals 1947 ski brochure advertises its year-round recreational activities on Echo Summit and included a map with instructions for skiers. Parking and a hand-crank telephone installed on the King's land at Highway 50 allowed patrons to call for snowcat service for transport to Echo Portals, Echo Chalet, or Nebelhorn. The owners of Nebelhorn were Gordon Stangland and Vic West. Their expert ski school instructor Lutz Aynedter's ski team called the Nebelhornets included ski champion Spider Sabich. (Courtesy Lake Tahoe Historical Society.)

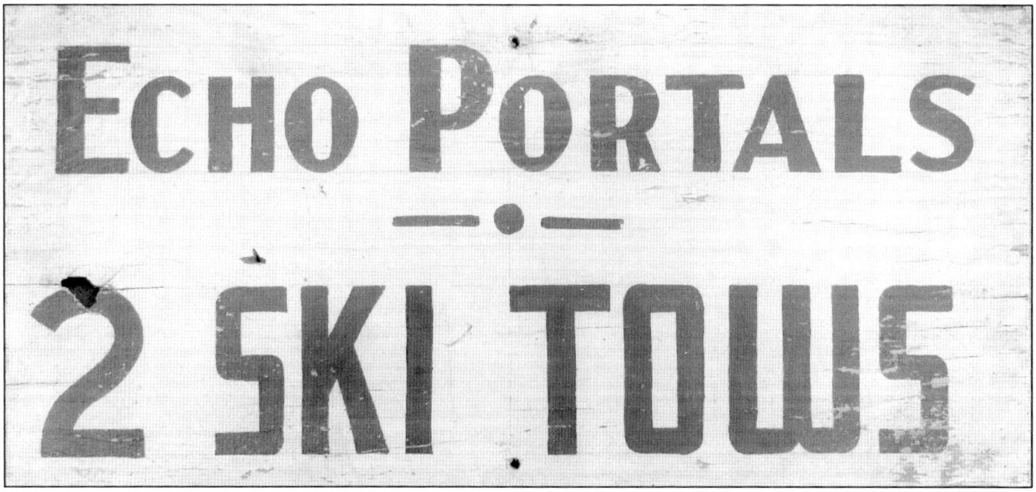

Shown here is one of the four signs Echo Portals posted along Johnson Pass Road, advising winter visitors of the distances to their two ski tows. Echo Portals Ski Area was open seven days a week for family skiing and winter recreation. Sleigh rides, pulled by employee Roderic McCuish's Alaskan husky dogs, were a popular attraction. The Echo Portals ski shop offered ski equipment and clothing for sale or rent, accessories, and minor equipment repair. (Courtesy of Robert King.)

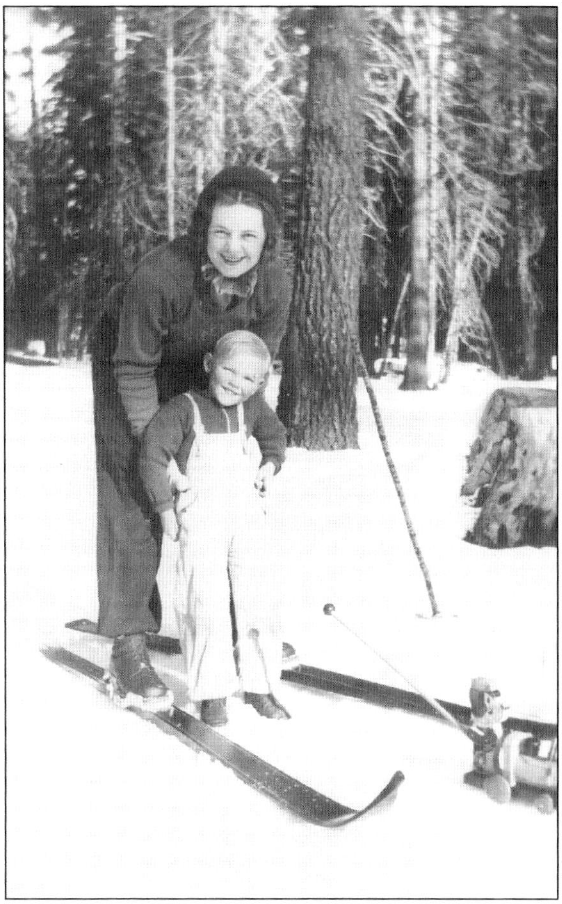

Shirley King and Donnie McCuish, with his push toy, are pictured at Echo Portals in the winter of 1935–1936 on this Frasher postcard. Ralph and Shirley King's recreational sports began with modest activities. Their location provided vacationers access to fishing, horse-back riding, boating, and more. Their cabin and rooms operated on the two-meal American plan. With the Depression and World War II's gas rationing, business and tourism was severely affected especially during winter. After the war, Echo Portals, Echo Chalet, and Nebelhorn partnered together to attract visitors to their ski operations on Echo Summit. (Courtesy of Dorothy De Mare.)

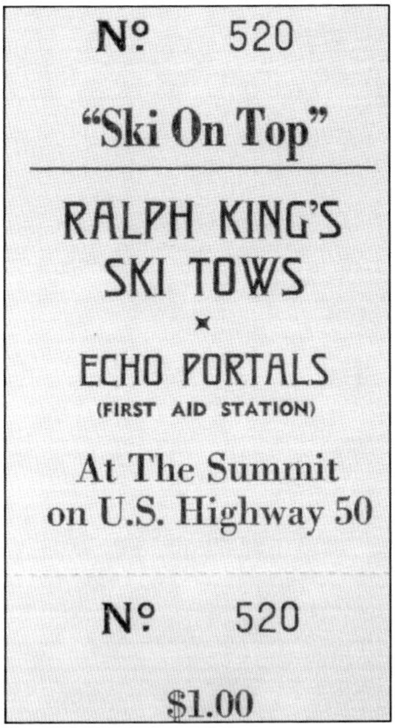

№ 520

"Ski On Top"

RALPH KING'S
SKI TOWS

ECHO PORTALS
(FIRST AID STATION)

At The Summit
on U.S. Highway 50

№ 520

$1.00

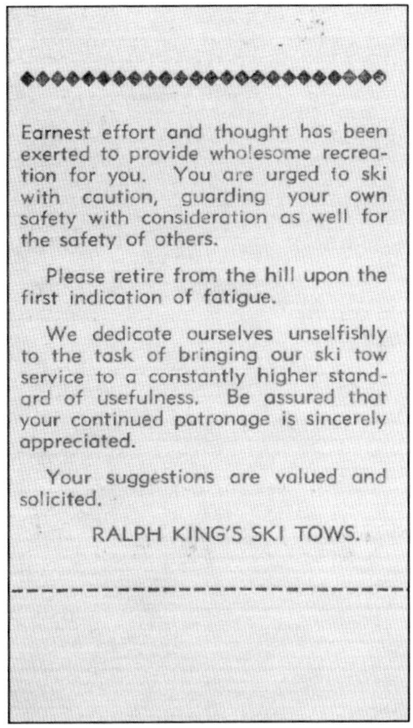

Earnest effort and thought has been exerted to provide wholesome recreation for you. You are urged to ski with caution, guarding your own safety with consideration as well for the safety of others.

Please retire from the hill upon the first indication of fatigue.

We dedicate ourselves unselfishly to the task of bringing our ski tow service to a constantly higher standard of usefulness. Be assured that your continued patronage is sincerely appreciated.

Your suggestions are valued and solicited.

RALPH KING'S SKI TOWS.

Shirley and Ralph King's Echo Portals ski tows provided ample parking nearby, with transportation to their resort. Reservations could also be made by writing care of Vade Post Office. Access to safe skiing, with all the comforts of home, was a priority. Guests enjoyed great customer service, with unlimited hot beverages, snacks, and a warm fire for their rest breaks. The bottom of the perforated ticket was the filet mignon dinner meal ticket. (Courtesy of Dorothy De Mare.)

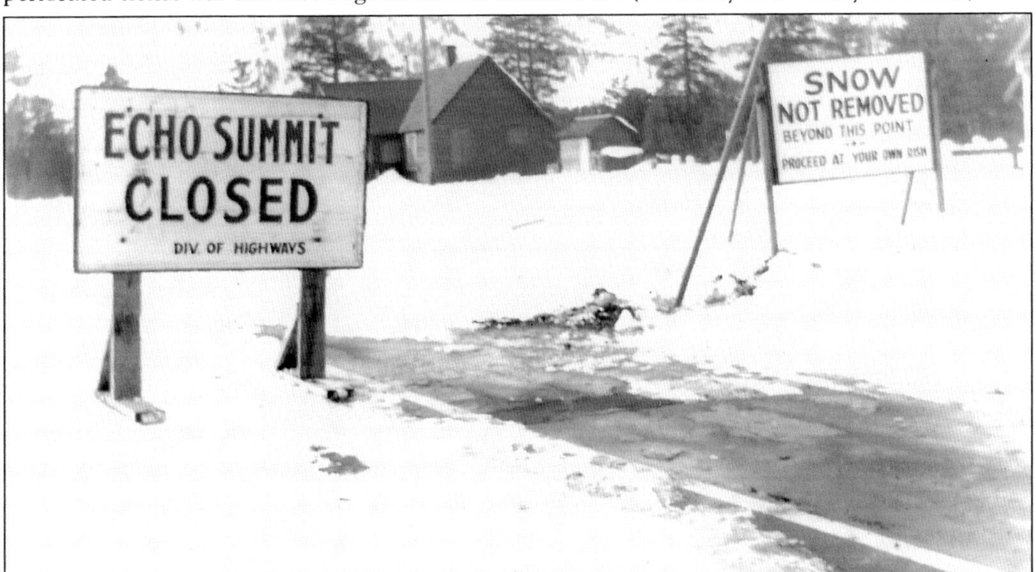

Portable 1930s road signs at Meyers advise westbound drivers of Highway 50's closure. Prior to World War II, no winter snow removal was provided over Echo Summit from Meyers to Kyburz. These winter closures caused extreme economic hardships and isolation for the Echo Summit and South Lake Tahoe communities. Successful lobbying by local merchants and volunteers brought approval for winter plowing in 1941; however, the outbreak of the war delayed plowing until 1946. (Courtesy of Dorothy De Mare.)

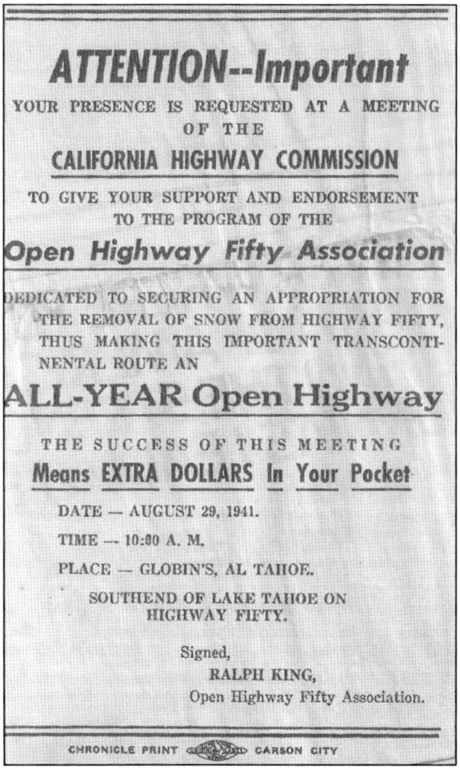

ATTENTION--Important

YOUR PRESENCE IS REQUESTED AT A MEETING OF THE

CALIFORNIA HIGHWAY COMMISSION

TO GIVE YOUR SUPPORT AND ENDORSEMENT TO THE PROGRAM OF THE

Open Highway Fifty Association

DEDICATED TO SECURING AN APPROPRIATION FOR THE REMOVAL OF SNOW FROM HIGHWAY FIFTY, THUS MAKING THIS IMPORTANT TRANSCONTINENTAL ROUTE AN

ALL-YEAR Open Highway

THE SUCCESS OF THIS MEETING

Means EXTRA DOLLARS In Your Pocket

DATE — AUGUST 29, 1941.

TIME — 10:30 A. M.

PLACE — GLOBIN'S, AL TAHOE.

SOUTHEND OF LAKE TAHOE ON HIGHWAY FIFTY.

Signed,
RALPH KING,
Open Highway Fifty Association.

CHRONICLE PRINT CARSON CITY

The California Department of Transportation road crews kept roads open in winter from Placerville to Kyburz. The remaining road over the Echo Summit to Lake Tahoe remained closed. Businesses and residents at the summit and in Tahoe valley faced extreme economic hardships without year-round access and tourism. Tahoe historian Jim Hubbard credits Ralph King's lobbying in 1939 for the first winter Highway 50 opening. King founded the Open Highway Fifty Association, appointing 12 friends as directors. John Keller and King met with Lt. Gov. Ellis Patterson, who ordered Donner Summit's public works to open Echo Summit on February 28, 1940, reluctantly done once. Continued lobbying and persuasion failed. Much hand-shoveling in the fall of 1941 finally proved the point; Governor Olson agreed, advising the state to begin plowing. (Courtesy of *Tahoe Daily Tribune*.)

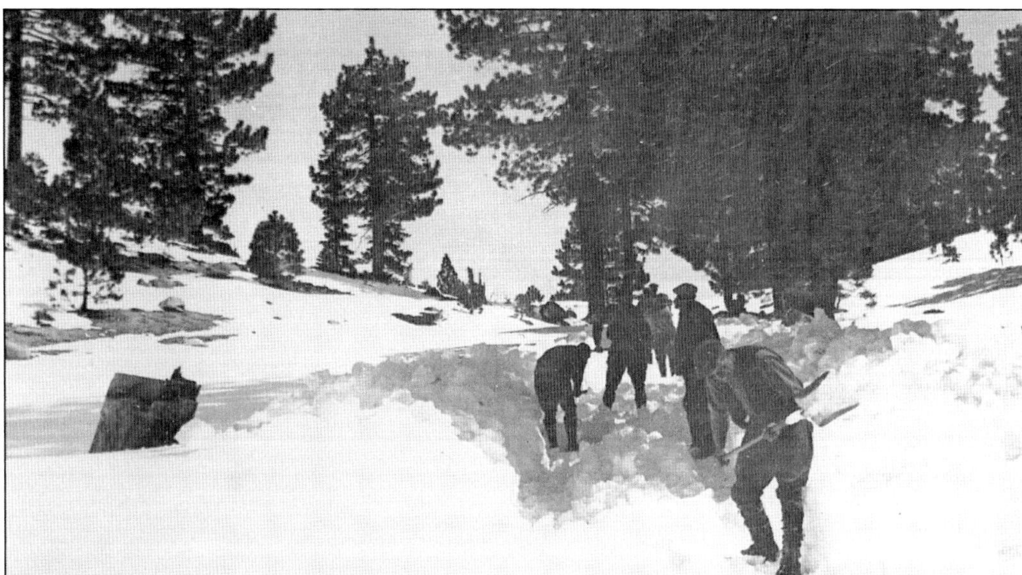

In the fall of 1941, South Lake Tahoe Chamber of Commerce charter members Ralph King, Al Lampson, Bode Martin, Frank Globin, and Ralph Plimpton, assisted by Vaughn Plimpton, Harvey Gross, Finn Barkley, and local residents, hand-shoveled Highway 50 many times. It was backbreaking work, yet festive. Lampson provided whiskey, and Gross brought the sandwich meats. Numerous phone calls of their progress impressed Governor Olson, who approved state plowing, which began after the war. (Courtesy of Lake Tahoe Historical Society Museum.)

Seven

ECHO SUMMIT LODGE

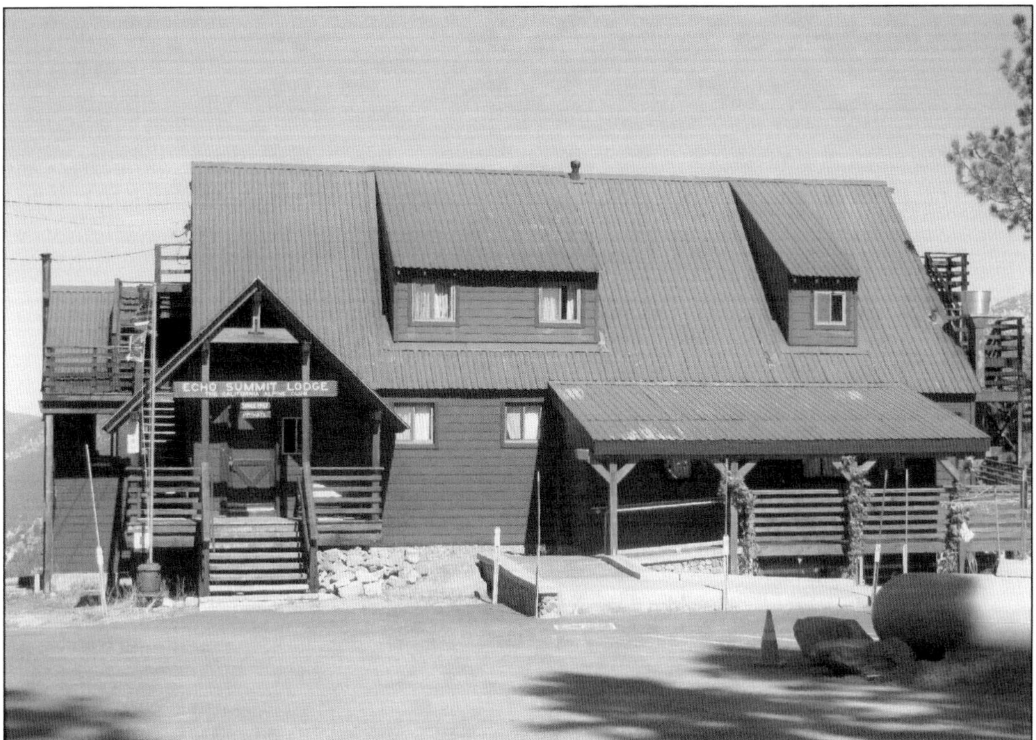

Echo Summit Lodge was established more than 90 years ago. Ever since its original construction, many changes have been made by each of its owners, lending to its current appearance. In the early 1950s, Shirley King of Echo Portals planted a hop vine at the lodge. Years later, members of the California Alpine Club made cuttings of Shirley's hop vine; five vines are growing at the lodge today. When the club bought Echo Summit Lodge in 1952, it was required to build fire escapes from the second and third floors. In the last decade, the club built a ramp for people to enter the lodge in their wheelchairs. These additions and changes would not have been possible without the initial planning and building of Echo Summit Lodge in 1922 by Theodore Clemens Wohlbruck. (Courtesy of Paul DeWitt.)

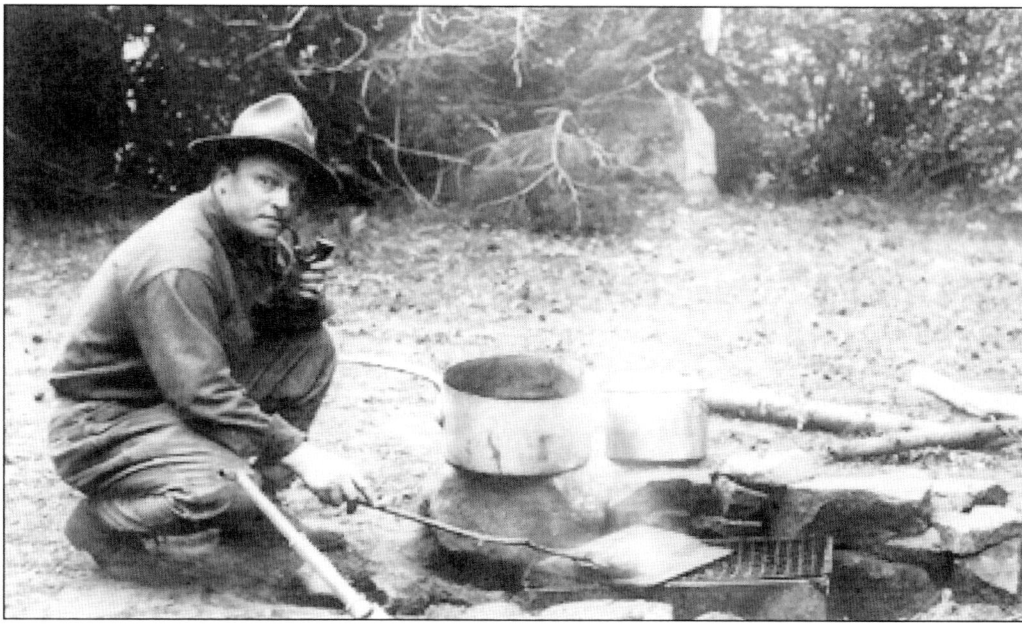

Theodore Clemens Wohlbruck was a prominent photographer, publisher, entrepreneur, and outdoorsman in California and Nevada for more than 20 years. He was an excellent school photographer. He took photographs of Yosemite, Marin County, and Mount Tamalpais, along the Lincoln Highway, Lake Tahoe, and parts of Nevada. In 1930, he created his own museum of early transportation in Redwood City that included Concord stagecoaches, surreys, carriages belonging to the Hearst and Stanford families, and early automobiles. (Courtesy of Norm Sayler.)

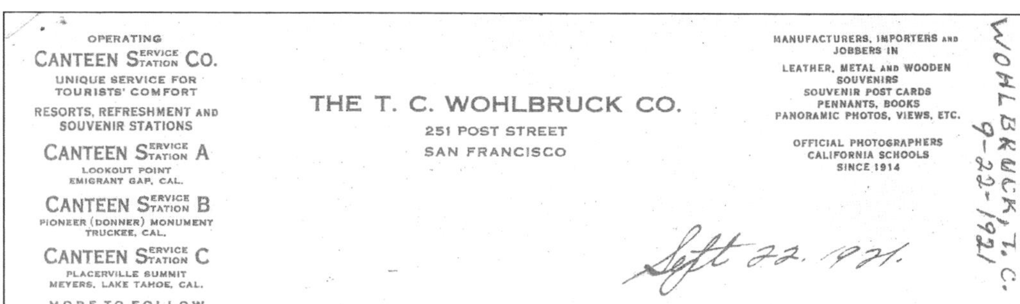

OPERATING
CANTEEN SERVICE STATION CO.
UNIQUE SERVICE FOR TOURISTS' COMFORT
RESORTS, REFRESHMENT AND SOUVENIR STATIONS
CANTEEN SERVICE STATION A
LOOKOUT POINT
EMIGRANT GAP, CAL.
CANTEEN SERVICE STATION B
PIONEER (DONNER) MONUMENT
TRUCKEE, CAL.
CANTEEN SERVICE STATION C
PLACERVILLE SUMMIT
MEYERS, LAKE TAHOE, CAL.
MORE TO FOLLOW

THE T. C. WOHLBRUCK CO.
251 POST STREET
SAN FRANCISCO

MANUFACTURERS, IMPORTERS AND JOBBERS IN
LEATHER, METAL AND WOODEN SOUVENIRS
SOUVENIR POST CARDS
PENNANTS, BOOKS
PANORAMIC PHOTOS, VIEWS, ETC.

OFFICIAL PHOTOGRAPHERS
CALIFORNIA SCHOOLS
SINCE 1914

T.C. Wohlbruck said much about what he did in his business letterhead. He wanted people to drive into the country and mountains to view the beautiful surroundings. To do this, he established what he called Canteen Service Stations, which provided resorts, gas stations, restaurants, and shops with his photographs and postcards, books, and souvenirs. All of his photographs and postcards had a distinctive style of block lettering, and most included his initials and his business address: T.C.W. Co., 251 Post, SF. (Courtesy of Art Sommers.)

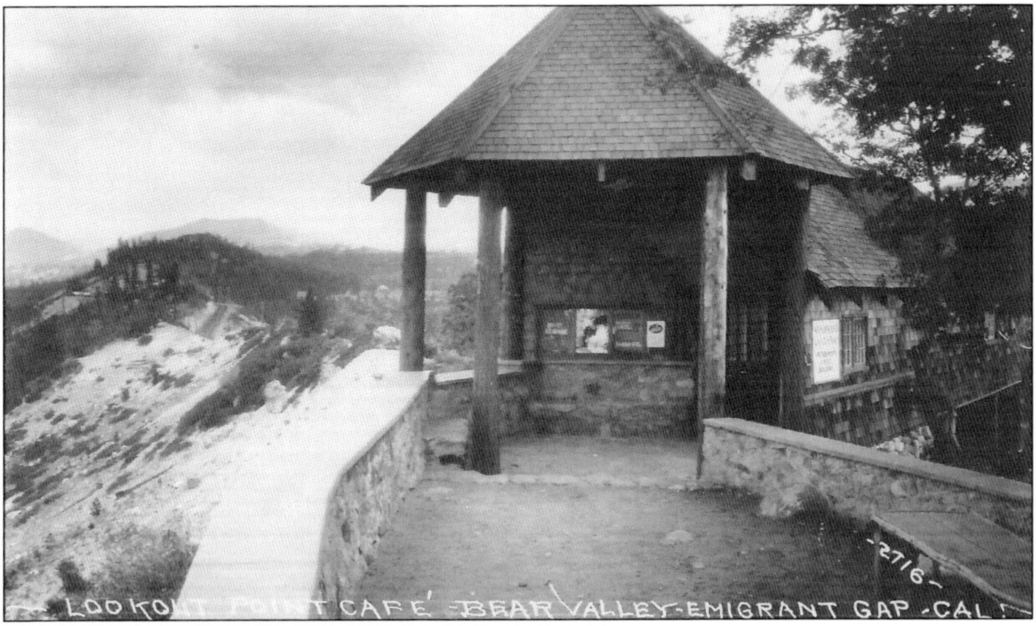

Wohlbruck's first Canteen Service Station was built in 1919 at Emigrant Gap along the Lincoln Highway, between Auburn and Donner Summit. From the lookout, visitors could see the panorama of Bear Valley, the Bear and Yuba Rivers, and Lake Spalding. The canteen had a coffee shop, soda fountain, and a store selling souvenirs, postcards, and books. Wohlbruck also built a small hotel and a gas station for his customers. (Courtesy of Norm Sayler.)

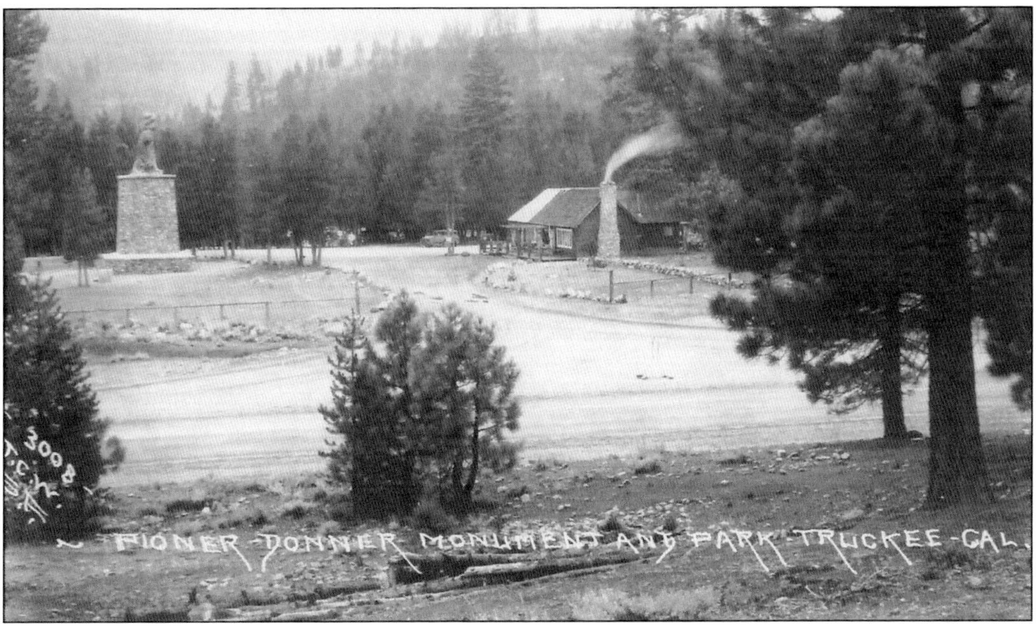

In 1920, Wohlbruck built Canteen Service Station B and a museum at the Donner Pioneer Monument. On the right is his lodge, where lunches and refreshments were served. It also had a soda fountain and a store selling photographs, postcards, books, and souvenirs. During its first summer season of 1920, more visitors came to the store and museum than all of the people who came to the monument during the previous two years. (Courtesy of Norm Sayler.)

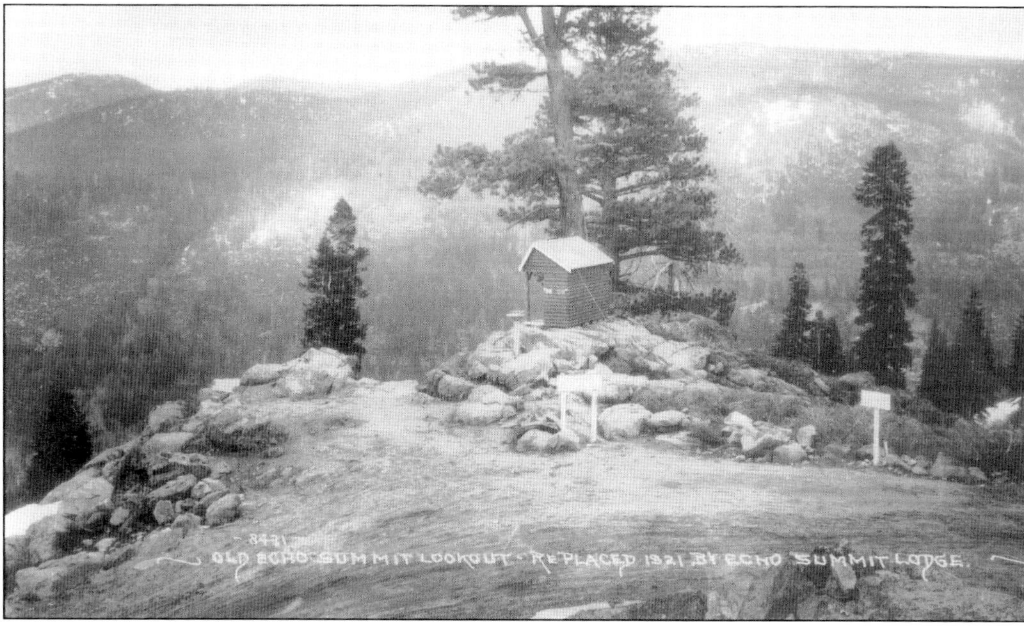

The US Forest Service built an observation deck at Echo Summit, overlooking Lake Tahoe and Lake Valley, in 1906. People could stop and take in the view using a US Forest Service Locator (a mounted telescope) and browse through maps and literature about the lake and valley. The telescope allowed viewers to get a closer look at different areas of the surrounding scenery. (Courtesy of Paul DeWitt.)

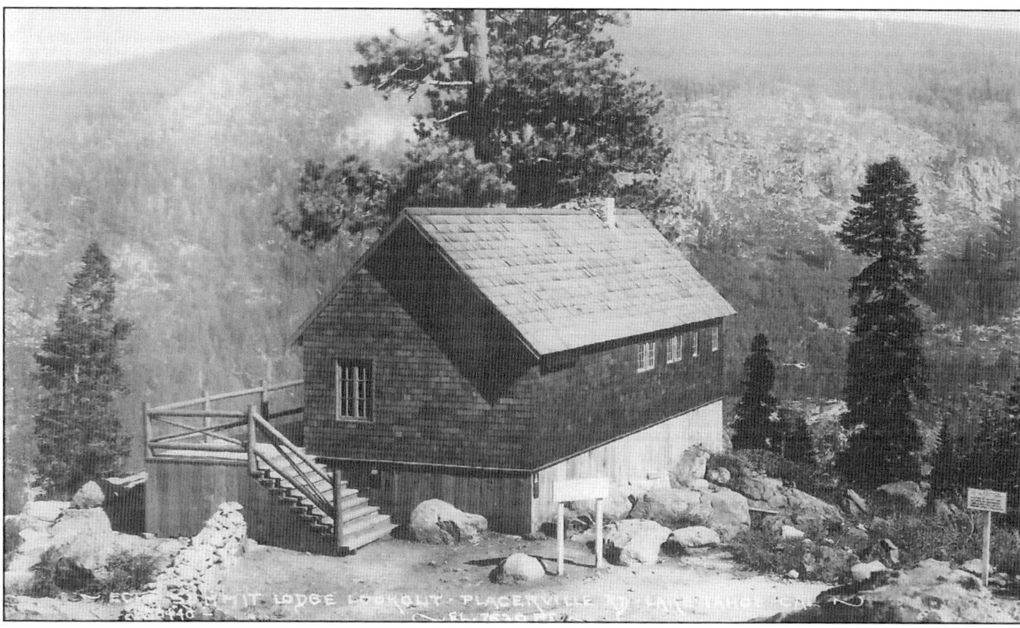

In 1921, Wohlbruck leased the land on which the US Forest Service observation deck was located. He built Canteen Service Station C and named it Echo Summit Lodge. The lodge was 40 feet long and 20 feet wide on the gable ends. There were two signs used by the US Forest Service to identify the lookout point that were kept by Wohlbruck as part of his lodge. The entrance to the lodge was on the deck facing the valley. (Courtesy of Paul DeWitt.)

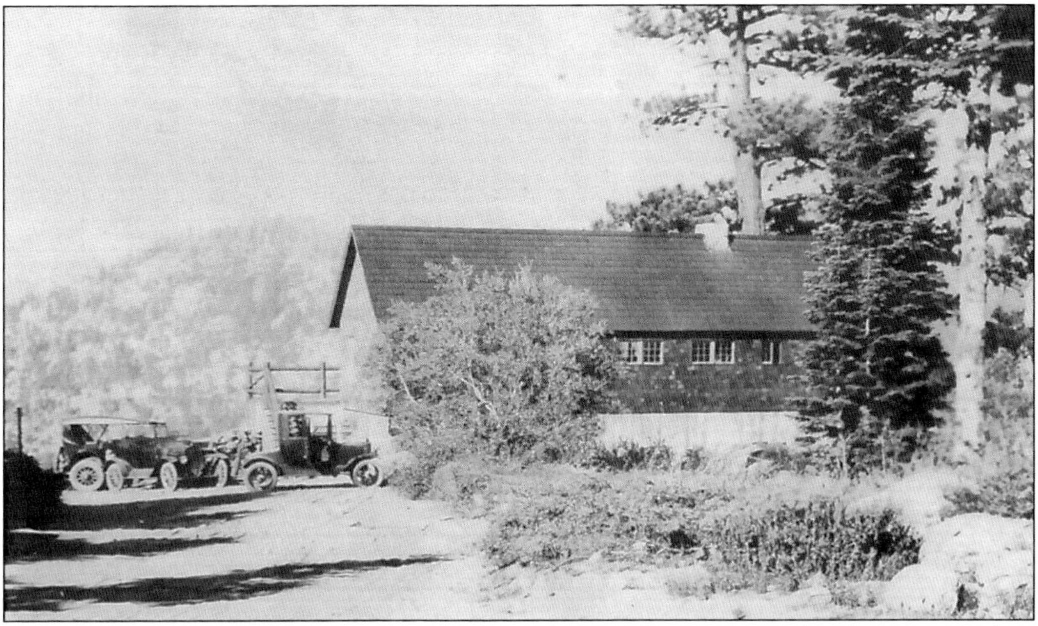

These early cars parked at Echo Summit Lodge indicate that it was immediately a popular place to stop for the view, get a meal, and shop in the store before driving down to Tahoe or Placerville. It was also a place to visit for the day. (Courtesy of Miles Celio.)

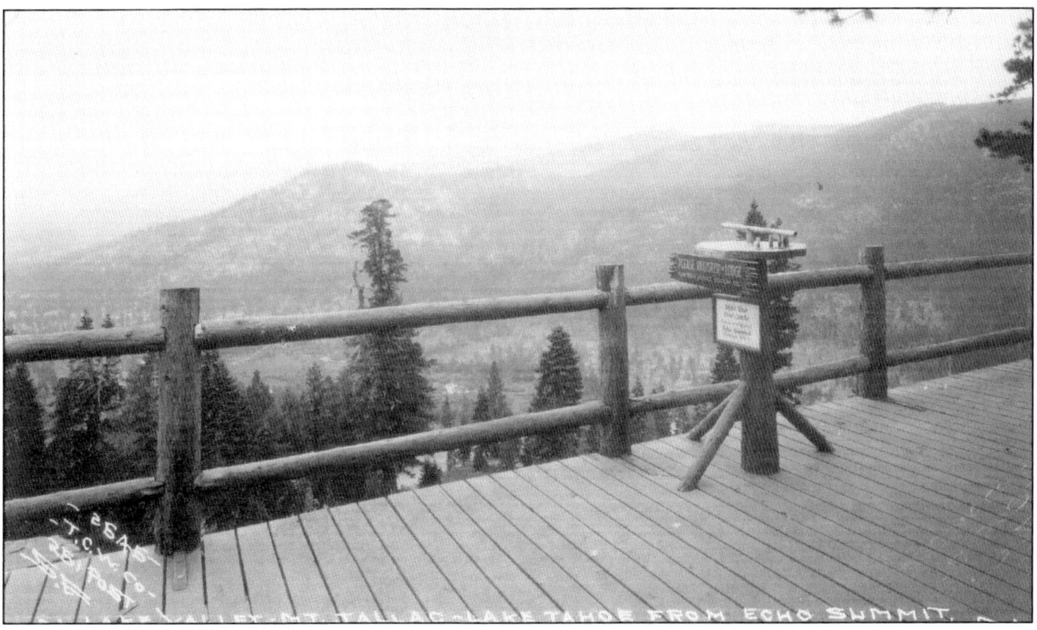

As part of his lease with the US Forest Service, Wohlbruck had to maintain the observation platform with the Forest Service Locator, a Forest Service Register, maps, and literature provided by the US Forest Service and maintained by the lodge. The observation telescope reads "Please Register at Lodge" and "Mail your Post Cards from the Top of the World—Echo Summit Elevation 7360 ft." The deck was to be open to the public at all times, even though the lodge was closed at night during the summer months and closed all winter because of the snow. (Courtesy of Dorothy De Mare.)

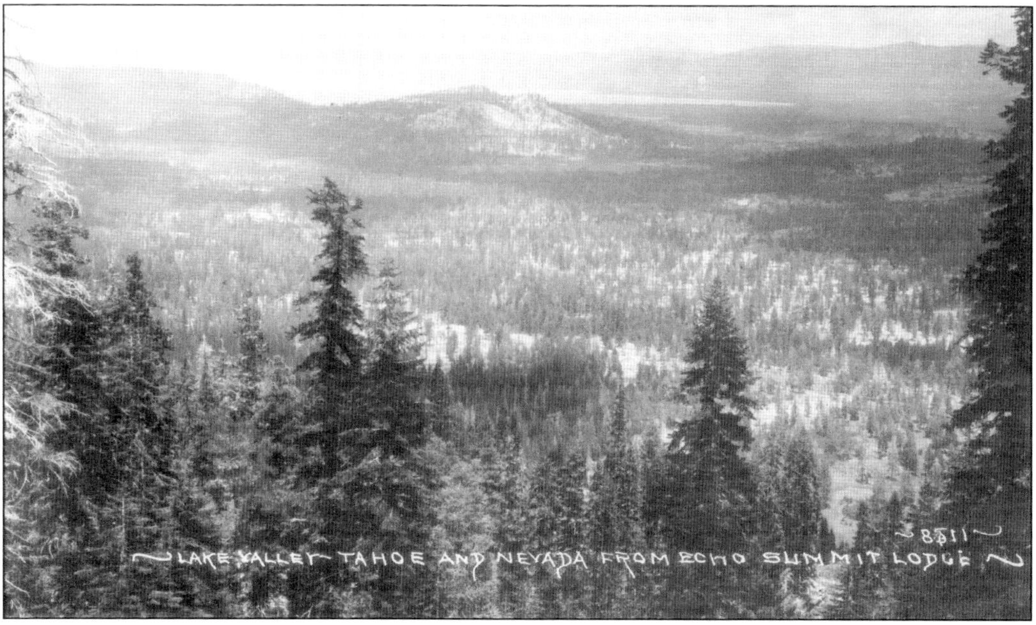

The views of Lake Tahoe, Lake Valley, and Nevada were spectacular from the deck of the Echo Summit Lodge. Guests could relax on deck chairs while taking in the scenery. Wohlbruck achieved what he wanted. People were coming into the mountains, stopping at his Canteen Service Stations, and enjoying the views and surroundings. He was able to make a profit at all three canteens. (Courtesy of Paul DeWitt.)

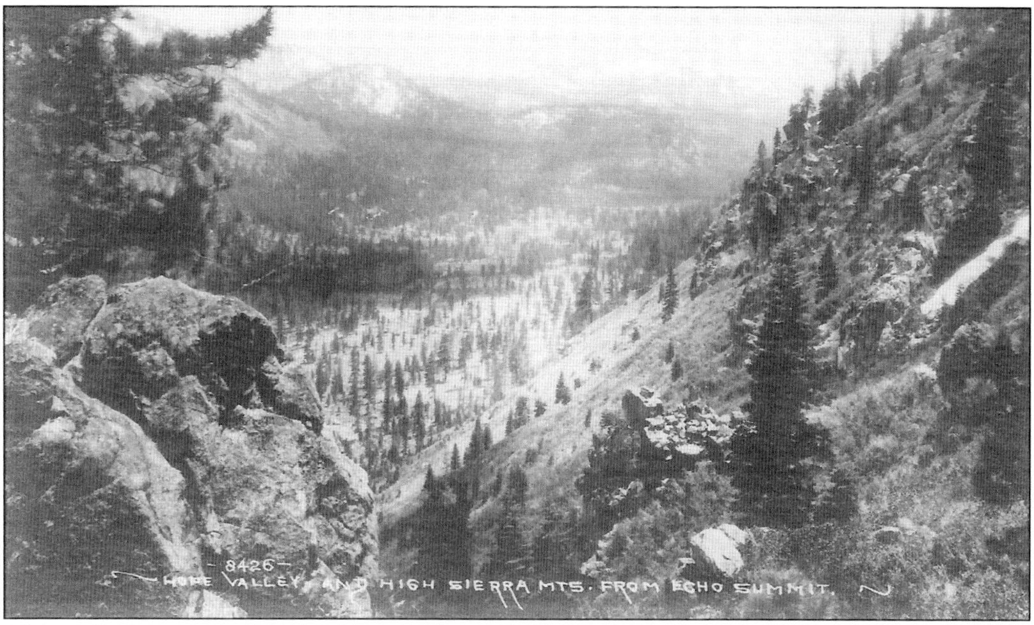

Although this postcard reads "Hope Valley and the High Sierra Mts," that is not correct. The photograph was taken from the far end of the Echo Summit Lodge deck, looking into Upper Lake Valley. To go to Hope Valley, a vehicle would drive up this valley, go through the gap to the left over Luther Pass, and then into Hope Valley. Echo Summit Lodge had a view of more than 180 degrees of the Tahoe and Lake Valley area. (Courtesy of Paul DeWitt.)

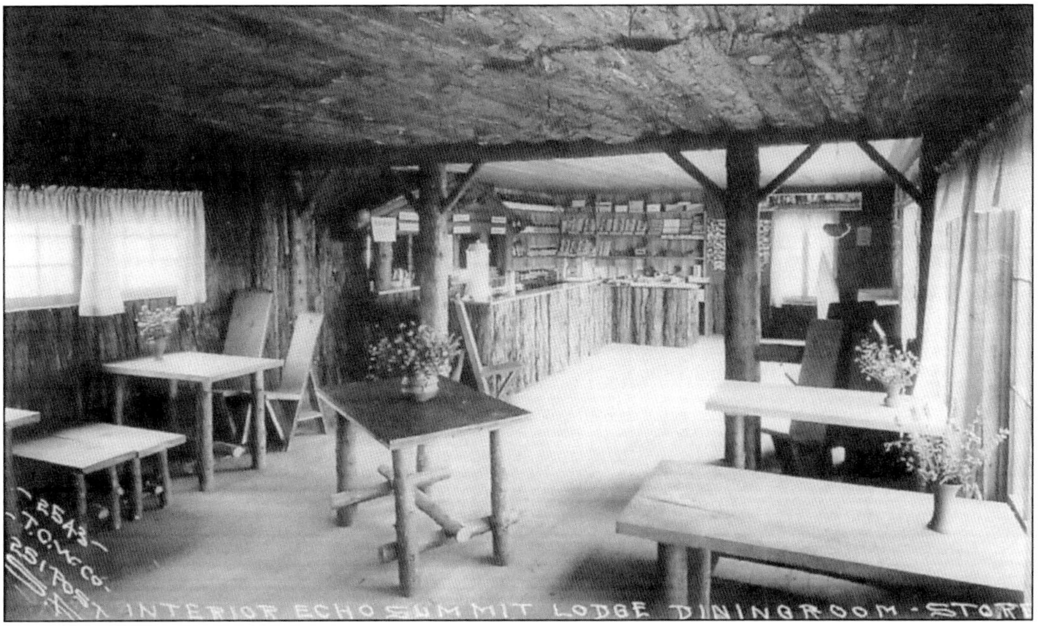

Coming into the lodge from the far right, customers entered the store area, displaying souvenirs, books, photographs, and postcards. In front of them was a counter for buying candy, ice cream, milk shakes, sodas, coffee, and other hot and cold drinks. Meals were served in the dining area. The tables and chairs were designed by Wohlbruck and made by hand. Today, three of these tables are still in use at Echo Summit Lodge. (Courtesy of Norm Sayler.)

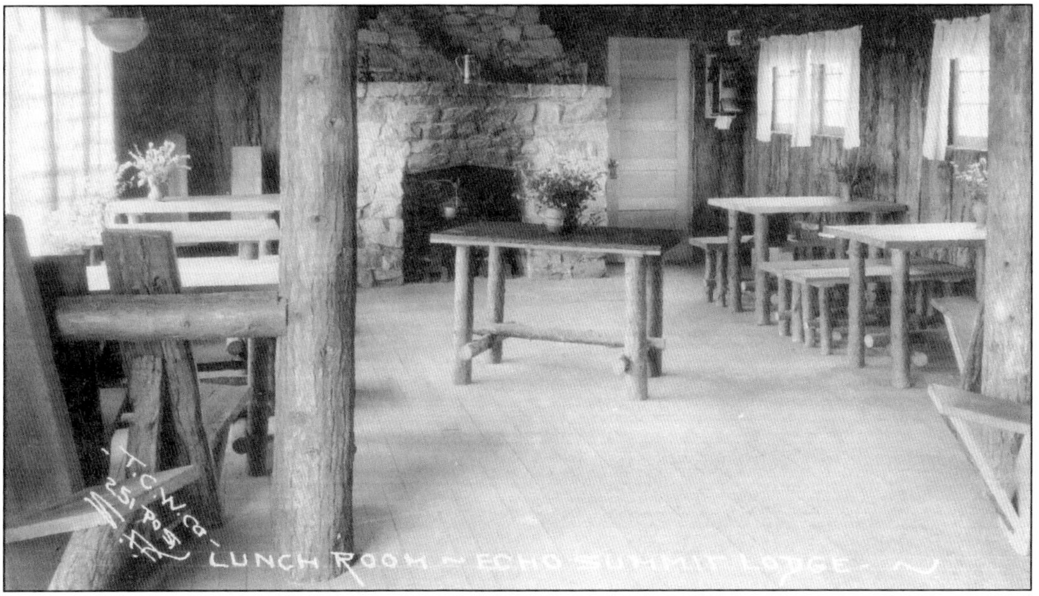

Echo Summit Lodge's lunchroom interior shows the simplicity of life at a mountain lodge situated within a beautiful forest. The granite fireplace and rustic furniture constructed from area pine trees highlight the natural resources and beauty of Echo Summit. Installed as extra structural supports for heavy snow loads, large pine tree posts about one foot in diameter help stabilize the lodge. Additional smaller posts with boards attached provide additional functionality and support. (Courtesy of Dorothy De Mare.)

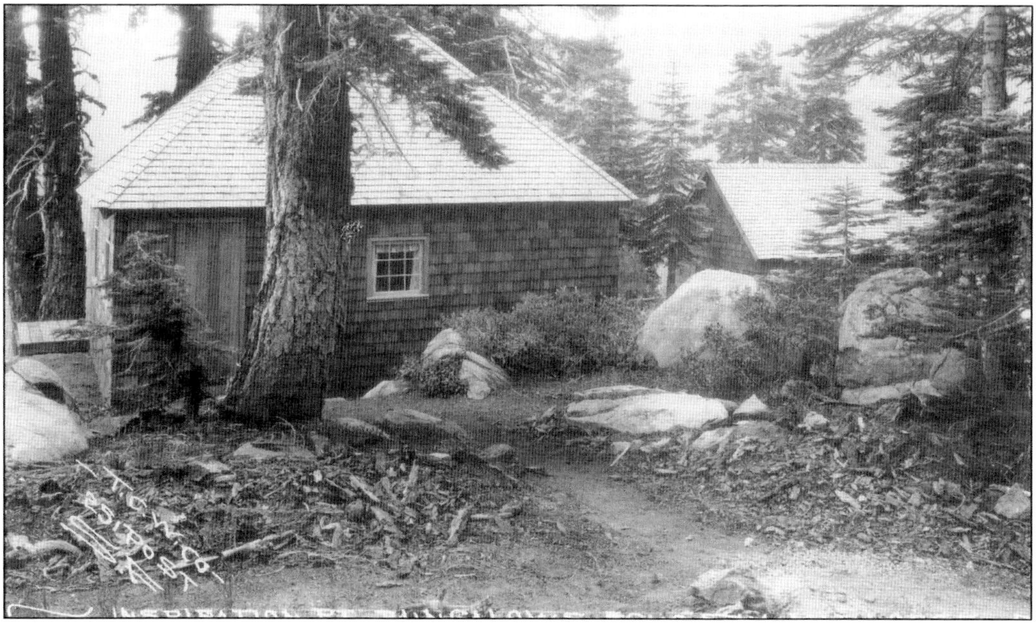

Besides building Echo Summit Lodge, Wohlbruck also built four small cabins on US Forest Service land that he rented for overnight and vacation guests. Wohlbruck advertised his cabins in the *Reno Evening Gazette*. In the early 1940s, when H.R. Matthias expanded Echo Summit Lodge, he gave these cabins to the contractor in lieu of paying him for the construction of the addition. These cabins still exist today. (Courtesy of Paul DeWitt.)

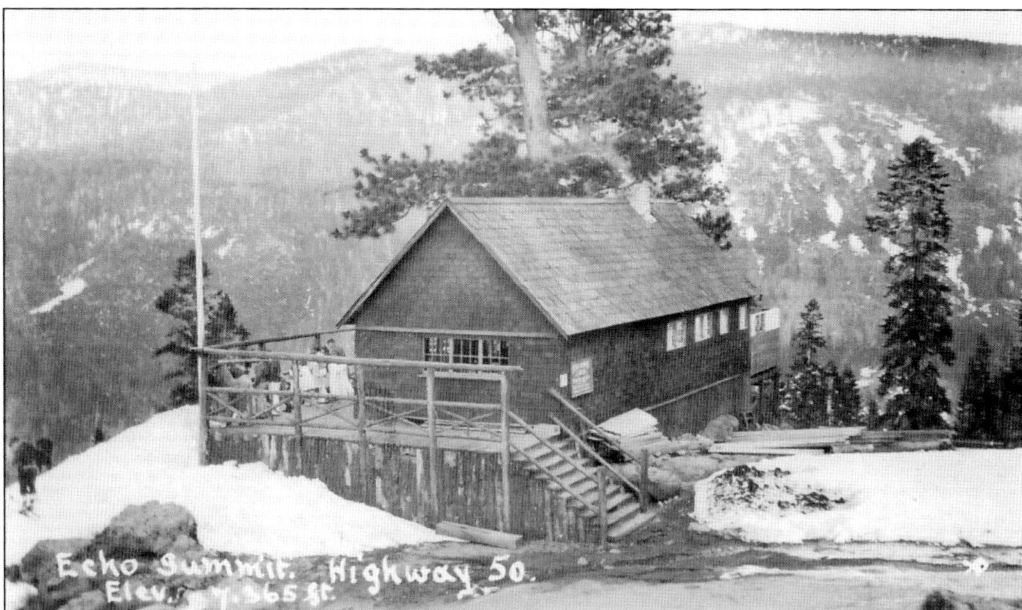

In 1929, Wohlbruck sold Echo Summit Lodge to John Jacob Smith for $8,000. Smith had already designed and built Echo Portals in 1926. He leased several other US Forest Service properties in the area. When the stock market collapsed in November 1929, Smith lost everything. He could not maintain any of his leases, and the US Forest Service took over his leases for Echo Portals, Echo Summit Lodge, and the other US Forest Service properties. (Courtesy of Paul DeWitt.)

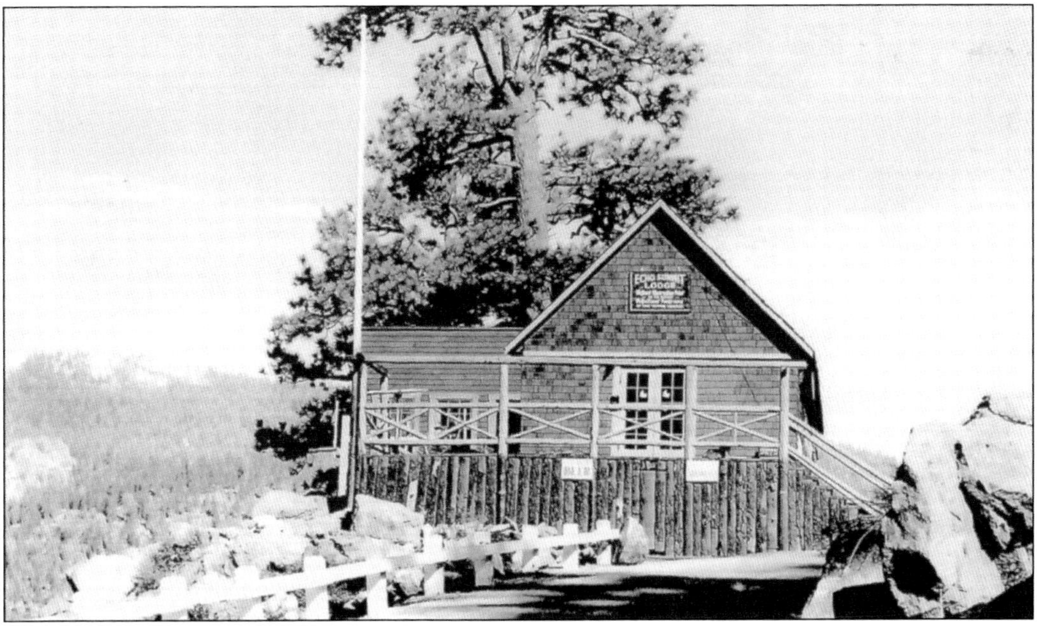

In the early 1930s, H.R. Matthias acquired the leases for Echo Summit Lodge and its rental cabins. He began remodeling the lodge by moving the deck out to the corner of the building, placing a double-door entrance on the gable end, and adding on to the dining area over the deck facing the valley. The sign over the new front door reads "Echo Summit Lodge, highest observation point on the mount. Highest local panorama of the Tahoe region." (Courtesy of Paul DeWitt.)

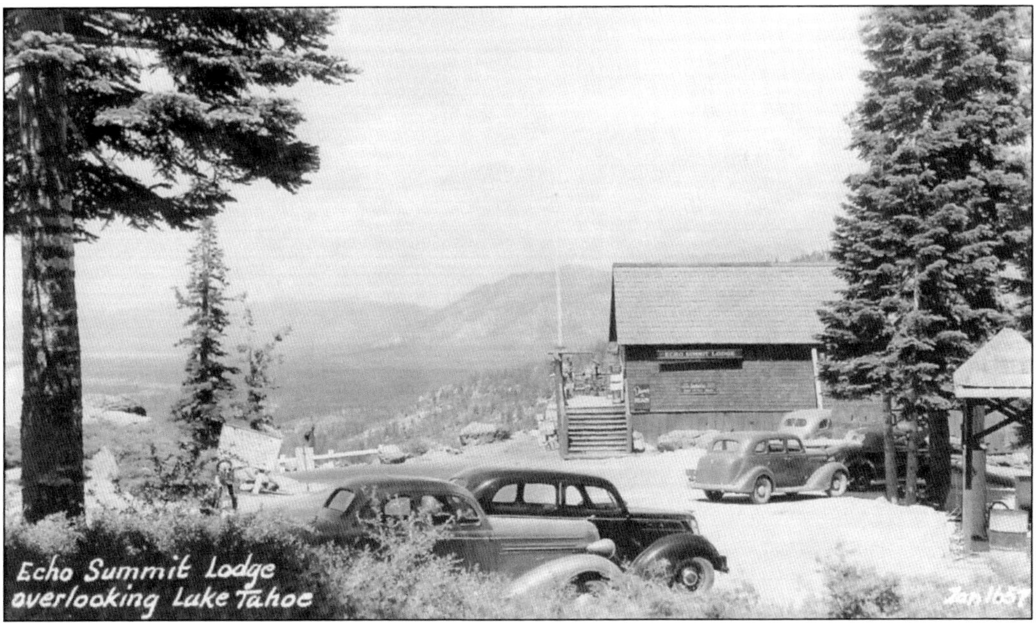

Echo Summit Lodge remained popular in the mid-1930s. Signs on the wall read "Dinner is Ready" and "Ice cream, sandwiches, good eats, beer and wine." The US Forest Service telescope was moved to the corner of the deck, and newspapers were sold at the top of the stairs. The guests shown here are looking at the view and through the telescope. The gas station is on the far right. (Courtesy of Paul DeWitt.)

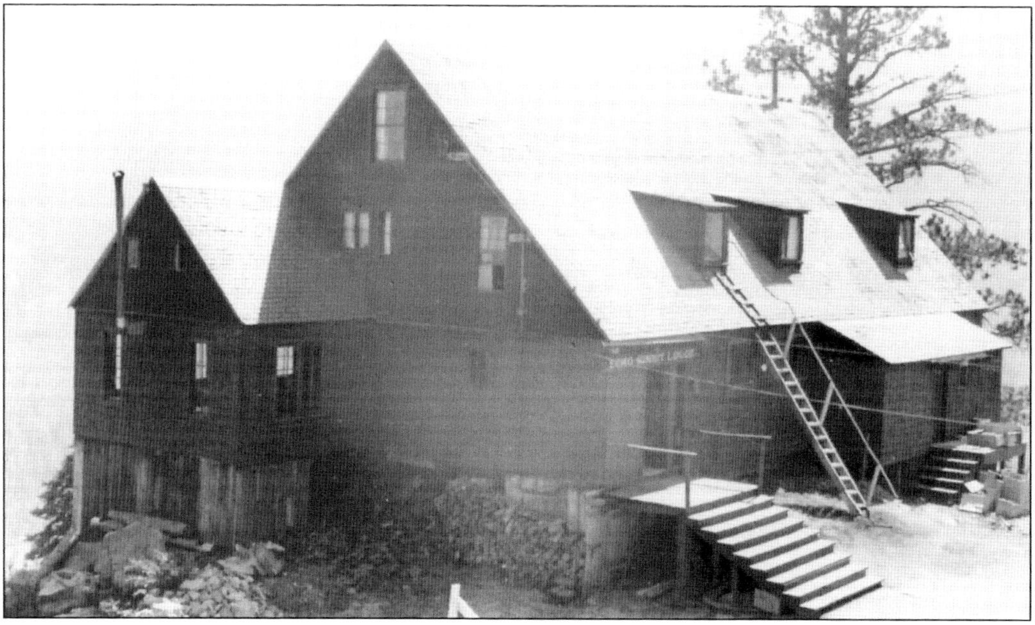

In the early 1940s, H.R. Matthias enlarged the lodge to about 40 feet by 80 feet. The double-door entrance was now an inside entrance to a large bar. There was now a large lobby and living room area with a wood-burning stove. Space was available for a small store selling groceries, gifts, and souvenirs. The dining and kitchen areas were increased in size. Added to a new second floor were nine sleeping rooms and two bathrooms. (Courtesy of the California Alpine Club.)

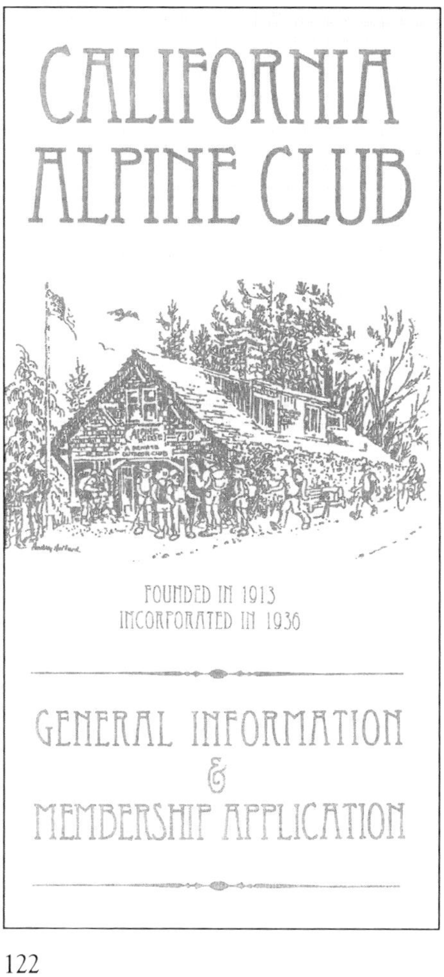

Roy and Catherine Butler bought Echo Summit Lodge in 1944. Because Highway 50 had been rerouted, the lodge had little business. In 1950, the California Alpine Club was looking for a ski lodge in the Sierras that could be used year-round. It heard about Echo Summit Lodge, and several members went to visit. They liked what they saw, and bought it for $10,000. (Courtesy of Dorothy De Mare.)

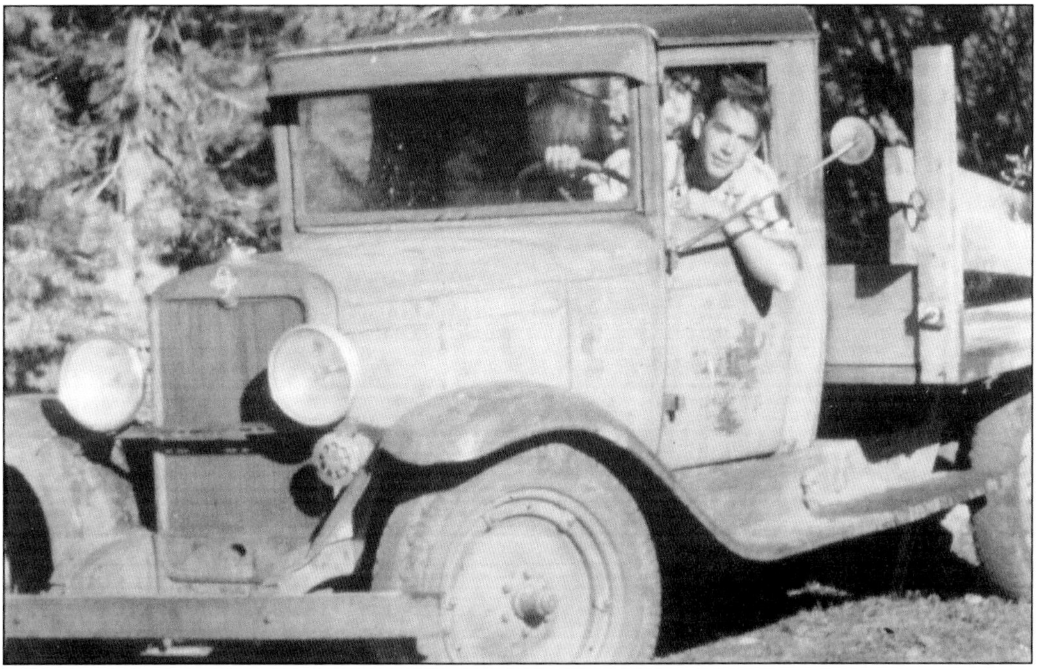

For another $10, the California Alpine Club bought all of the furniture and beds, kitchen facilities, eating utensils, tools, and equipment that were part of the lodge. Also included was a 1929 Chevrolet truck that was used to haul loads of trash to the dump in Lake Valley. Shown here driving the truck is Harry Walter West. He was one of the first Echo Summit Lodge Trustees, serving for 35 years. (Courtesy of the California Alpine Club.)

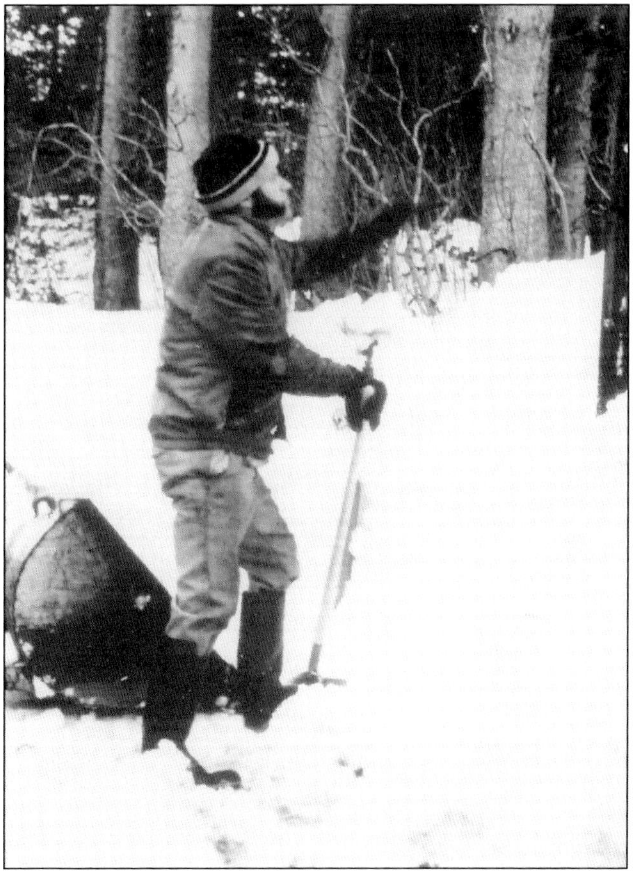

For more than 40 years, Robert King performed numerous jobs for the lodge, including serving as a plumber. He is seen here searching for frozen water pipes that needed to be fixed for the winter. He also cut logs for firewood. Club volunteers split the logs into smaller pieces for the lodge stoves. Today, all the work at the lodge is done be volunteers during the week and on work weekends. (Courtesy of the California Alpine Club.)

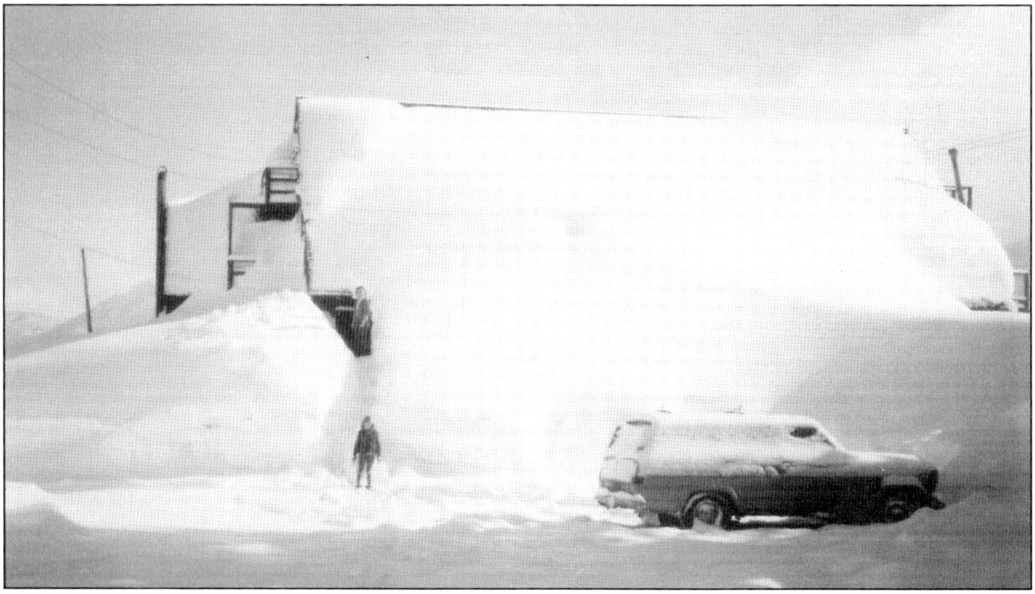

This snowfall at Echo Summit Lodge on March 1, 1969, was typical of heavy-snow years. The road had been cleared to the lodge. On most occasions, California Alpine Club members would leave their cars in the snow park at the junction of Johnson Pass Road and Echo Lakes Road and ski or snowshoe the half mile to the lodge. (Courtesy of the California Alpine Club.)

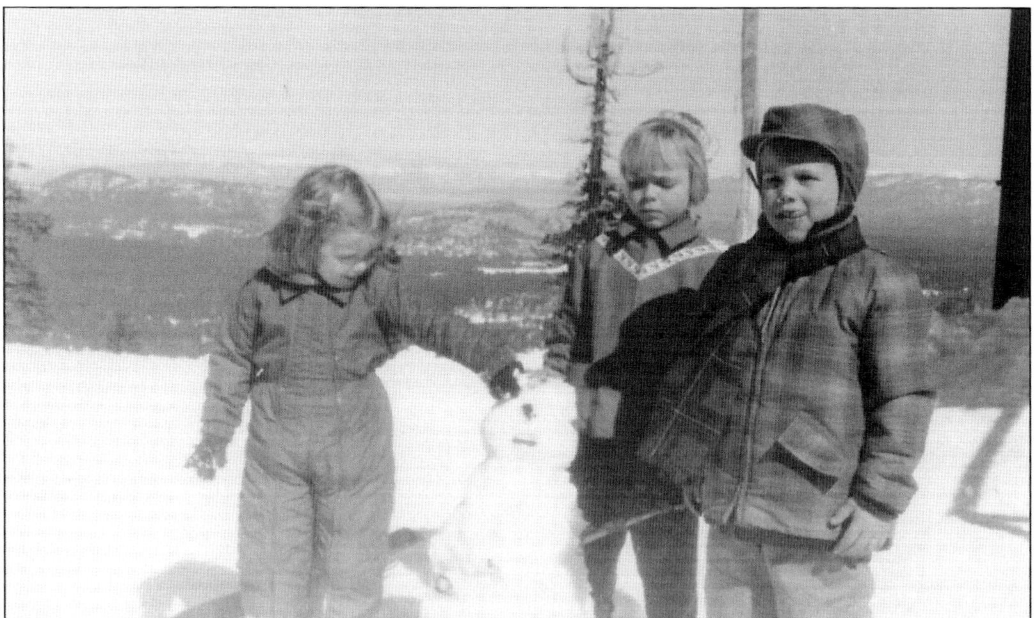

Families have always come to the Echo Summit Lodge in the winter. Seen here in February 1960, (standing from left to right) Donna and Judy West and Grahame Crawford are playing with a snowman. In the background is Lake Tahoe and Lake Valley. By the 1990s, four generations of California Alpine Club members were visiting the lodge and skiing, snowshoeing, or playing in the snow. Some members would go to the ski resorts close to the lodge, like Sierra at Tahoe and Heavenly Valley. (Courtesy of the California Alpine Club.)

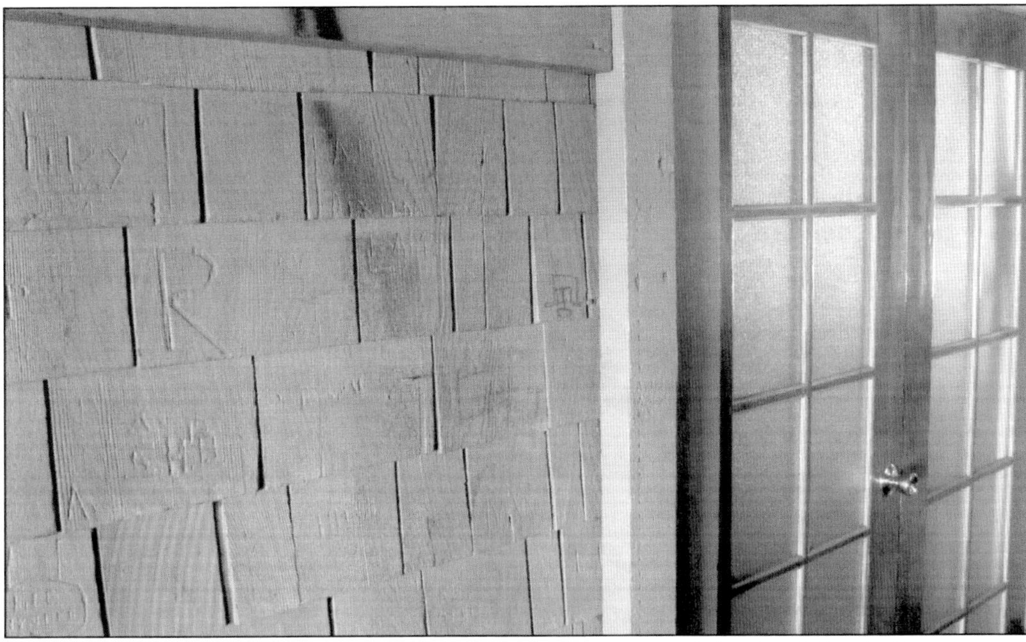

When coming into the Echo Summit Lodge today, a guest enters an 8-foot-by-20-foot hallway designed to store skis, snowshoes, a toboggan sled, and other snow equipment. The right wall was the original exterior wall of the lodge before remodeling in the 1940s. Before the 1940s, the two doors were the entrance to the lodge. The shingles were the exterior siding on which visitors carved their initials. At one place, the year "1941" is carved into the shingles. (Courtesy of Paul DeWitt.)

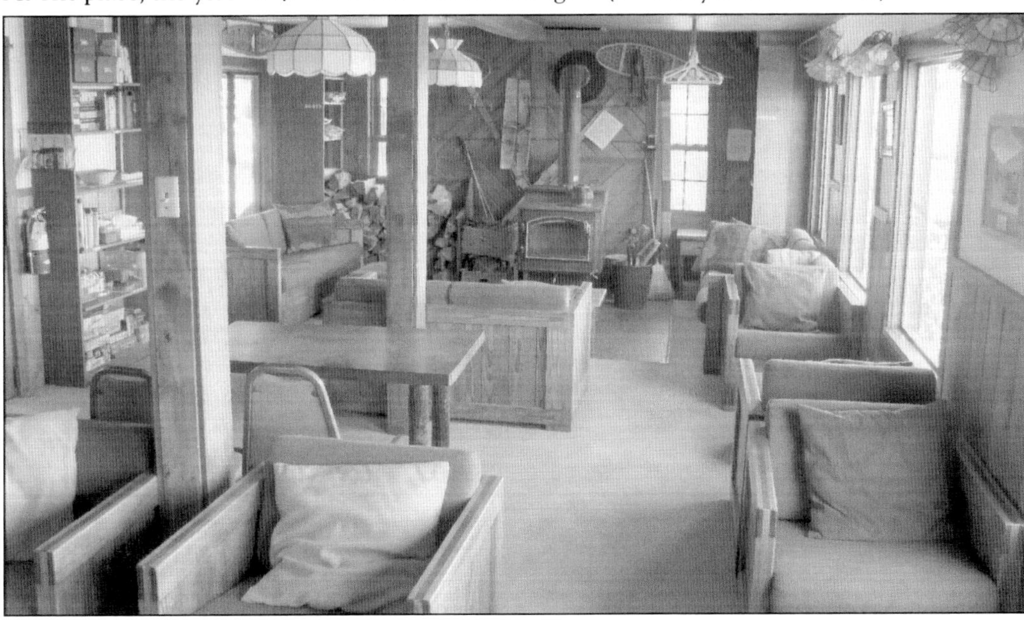

This is the living room of Echo Summit Lodge as it looks today. The door from the front hallway is on the left. The windows on the right look out on the Lake Tahoe Basin. The living room seats about 20 guests comfortably. The dining room, behind the camera, can seat about 40 people for meals. With the two dormitory rooms and nine sleeping rooms, the lodge can sleep about 50 visitors at any time. (Courtesy of Paul DeWitt.)

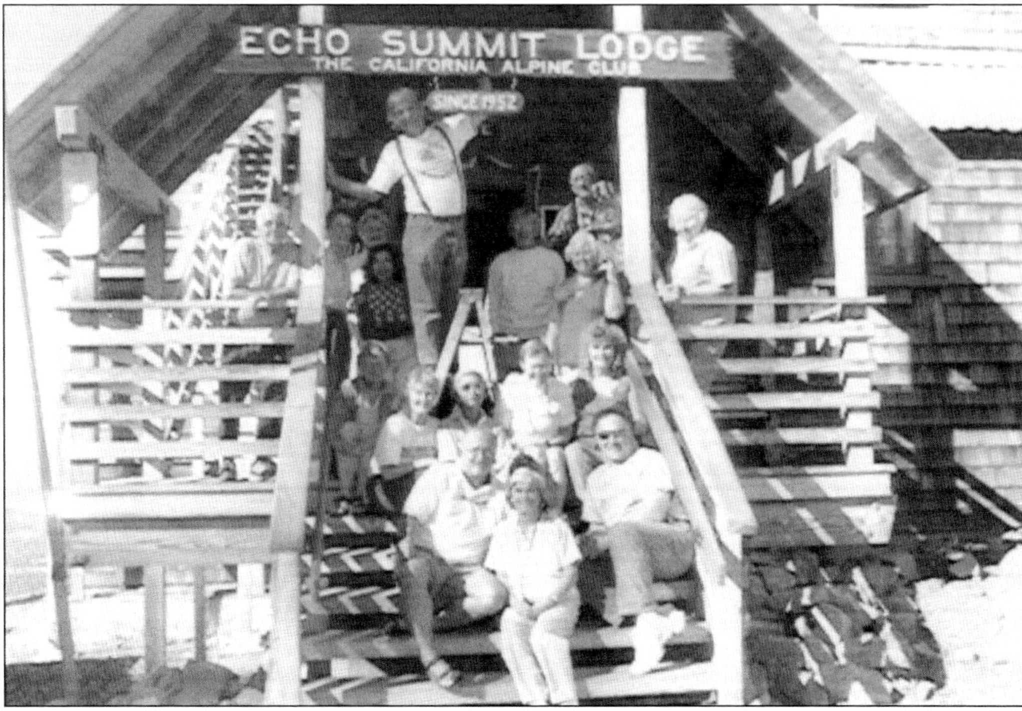

On the July Fourth weekend in 2002, the California Alpine Club celebrated its 50th anniversary of ownership of Echo Summit Lodge. The club invited all of the cabin owners along the ridge to celebrate with them. The lodge was full with its own members, and cabin owners came in and out the whole day. About 80 people attended the event. Many of the club members sat on the front porch to have their picture taken. (Courtesy of the California Alpine Club.)

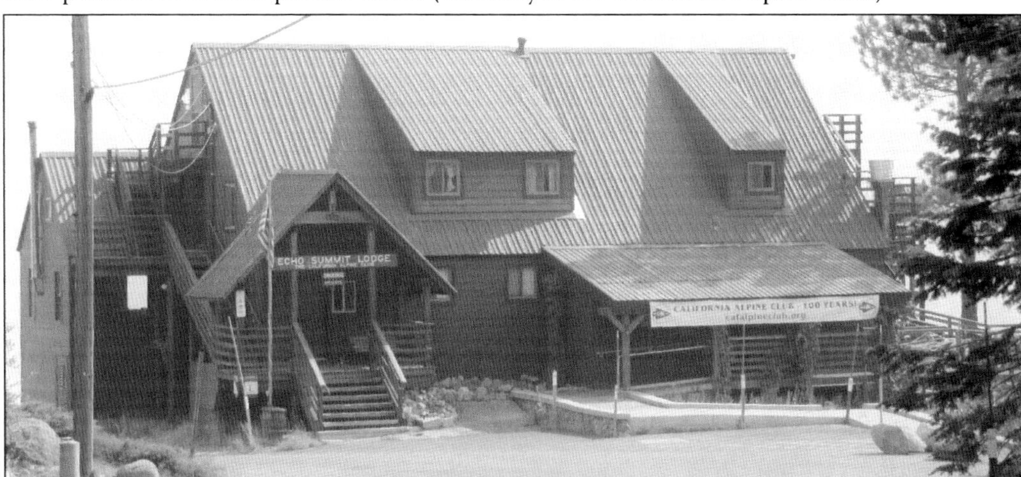

In the summer of 2013, the Alpine Club celebrated its 100th anniversary. Echo Summit Lodge played a major role for the occasion. Cabin owners were invited to a party at the lodge on August 17. This time with a full house of club members and cabin owners attending. More than 100 people showed up for the celebration, including Paul and Jayne DeWitt and Dorothy De Mare. The California Alpine Club continues to operate the Echo Summit Lodge throughout the year for its members and guests. (Courtesy of Jayne DeWitt.)

BIBLIOGRAPHY

"CHP Gets Its Feet Wet." *Tahoe Daily Tribune*. South Lake Tahoe, CA. August 13, 1962.

Frickstad, Walter N. *A Century of California Post Offices 1848 to 1954*. Oakland, CA. Philatelic Research Society, 1955.

Jackson, Robert J., BioSystems Analysis, Inc., and Mary Maniery. PAR Environmental Services, Inc. *Echo Lake Chalet Evaluation Draft Report* and *A Consideration of Cultural Resources for PG&E's Echo Lake Reservoir Monitoring Facilities Project*. Sacramento, CA. December 1990 and May 1991.

Lekisch, Barbara *Tahoe Place Names: The Origin and History of Names in the Lake Tahoe Basin*. Lafayette, CA. Great West Books, 1988.

Reynolds, G.E. "Cagwin's Museum at Echo Lake." *Stockton Daily Evening Record*. Stockton, CA, July 21, 1913.

Salley, H. E. *History of California Post Offices 1849–1990*. Second ed.; the Depot, 1991.

Schaefer, Lynn and Tom Schaefer. *Little Echoes: Echo Lakes Newsletter*. Echo Lake and South Lake Tahoe, CA. Tom and Lynn Schaefer, 1988–1998.

Scott, Edward B. *The Saga of Lake Tahoe: Volumes I and II*. Crystal Bay, NV, and Carmel, CA: Sierra-Tahoe Publishing Company, 1957 and 1973.

Sioli, Paolo. *The History of El Dorado County*. Paolo Sioli, 1883.

Smith, Gladys L. *A Flora of the Tahoe Basin and Neighboring Areas*. San Francisco: The University of San Francisco, 1984.

Snyder, Steffanie. *For a Greater Picture in Nevada County*. Nevada City, CA. Nevada County Historical Society, April 2004.

Trussell, Margaret E. *Sierra Summers: Fireside Tales to Share with Young and Old*. Bodega Bay, CA: Talking Mountain Press, 1989.

Upton, Charles E. *Pioneers of El Dorado*. Placerville, CA. Charles Elmer Upton, 1906.

Vestal, Lee. *The Celio Family in Lake Valley*. South Lake Tahoe, CA. Lake Tahoe Historical Society, August 2013.

Yohalem, Betty. *"I Remember . . ."*: *Stories and Pictures of El Dorado County Pioneer Families*. Placerville, CA: El Dorado County Chamber of Commerce, 1977.